PRAISE FOR *LEVERAGING DEEP LEARNING*

"This book is a vital resource for educators committed to shifting from a content-driven curriculum to one focused on conceptual understanding. It masterfully bridges theory and practice, guiding readers from foundational ideas to hands-on applications. The authors tackle the complexity of assessing conceptual learning, offering practical tools, such as the Rubric for Understanding, which functions as both a planning and assessment guide. With authentic examples across disciplines, this book is grounded in real-world classroom practice and offers clear, actionable strategies for continuous assessment. A must-read for educators aiming to deepen student engagement and transferable understanding."

—Pam Ryan, PhD, Education Consultant

"As the Head of School, I wholeheartedly endorse *Leveraging Deep Learning: Strategies and Tools for Continuous Assessment of Conceptual Understanding*. This invaluable resource empowers educators to transform their assessment practices by placing learners at the centre of the process. The book's clear and engaging approach demystifies the creation of assessments that foster conceptual understanding, making it accessible for teachers at all levels. What sets this book apart is its emphasis on cultivating assessment-capable learners. By encouraging active involvement in their own learning and that of their peers, it promotes a culture of collaboration and continuous improvement. The step-by-step guide for developing effective rubrics is particularly noteworthy, as it equips educators with the tools they need to assess understanding meaningfully and constructively.

"I highly recommend this book to all educators seeking to enhance their assessment strategies and create a more engaging learning environment. It is a must-read for anyone committed to fostering deep learning in their classrooms."

—Tom Egerton, Head of School, Beijing City International School, Beijing, China

"In a world where traditional grading often falls short, this book provides an invaluable framework for continuous assessment that honours each student's unique journey. It equips educators with practical assessment strategies for learning, not just *of* learning. It is a must-read for any teacher committed to deep, impactful education."

—**Julian Edwards,** Director of Learning and Innovation, The KAUST School, Jeddah, Saudi Arabia

"This book will be an invaluable resource and guide for educators aiming to foster deep understanding and purposeful learning in their learners. The *why* of education is clear from start to finish, equipping educators with the understanding and tools to help learners build meaning through authentic assessment practices. Through the many models, ideas, and strategies that can be applied directly in the classroom, the book clearly encourages educators to partner with their learners. I especially loved the chosen quotations and voices of educators woven throughout, as it makes the reading relatable. The detailed guide that steps through the process of creating a Rubric for Understanding is invaluable, and I love the idea of the shift from using summative assessment to transfer and application. It requires educators to really think about the why and purpose of the learning. As a result of reading this book, my understanding of continuous assessment has grown greatly."

—**Renee Wehner,** Education Leader, Lutheran Education SA, NT, and WA, Adelaide, Australia

"Andrea and Tania have crafted an essential teacher guide in *Leveraging Deep Learning*. As educators, we are familiar with the assessment of information and progress within a particular subject or inquiry. Many schools have excellent processes in place for students to also be able to assess where they are, what their next steps are, and what they need to do to move forward. The notion of enabling students to assess their and others' understanding of concepts, however, is tricky for the best of us. This book guides us through the importance of conceptual learning as well as practices that we and our students can use. The authors present concrete examples using rubrics that all educators and schools can understand and apply. This book is one that will support teachers, and through transference, students, to be capable of conceptual assessment."

—**Mark Beach,** Interim Head of School, United World College Thailand, Phuket, Thailand

"'Yes, but what about assessment? How can we assess this kind of deep learning?' Over several decades of working with schools, the issue of assessment continues to be one that I most often hear raised by educators. What and *how* we assess communicates to learners, their families, and the community at large what we value. If we value deep conceptual understanding, learner agency, and differentiation, then it follows that assessment practices should mirror those values. This is no easy task, but Tania Lattanzio and Andrea Müller's book provides educators with a thorough, practical guide that will be a wonderful addition to any educator's professional library.

"*Leveraging Deep Learning* draws on an impressive body of literature in the fields of assessment, inquiry, concept-based curricula, and teaching for understanding. The book artfully synthesises this work and offers clear, well-informed advice and tools that have been trialled and shared with practicing teachers. At a time when popular discourse around education seems to have reverted to a teacher-centred, one-size-fits-all model of instruction, this resource champions assessment strategies and approaches that recognise the right of the learner to participate in decisions made about and for their learning. In addition, the explanations and examples make such a valuable contribution to nurturing an assessment-capable educator."
—**Kath Murdoch,** Author and Education Consultant, Seastar Education, Melbourne, Australia

"This book really identifies how the continuous assessment of conceptual understanding is a crucial part of the learning process. The model offers clarity and guidance on the development of a rubric for understanding and the collection of related evidence. The book is full of examples and ideas, and I envisage it being a great go-to resource to enhance conceptual understanding and ensure consistency across the school. It is certainly a resource I would have in my school!"
—**Sue Cattell,** Head of Junior School, Diocesan School for Girls, Auckland, New Zealand

"*Leveraging Deep Learning: Strategies and Tools for Continuous Assessment of Conceptual Understanding* is not a book like any other. If you like reflection questions, if you like quotations from great educators, if you like charts and graphic organisers, if you like to hear about the experience of others, if you like photos and real-life connections, if you are looking for practical tools and strategies, you will find all of this and more. The book provides examples for all teachers, all disciplines, and a variety of grade levels. The four levels of understanding are helpful and practical. The book is a journey. You don't just read it; you interact with it while enjoying the hints provided and the spaces for reflection."

—**Ali Ezzeddine,** Author, Educator, Coach

"*Leveraging Deep Learning: Strategies and Tools for Continuous Assessment of Conceptual Understanding* is a brilliant resource for educators committed to fostering meaningful learning. This book masterfully bridges theory and practice, providing clear, actionable strategies for integrating continuous assessment into everyday teaching. With its innovative Rubric for Understanding and step-by-step guidance, it empowers educators to collaboratively create assessment criteria with students, fostering collaboration, critical thinking, and authentic engagement. Packed with practical examples, reflective prompts, and adaptable tools, this book is an essential companion for any educator looking to deepen conceptual understanding and inspire lifelong learning in their students. A must-read for advancing teaching and learning practices!"

—**Bernadette Scott,** Religious Education Leader, Catholic Education, Archdiocese Canberra, and Goulburn

"*Leveraging Deep Learning: Strategies and Tools for Continuous Assessment of Conceptual Understanding* has been invaluable in clarifying my thinking around assessment practices. Thank you! I believe it will greatly support our teachers in moving beyond simply assessing recall to focusing on deeper learning. The step-by-step guides to developing rubrics centred on conceptual understanding will empower teachers to provide more effective real-time feedback, foster student collaboration, and better differentiate instruction. A great resource to help personalize learning and ensure students can apply their knowledge in meaningful, real-world contexts. Thank you to Tania and Andrea for leading the way in best assessment practices."

—**Justine Smyth,** Elementary Principal, Jakarta Intercultural School, Jakarta, Indonesia

"All the noise surrounding the clear and critical need to transform education can arguably be distilled into the relative simplicity of this: we need to start with the end in mind. We need to concentrate our finite energies on the things learners will carry away from their learning experience. We need to focus on building deep, transferable, conceptual understanding, on how to teach for it, and on how to know whether we are achieving it. Lattanzio and Müller have focused squarely on this need and have addressed it in a comprehensive guidebook that is not only accessible and engaging but also eminently practical. To do great work, we need the right tools. This new contribution to the field is not just a 'nice to have.' It is a necessary, enduring addition to any serious educator's transfer toolkit."

—**Kevin Bartlett,** Founding Director, Common Ground Collective, Panama City, Panama

"The concept of continuous assessment resonates deeply with me because it places the learner at the centre of the educational process, valuing their unique journey and personal growth. This approach empowers learners by actively involving them in the assessment process, particularly through the co-creation of rubrics for understanding alongside teachers. In the age of AI, this becomes even more crucial. In this way, assessments reflect the true progression of each student, valuing evidence of understanding gathered over the course of their learning journey instead of just results at the end. Additionally, continuous assessment fosters a growth mindset by emphasizing progress and effort over fixed abilities, motivating learners to embrace challenges.

"The book provides a variety of tools and strategies for continuous assessment. For example, they describe how to use 'invitations' (provocations) to elicit student thinking and prior knowledge. They also discuss a range of formative assessment strategies, such as concept maps, placemats, and exit tickets, which educators and learners can use to gather evidence of understanding throughout a unit. Additionally, it explains the role of rubrics in defining learning criteria and helping students understand expectations.

"This book is a valuable resource for educators aiming to enhance conceptual learning and student-centred assessment. Practical strategies in the book encourage meaningful engagement and personal growth, making it essential in AI-driven education."

—**Alison Yang,** MYP Coordinator, ESF, Discovery College, Hong Kong

"As someone who experienced the limitations of rote memorization and content-heavy instruction, I deeply appreciate the value of this book, *Leveraging Deep Learning: Strategies and Tools for Continuous Assessment of Conceptual Understanding*. Written by Tania Lattanzio and Andrea Müller, this book offers a much-needed shift towards developing meaningful, transferable learning for students.

"Tania and Andrea present actionable tools and strategies to help educators develop and assess deep learning in their students, ensuring that knowledge, skills, and understandings are transferable and authentic. This book is not just a resource; it is an essential guide for teachers committed to making a lasting difference in the lives of the thousands of students they influence over their careers.

"Every single chapter in the book makes a significant contribution by empowering educators to move beyond mere acquisition of knowledge, developing learners who can think critically and thrive in a complex, ever-changing world."

—**Ashish Trivedi,** Head of Government Partnerships, International Baccalaureate, Singapore

"*Leveraging Deep Learning: Strategies and Tools for Continuous Assessment of Conceptual Understanding*, provides a firm foundation for deep, rich, and focused discussions within learning communities to make assessment purposeful and relevant in ways that are respectful to learners and all their ways of being, knowing, and understanding.

"Tania and Andrea set a tone for curating a culture of learning that is reflective, values the learning process as learning itself, and creates safe spaces for mistake-making and growth.

"This book's human-centred approach will elevate decision-making and conversations to keep the priority on students and their learning and will become a go-to resource around collaborative planning tables all over the world."

—**Katherine Williams,** Kindergarten Teacher, United World College South East Asia, Singapore

CONCEPTS IN ACTION

LEVERAGING
DEEP LEARNING

Strategies and Tools for Assessment of
Conceptual Understanding

Tania Lattanzio   Andrea Müller

Leveraging Deep Learning
© 2025 by Tania Lattanzio and Andrea Müller

These books are available at special discounts when purchased in quantity for use as premiums, promotions, fundraising, and educational use. For inquiries and details, contact the publisher at elevatebooksedu.com.

Published by Elevate Books EDU

Library of Congress Control Number: 2024947408
Paperback ISBN: 979-8-9913909-0-3
eBook ISBN: 979-8-9913909-1-0

Contents

Acknowledgements

We are indebted to many people in the process of writing this. We owe huge thanks and much gratitude to Jackie Becher, whose dedication in providing continual feedback ensured the authors (us) kept on track and what we're saying made sense to the reader. Her contributions have been so appreciated and *needed*. Thank you.

Further thanks to Lucy Allsopp, who provided a secondary lens when reviewing the book to ensure that it connected to a wider audience and used the ideas presented in the book in her role at her school.

To all the educators we have collaborated with, we cannot thank you enough for guiding us in the writing of this book. It is your research of assessment and feedback of your own practices that has enabled us to write this book. We want to acknowledge the many educators who have also contributed to various Innovative Global Education (IGE) professional learning contexts—planning conceptual units, developing Rubrics for Understanding, and analysing the effectiveness of continuous assessment in practice.

Throughout the book, we have acknowledged educators, their ideas, and examples of concepts in action. We are incredibly grateful to these wonderful educators for being open and sharing their thoughts with us.

Many educators have paved the way for this book. We are thankful for the educational thinking and theories of David Perkins, Guy Claxton, Lynn Erickson, Jay McTighe, Grant Wiggins, Geoff Masters, Tina Blythe, Dylan Wiliam, Jerome Bruner, Carol Anne Tomlinson, Jo Boaler, Kath Murdoch, John Hattie, Mark Treadwell, Rick Stiggins, and others who have inspired and informed us as educators who strive to make a difference. Without their extensive research around education, this book would not be possible.

Introducing the Concepts in Action Series

> If you do not know why the curriculum prescribes particular standards and objectives, it should be no surprise when your learners cannot see the purpose of the content presented.
>
> A conceptual framework can provide students with context and a compelling reason to learn.

As educational consultants at Innovative Global Education (IGE), we deliver a range of professional learning services to schools and educators around the globe. Our aim is to facilitate creative, practical, and flexible solutions that build capacity for sustainable educational innovation and development.

Our primary areas of expertise are curriculum, instructional pedagogy, and assessment, with a focus on conceptual learning. We're writing the books for the Concepts in Action series to equip educators to bring conceptual understanding and learning to the forefront of teaching. The goal is to bring conceptual learning and understanding to life for learners.

The three books in this series focus on the role of concepts. Here's a summary of each of the books.

This book, *Leveraging Deep Learning: Strategies and Tools for Continuous Assessment of Conceptual Understanding*, examines the role of continuous assessment of conceptual understanding. It places the emphasis on learners as being assessment capable and calls on educators to actively involve students in the assessment of their and their peers' learning. We provide a step-by-step guide to assist educators in developing a rubric that promotes assessment as continuous and assesses learners' conceptual understanding. Using numerous examples, we explore and explain both the rubric and the role of continuous assessment.

Designing for Wonder: Strategies and Tools for Framing the Inquiry for Conceptual Learning focuses on building conceptual understanding. Recognising the purpose of scope and sequence documents, or curriculum standards, this book offers guidance on how to shift from content to concepts when designing units of learning. We look at what makes something worth learning as well as at the design components that promote understanding, inquiry, and agency. This book is about how to frame the learning to be conceptually driven and promote inquiry. It also considers the skills and larger conceptual ideas we want as throughlines for a school.

Engaging Wonder: Strategies and Tools for Implementing the Conceptual Inquiry Process focuses on a model we have developed to guide the conceptual inquiry process. Within this model, we provide explanations and examples of how to connect learners to concepts, the role of curiosity through invitations, and how to design learning that moves beyond activities. We show educators how to craft broader learning experiences that provide diverse, meaningful, and engaging pathways to building understanding through conceptual inquiry.

We are writing this series for educators who work with learners who are six to sixteen years old. That is not to say that many of the ideas in the book could not be used in the early years or in the final two years of schooling, simply that the examples provided take into consideration the learning needs and development of learners in this age range. We believe the ideas represented in this book can be used at every grade level, but we acknowledge that some external assessment practices could impact the way educators apply the ideas presented in this book.

CHAPTER ONE

Why Conceptual Learning?

In a complicated, fast-changing world, the intelligent path is to let go of being a Knower and embrace being a Learner.

——————— Guy Claxton, *What's the Point of School?* ———————

In the world of education, a concept acts as an umbrella, linking the details and characteristics that form the main parts of an idea. A concept can be expressed in a single word or a phrase, such as *power* or *points of view*. In *A Study of Thinking*, educational researchers Bruner, Goodnow, and Austin defined *concepts* as the mental categories we use to classify information according to its common features; they help us make sense of the world.

This act of linking differentiates conceptual learning from the practice of using topics or themes to organise learning for students. Topic-based learning narrows the curriculum focus on facts. In contrast, conceptual learning links learners' understanding of topics, allowing them to develop a broader understanding of the world.

Consider the characteristics of concepts versus the characteristics of facts or topics:

A concept is . . .	A topic is . . .
Abstract	Concrete
Broad	Verifiable
Universal	Specific
Timeless	Observable
Transferable	
Represented by a variety of examples	

If you currently use topics or themes to plan your units of study, you'll be happy to know that transitioning to a conceptual curriculum does *not* require you to discard your current units. You simply expand existing topic-based units by reframing them, using a conceptual lens. The list below offers an example of how unit topics can be adapted and broadened when viewed through this lens.

Topic	Concepts
Dinosaur	extinction, loss, adaptation, survival
Fashion	trend, material, identity, pattern, production
War	conflict, causality, impact, power
Celebrations	culture, belief, value, symbolism
Games	rule, strategy, space
Number	pattern, operation, sequence, equivalence
Painting	interpretation, texture, theme, balance

Please note that in this book, the shift to conceptual learning is explored through the lens of continuous assessment. This shift will be further examined and explained in greater detail in the book *Designing for Wonder: Strategies and Tools for Framing the Inquiry for Conceptual*

Learning. In this book, we'll focus on the fundamentals of conceptual teaching and learning that explain the *why* behind this teaching practice as well as *what* makes it effective.

Six Fundamentals of Conceptual Teaching and Learning

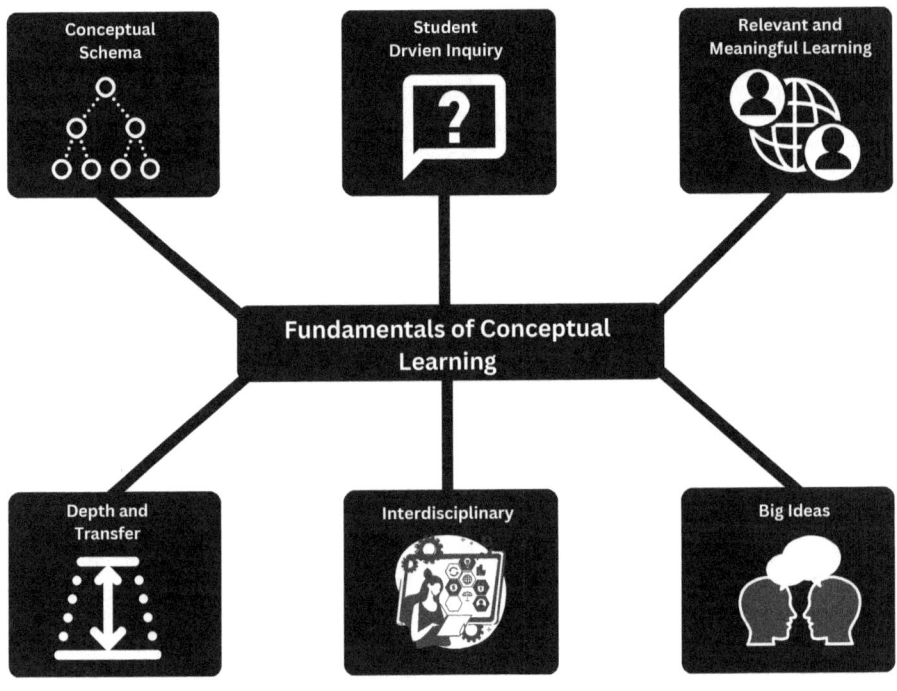

Fundamental 1:
Developing a Conceptual Schema

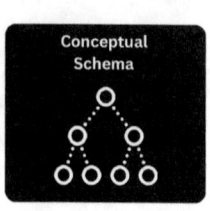

> *"Concept framework(s) . . . includes knowledge, ideas, and concepts that are all linked to each other as a learning package within our brain.* Most of our thinking involves concept frameworks. In our brain sits an unfathomable number of the most extraordinary complex and re-usable knowledge, ideas, concepts, and concept frameworks that we combine in numerous different ways allowing us to predict and create new possibilities for additional contexts we may have never experienced before."
>
> — Mark Treadwell, *The Future of Learning*

"Schemas are neural networks, and the way those networks get created and connected ends up defining your concept, or understanding of the topic," explains Eric Sbar in his article, "Schemas Are Key to Deep Conceptual Understanding." These mental constructs are a lens through which new information is interpreted and integrated with existing knowledge. They provide a framework that helps people make sense of their world.

The shift from content-based curriculum to conceptual teaching and learning helps to ensure that developing schemas becomes an intentional aspect of instructional practice. As learners explore concepts, they use the conceptual schema to connect new learning to previous knowledge. Our approach is built on the *connections* that link facts in the form of concepts. This method differs from content-driven instruction in that it leverages the full potential of conceptual schemas for improved learning.

Fundamental 2:
Focuses on Big Ideas

> *"Educators should move away from trying to cover excessive factual material, and instead orient their curriculum around a smaller number of conceptually larger, transferable ideas. Focusing on fewer, bigger ideas is critical to avoiding superficial coverage, and it allows more time to engage learners in the kinds of active meaning-making processes that are necessary for understanding the relevant content."*
>
> — McTighe and Silver, "Instructional Shifts to Support Deep Learning"

In *The Process of Education*, Jerome Bruner stated, "A curriculum ought to be built around the great issues, principles, and values that society deems worthy of the continual concern of its members." Jo Boaler reiterated this idea in her article, "Big Ideas": "I always recommend that teachers focus on 'big ideas' instead of isolated standards." Conceptual understanding focuses on those *big ideas*.

Organising and reframing content under conceptually driven big ideas shifts the attention from simply acquiring content knowledge to building understanding. Learners use knowledge to explain and verify their current understandings building and developing their conceptual schema. Using the school's prescribed standards and objectives as the starting point for conceptual learning, we can set our aim at developing meaningful, purposeful, and engaging units in which the content supports a deeper understanding of big ideas. We refer to this as *conceptual understanding*.

Conceptual understanding occurs when concepts are embedded in big ideas. Big ideas are broadly written and provide scope for learners to build understanding over time. Big ideas (conceptual understandings) will be explored more in *Designing for Wonder: Strategies and Tools for Framing the Inquiry for Conceptual Learning,* the next book in the Concepts in Action series.

Examples of Conceptual Understandings

Each of the statements below represents a conceptual understanding. By embedding and explicitly articulating the concepts (highlighted by the bold type), conceptual understandings take shape. To make meaning, it's necessary to understand the concepts within the statement.

1. Through interpreting and **representing** numerical **expressions,** mathematicians see and explain **patterns.**
2. Through **experimentation,** people develop and test **theories.**
3. Improving **performance** in individual pursuits involves **refinement** and **reflection.**
4. **Systems** have **interdependent** parts and **impact** the world in which we live.

Fundamental 3:
Promotes Meaningful and Relevant Learning

"Establishing relevance was the most prominent and often cited learner response. Relevance is a key component to intrinsically motivating learner learning. By establishing both personal and real-world relevance, learners are provided with an important opportunity to relate the course subject matter to the world around them, and to assimilate it in accordance with their previously held assumptions and beliefs. Relevance is a key factor in providing a learning context in which learners construct their own understanding of the course material."

"How to Make Learning Relevant to Your Learners," OpenCollege.edu.au

Conceptual learning puts an end to teaching content out of context. We are not implying that content is unimportant; we are saying that context and connections are essential for deeper learning. Teaching content out of context leaves learners with isolated facts. They know about the material but may not have an understanding of it that allows them to apply and use what they have learned. Concepts provide relevance and significance to the learning.

David Perkins (cited by Nigel Coutts) notes that with factual learning, "we might finish the unit with a detailed understanding *of* the (topic), but we have learned little else." He suggests a shift toward understanding *with*, "where we finish the topic with an understanding of the essential information about the (topic) and we also exit with a broader perspective on the world and a new way of understanding many interrelated topics. We have developed understandings with our study . . . rather than merely developing an understanding of the (topic)."

Concepts are in our world; they are all around us. As we delve into concepts with learners, we can make connections to their existing understanding and schema by including concepts from outside the classroom. As Casey Pettit and Claudia Bicen explain, "For learners to achieve deeper learning, they must be able to connect lessons to their own experiences, current interests, and future pursuits." It is important to understand that relevance may differ among learners, so we want them to make their own connections and consider what is relevant to them.

Fundamental 4:
Provides Opportunity for Learner-Driven Inquiry

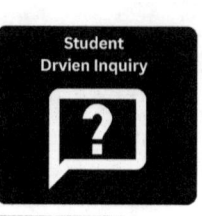

> *"The best contexts for inquiry lend themselves to learning that goes beyond the content of the inquiry itself. Great contexts for inquiry have some 'conceptual congruence' and give students insights into big ideas that they will, ideally, visit, time and time again across their learning."*

— Kath Murdoch, *The Power of Inquiry*

Another important aspect of conceptual teaching and learning is that it provides opportunities for learners to follow their questions, wonders, and inquiries. We design learning in response to learners, not for learners. When concepts are the language of the learning and are explored through a range of relevant, significant, and intriguing contexts, resources, and locations, learners engage. They are curious about their learning and recognise that there are questions, theories, and interests they would like to pursue.

Using a wide conceptual lens, a topic of the rainforest can shift to an exploration of the concepts relevant to systems and interdependence. Pursuing the concepts of systems and interdependence, learners could venture beyond the rainforest to an area of personal interest. In other words, a focus on conceptual understanding reveals new possibilities for learner-driven inquiry.

Topic	Conceptual Focus: Opening Possibilities for Learner Interest
Ancient Egypt	civilization, influence
Electricity	sustainability, transformation
Christopher Columbus	exploration, discovery, impact
Plants	growth, needs

Rainforest	interdependence, system, balance
World War II	conflict, power, impact
Transport	systems, interdependence, process
Natural disasters	process, change, adaptation

Fundamental 5:
Promotes Depth and Transfer of Learning

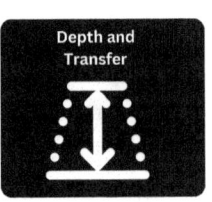

> *To understand exploration, we need to view the concept of exploration through more than one explorer, more than one lens. We need a variety of perspectives and explorations, including those taking place today.*

When planning and mapping out units of learning with an emphasis on concepts, core knowledge will underpin the subjects being taught. Learners must have this knowledge both to make conceptual connections and to articulate how that knowledge builds their understanding of the concepts. Accessing the knowledge that supports the learners' understanding of the concepts enables them to think in specific ways about the big ideas of the discipline. There can be transfer within the discipline and beyond the discipline. Refer to the examples below.

In *How People Learn*, educational researchers Bransford, Brown, and Cocking explain the importance of connections to knowledge transfer:

> *A key finding in the learning and transfer literature is that organizing information into a conceptual framework allows for greater "transfer"; that is, it allows the learner to apply what was learned in new situations and to learn related information more quickly. . . . Transfer is affected by the degree to which*

people learn with understanding rather than merely memorize sets of facts or follow a fixed set of procedures; the research also shows clearly that usable knowledge isn't the same as a mere list of disconnected facts.

An Example of Knowledge Transfer Within a Discipline

Consider how the concepts of strategy, space, and cooperation come into play during various games in Physical Education. While playing basketball, for example, these concepts unfold as learners practise the sport. Because those concepts are equally essential to other team sports, learners can transfer their knowledge and experience to other games, such as football. When we ask learners to consider how the concepts of strategy, space, and cooperation apply to both sports, we help them deepen their understanding of those concepts and transfer them to other games.

The following example demonstrates how concepts provide a vehicle for transferring learning through conceptual links.

Conceptual Link	Topical Link	Transferring Learning trough Conceptual Links
Concept: System		
Social Studies— Examining systems in the community and how they are connected, including transport systems.	Physical Education— Moving like trains	Physical Education— Examining the systems involved when organising a game
Concept: Interdependence		
Science— Examining the interconnected relationship between living and nonliving things in a rainforest.	Art— Making a collage of an animal from the rainforest	Art— Using collage, examine how the pieces of the collage come together to form a piece of artwork, how the parts are interconnected in making the art piece.

Fundamental 6:
Promotes Interdisciplinary Learning

"An interdisciplinary thematic learning environment centered on real-world challenges fosters students' creative thinking in open practice while also encouraging group communication and collaboration. Students also gain critical thinking skills through questioning and critique."

Ye, Peiqi, and Xionghu Xu, "A Case Study of Interdisciplinary Thematic Learning Curriculum to Cultivate '4C Skills'"

When we present concepts in different contexts, learners practise transferring their understanding. Exposing learners to concepts through various perspectives is important for promoting deep learning. This is interdisciplinary learning.

Interdisciplinary study, note Weller and Appleby, "allows the learner to learn by making connections between ideas and concepts across different disciplines. Learners learning in this way are able to apply the knowledge gained in one discipline to another different discipline as a way to deepen the learning experience."

Teaching through a conceptual lens expands opportunities for interdisciplinary learning. As we move from teaching topics to teaching concepts, learning takes on a broader scope. Although the context of the knowledge emphasised may vary across disciplines, concepts connect that knowledge. In other words, the interdisciplinary links promote the depth and transfer of learning. Consider this example: The concepts of conflict and cause and effect can be viewed through the lenses of personal and social conflict (social–emotional learning [SEL]), conflict over resources (economics), or conflict as represented in literature and the arts (language arts). As learners learn to transfer and apply their understanding of conflict and cause and effect to various situations, they simultaneously develop a deeper understanding of the concepts.

Note that for this type of study to be effective, there must be a **genuine connection through a conceptual lens.** When a link is topic driven, the focus on knowledge may make the connection seem forced or weak. Understand also that not all subject areas will connect to every concept, so don't try to force it. The goal is not to make links between subject areas simply for the sake of calling the learning interdisciplinary. The true value of these links across subjects comes from their ability to support and build learners' schema, understanding, and ability to transfer the learning.

Note that it is important to make links clear so learners can see and use the connections to develop and build on their schema.

Concepts: Properties and Change Interdisciplinary Possibilities	
Math	Classify different materials based on their geometrical properties.
Music	Compare and contrast musical instruments, the materials they are made from, and the sounds they make.
Art	Compare and contrast different tools and materials and note the varied effects they make. Manipulate and change the materials to create artworks.
Science/Art	Explore the properties of materials and how they can be changed and transformed.
Physical Education	Explore the uses of different sporting equipment. Connect the uses of each piece of equipment to the properties of the material from which it is made.

Concept: System Interdisciplinary Possibilities	
Math	Unpack number systems from different cultures, including the base 10 number system.
Science	Explore ecosystems and how they are interdependent.
Social Studies	Explore governance systems from different countries. Explore systems in the community and how they function and who is involved.
Health	Examine body systems. Consider how they are interrelated and how to keep them healthy.
Design	Create a functional mechanical system.

A FOCUS ON ASSESSING CONCEPTUAL UNDERSTANDING

Understanding is different from knowing. When referring to knowledge we are referring to factual knowledge.

Knowing is about *collecting* information and facts. Understanding is about *connecting* facts and creating relevance between that information and one's preexisting knowledge. Understanding takes learning further because, as David Perkins explains in *Teaching for Understanding*, it involves "the ability to think and act flexibly with what one knows."

It is in this active state of mind that learners construct meaning and gain a wider perspective of the world around them. Equally important, they are able to transfer and apply their learning to different contexts; for example, when learning about sustainability and the environment, learners are encouraged to consider sustainability issues in their community and how they might develop solutions to solve them. This shift gives meaning *to the learning **for** the learners* and often sparks an increased desire to learn. In *The Conceptual Age and the Revolution*, Mark Treadwell puts it this way: "Suddenly the purpose of education is not just to consume knowledge for survival but rather to appreciate the learning journey, the company on the journey, to enjoy the event and to leave satisfied; intellectually and emotionally, inspired to take the new understanding and make a difference in an increasingly complex world."

Understanding is based on knowledge but is more holistic than simply learning facts.

Understanding is personal in that it draws on and connects with each learner's previous experiences and knowledge. This personal relevance increases the retention of learning.

5 Characteristics of Understanding

Understanding is contextual. Anchoring information in context enhances the likelihood that learning will be retained.

Understanding is flexible in that learners can apply it to new educational contexts and real-world situations.

Understanding takes into account the connections between facts and details.

Conceptual understanding empowers learners to develop essential skills:

- Make connections
- Notice patterns
- Consider different perspectives
- Reason
- Explain
- Transfer understanding
- Theorise
- Retrieve learning

For all of the benefits listed above and more, we wrote this book with a focus on assessing learners' conceptual understanding. In other educational settings, conceptual understanding may be referred to as *enduring understandings, central ideas, big ideas,* or *statements of inquiry.* Regardless of the terminology used, the goal is for learners to develop a deep comprehension of concepts so they can apply them to real-world situations. By continually assessing conceptual understanding, educators can enhance and personalise learning.

The assessment phase of conceptual learning begins once educators have collaborated to *frame the inquiry.* This means they've collectively identified the key understanding questions, clarified what they want learners to understand as a result of the learning, and determined the core concepts and conceptual understandings that will guide the inquiry. This ensures that the learning remains focused on its conceptual foundations. We explore this in our book *Taking the Complexity out of Concepts* and will elaborate further on framing the inquiry in the next book in this series, *Designing for Wonder.*

> *Continuous assessment honours the learner and their journey. It is about putting the learner at the centre. Educators co-constructing the process with learners to empower them.*

A Focus on Continuous Assessment

The chapters that follow will equip you to bring continuous assessment of conceptual understanding into action in your classroom. Notice that we promote *continuous* or ongoing assessment. This kind of assessment is integrated into the teaching and learning process. Rather than relying on summative assessment or even periodic evaluations of educator-determined checkpoints for knowledge, we believe that involving learners to co-construct assessments designed for continuous use can inform and improve current and future learning.

To that end, one of the tools we offer is an IGE-designed Rubric for Understanding. In Chapter 3, we explain this model, which provides a step-by-step process you and your learners can employ to co-construct a rubric for conceptual understanding. Together, you will identify and demonstrate what evidence of understanding might look like at different stages in the learning process.

> *Evidence*—In some settings, evidence is referred to as *data*. The most important thing to recognise is that data, or evidence, comes in many different forms.

HOW TO USE THIS BOOK

We invite you to use this book as a guide. It is packed with practical models, strategies, and ideas for assessing concepts and conceptual understanding. In addition to the tools you will find throughout the book, the final chapter includes checklists and resources to assist in your efforts to revise or refine your assessment practices.

 Additionally, we've made space for reflection. We hope that when you come across the Transfer and Apply icon, you will pause to consider what you have read and how you might use the concepts in your context. You can do this on your own; however, we encourage you to use this book, and in particular the Transfer and Apply sections, with your teaching team or professional learning network.

Watch for the HINT icon as well. These will highlight key ideas, strategies, and practices for consideration and easy reference.

CHAPTER TWO

Setting the Scene for Assessing Conceptual Understanding

Assessment in this spirit does not concern assignment of grades or evaluation of whether instruction was effective. It's assessment designed squarely to feed into the learning process and make the learning stronger.

—— David Perkins, *Making Learning Whole* ——

In this chapter, we will explore the purpose of continuous assessment and its benefits for both educators and our learners. We will identify principles of integrating assessment of conceptual understanding in the learning process and discuss its connection to differentiation. Additionally, we will introduce two models for effective assessment: the "Model for Continuous Assessment for Conceptual Understanding," which will be examined throughout the book and the "Process Model for Assessing Understanding," which is examined in detail at the end of the book.

Let's start by defining continuous assessment and its role in the learning process.

THE ROLE OF CONTINUOUS ASSESSMENT

In their 2021 study of assessment-informed differentiation in the classroom, Eysink and Schildkamp note that "formative assessment can be defined as a *continuous* and cyclical process of gathering evidence about learning and using that evidence to guide the learning process of learners through clear and detailed instruction, together with feedback" (emphasis added).

EDUCATOR'S VOICE

"Continuous assessment is ongoing, in real time, through observation, dialogue, photographic and video evidence within the context of the learning. Learning is a process and not a product. It is fluid and can take place between students or teacher/students. The process of assessing is reflecting on what you're doing and looking for next steps."

— Rachel Gonin, Language Curriculum Lead and Grade 2 and 3 teacher, ACS Egham, Surrey, England

Like formative assessment, continuous assessment occurs throughout the learning process. We stress the phrase *continuous* to reinforce its real-time nature. Rather than waiting until the end of a unit or even the end of the week, continuous assessment involves ongoing observation, feedback, and documentation of the learners' inquiry, investigations, and dialogue. It is a means of determining learners' current thinking and continually changing understanding.

We view continuous assessment as being interwoven into the learning process. When teachers and learners co-construct the rubric for assessment, the shared responsibility honours the learners and their journey. As we noted in *Taking the Complexity Out of Concepts,* the trust that develops through this collaborative effort promotes positive relationships between educators and their learners." It also promotes better academic achievement. Stiggins and Chappuis in their research noted, "Evidence gathered over decades from around the world reveals strong achievement gains and reduced achievement score gaps when teachers implement student-involved classroom assessment practices in support of student learning in their classrooms."

EDUCATOR'S VOICE

"We can use the criteria in order to empower students to identify where they are in the learning process. It allows students to have clarity and to see how everything in the classroom is important to develop their understanding. This promotes student autonomy which in turn promotes differentiation. When students see that assessment is ongoing and not isolated it gives them a road map for improvement. This means that no matter where students are in the learning process (in early stages or later stages) they know where they are heading and don't need to be stressed. They can extend or follow."

Claire Margaret Cotton, Head of Department: Arts,
Middle School Teacher, Drama and English A,
Stonehill International School, Bangalore, India

Although research validates the academic benefits of continuous, co-constructed assessment, our focus is not solely on higher scores but on better teaching and deeper understanding. Quality teaching demands that educators use their professional judgement to assess what is necessary to help learners achieve. By assessing learners in real time, educators can immediately identify areas where learners need improvement.

Continuous assessment relies on educators and learners working together to gather evidence of learning over time. The collaborative nature of the assessment ensures everyone is aware of the expectations for the evidence and the goals for understanding. The evidence can then be used to enhance learning opportunities, which leads to another benefit of continuous assessment: when learners feel supported and can see their progress in real time, over time, they are more likely to stay engaged and motivated.

> **HINT!** Rather than a few formative assessments, provide tools that learners can use throughout the learning process to check their understanding.

Finally, continuous assessment increases the reliability of evidence of true learning. "Concerning reliability, continuous assessment would lead to more stable judgements of learner achievement (through collection of more extensive information over time and consultative judgements among teachers)," stated researchers Maxwell and Cumming in their work on assessment reform. With multiple data entry points collected and moderated over time, the assessment focuses less on memory and test-taking skills and puts the emphasis on understanding, including the ability to transfer and apply learning.

EDUCATOR'S VOICE

"(Continuous assessment) allows me to adjust my teaching—learning where students are on an ongoing basis. It gives me more information to see growth."

— Susan Bartley, Grade 5, The International School, Ho Chi Minh City, Vietnam

Why Continuous Assessment?

To summarise, here are the main purposes and benefits of continuous assessment:

- Provide timely feedback
- Identify areas for improvement
- Improve teaching
- Enhance student engagement
- Support evaluation

PROVIDE TIMELY FEEDBACK	**IDENTIFY AREAS FOR IMPROVEMENT**	**IMPROVE TEACHING**
Timely and ongoing feedback can assist learners to identify areas where they need to clarify concepts by making adjustments to their learning strategies.	Educators and learners use continuous assessment to identify current understanding and what is required to further challenge learners in their conceptual thinking.	Educators can use evidence to reflect and plan for how they might revisit the concepts to assist learners in deepening their understanding of the learning outcomes.

PROVIDE STUDENT ENGAGEMENT	**SUPPORT EVALUATION**
By providing frequent and varied opportunities for learners to demonstrate their understanding of concepts, continuous assessment increases engagement and motivation. The learner is involved.	Continuous assessment provides evidence of learning that both the learner and educator evaluate in order to consider where the learner is in the learning journey.

THE CONNECTION BETWEEN CONTINUOUS ASSESSMENT AND ASSESSMENT FOR UNDERSTANDING

Assessment for understanding focuses on evaluating the learners' depth of comprehension and how well they can transfer and apply the concepts and knowledge they are learning. Continuous assessment allows educators to see that understanding develops and deepens over time.

"Deeper learning seeks to empower students to think deeper, collaborate better, and problem-solve meaningfully. It goes beyond surface-level understanding and memorization and focuses on developing students' higher-order thinking skills and abilities, enabling them to understand and apply knowledge in meaningful ways."

Chris Bronke, "Deeper Learning: Empower Students
to Think, Collaborate, and Problem-Solve"

As we engage learners in activities that foster understanding, continuous assessment allows us to determine where they are in that development process. The evidence we and learners collect enables us to identify the next steps for building on their schema and deepening their learning. When used effectively, this ongoing assessment provides comprehensive insight into our learners' progress toward understanding.

One might argue that all assessment measures understanding. Consider the differences between continuous assessment and assessment as outlined in Figure 2.1. Note the valuable distinctions. When we regularly and consistently check for evidence of understanding, we can meet our learners where they are and provide the support they need to succeed.

Continuous Assessment	Assessment
Concept map that learners revisit and add to throughout the learning, showing theirs and the educator's new learning and new understandings	A quiz administered partway through the learning to test knowledge
A Rubric for Understanding providing a continuum of understanding that both learners and educators use throughout the learning to provide feedback and plan next steps	A rubric based on proficiency used to assess a product at the end of the learning
A range of assessment tools and strategies designed and scaffolded for all learners individually	The same single assessment tool or strategy used for all learners

Using multiple examples of evidence to understand that all learning is an opportunity for both learners and educators to evaluate where learners are in their understanding	Two formative assessment tools used in the learning to assess where learners are

Figure 2.1 Differences Between Continuous Assessment and Assessment

Can you think of a time when you used continuous assessment?

What was the assessment?

_____

_____

What were you assessing?

_____

_____

How did you know it was continuous?

_____

_____

How did using continuous assessment impact your ongoing planning and teaching?

_____

_____

What were the benefits of using continuous assessments? What were the downfalls or things to consider?

_____

_____

6 PRINCIPLES FOR ASSESSING CONCEPTUAL UNDERSTANDING

The following principles outline the *what* and the *why* of assessment for conceptual understanding. We've listed them here for your reflection and so that you can easily share these key ideas with your colleagues. As you read each principle, consider what you might want or need to do more (or less) of to effectively and continuously assess understanding.

Assessing for conceptual understanding is a shared process between educators and learners in documenting, collecting, and evaluating learning to inform progress.	Assessing for conceptual understanding involves clear criteria that focuses on building understanding over time. These can be designed by the learner and/or educator.
Assessing for conceptual understanding is a collaboration between educators, learner and educator, and between learners.	Assessing for conceptual understanding involves high levels of learner self reflection, goal setting, and regulation.
Assessing for conceptual understanding is diverse and differentiated to meet the varying learner needs going beyond "one size fits all" to tasks that are designed to provide authentic opportunities for valid assessment.	Assessing conceptual understanding is evaluating a learner's understanding of fundamental concepts and their ability to transfer and apply that knowledge and understanding to authentic situations.

1. **A shared process between educators and learners in documenting, collecting, and evaluating learning to inform progress**
    - Ongoing monitoring of progress ensures that both the educator and learners are aware of how they are developing a deep understanding of the concepts.
    - Documentation of learning takes place throughout the learning around the levels of understanding. Ongoing evaluation ensures effective evidence of understanding and informs the planning for next steps in the learning process.

2. **Involves clear criteria that focuses on building understanding over time. These can be designed by the learner and/or educator**
   ◦ Educators and (where appropriate) learners develop levels of understanding around the understanding questions. These levels form the criteria for the learning and give both educators and learners clear guidelines on how to build conceptual understanding over time.

3. **A collaboration between educators, between the learner and educator, and between learners**
   ◦ Learners and educators both need clarity regarding the levels of understanding. Making everyone aware of the expectations promotes collaboration of learning and assessment.
   ◦ Collaboration involves co-construction of the criteria through peer assessment, year-level moderation, feedback, dialoguing, and conferencing.

4. **Involves high levels of learner self-reflection, goal setting, and regulation**
   ◦ The ability to self-regulate, set goals, and plan for next steps for learning is core to developing an assessment-capable learner. Building the capability for self-assessment involves providing opportunities for learners to develop the skills to engage in deep self-reflection.
   ◦ Clear criteria for various levels of understanding enable learners to consider questions such as *Where is my current understanding? How do I know? What can I do to deepen my understanding?*

5. **Diverse and differentiated to meet the varying learner needs, going beyond "one size fits all" to tasks that are designed to provide authentic opportunities for assessment**
   ◦ Ensure the evidence collected is a reliable gauge of understanding by offering options for how learners can demonstrate their learning.

- ◦ Use the Rubric for Understanding to guide decisions on how to best gather evidence and differentiate assessment tasks.
- ◦ Provide a range of options with established and clear criteria to encourage optimal participation and opportunities for personalised learning.

6. **Evaluates a learner's understanding of fundamental concepts and their ability to transfer and apply that knowledge and understanding to authentic situations**

- ◦ Authentic assessment involves creating assessments that reflect authentic application and require critical thinking and problem-solving skills.
- ◦ Using continuous assessment, educators and learners assess conceptual understanding and the ability to transfer and apply that understanding to authentic contexts.

 Consider the questions below as you reflect on the 6 Principles of Assessment to consider how you can transfer and apply these to your teaching.

When have you used the assessment principles?

What did it look like? How do you know?

or

What might these principles in action look like?

What might the learner be doing? What might the educator be doing?

1　**Assessing conceptual understanding is evaluating a learner's understanding of fundamental concepts and their ability to transfer and apply that knowledge and understanding to authentic situations.**

_____

_____

2   Assessing for conceptual understanding involves clear criteria that focuses on building understanding over time. These can be designed by the learner and/or educator.

3   Assessing for conceptual understanding is a collaboration between educators, the learner and educator, and between learners.

4   Assessing for conceptual understanding involves high levels of learner self-reflection, goal setting, and regulation.

5   Assessing for conceptual understanding is diverse and differentiated to meet the varying learner needs, going beyond "one size fits all" to engagements that are designed to provide authentic opportunities for valid assessment.

6   Assessing for conceptual understanding is a shared process between educators and learners in documenting, collecting, and evaluating learning to inform progress.

> *In planning for conceptual understanding, assessment is key. Without assessment and evaluation, we cannot respond to the needs of our learners. It is through our continuous assessment that we adapt the learning. We plan in response to our learners and not for them.*

THE RELATIONSHIP BETWEEN CONTINUOUS ASSESSMENT AND DIFFERENTIATION

> *"If we say we value student thinking and understanding but largely assess 'right answers' and spend most of our class time doing rote drills on information and skills, the goal of developing students who are engaged thinkers is merely a delusion."*
>
> — Carol Anne Tomlinson, Tonya Moon, and Marcia B. Imbeau, "Assessment and Student Success in a Differentiated Classroom: White Paper"

Continuous assessment is linked to differentiation through its design and the activities in which learners engage. Because the evidence we collect reveals current understanding as well as our learners' diverse needs, it can be used to guide our teaching.

Our learners' self-assessment and ability to recognise and analyse evidence of conceptual understanding also provide valuable insights to further inform our instruction.

The central purpose of continuous assessment is to enhance our teaching and improve the learning that happens in our classrooms. It is essential, therefore, to allow time to pause, reflect, and then to adjust the learning according to the needs indicated by the evidence. As Carol Anne Tomlinson states, "Assessment is today's means of modifying tomorrow's instruction" (2003).

In a learning environment where differentiated assessment of understanding is utilized, we would see the following:

- Questions that identify what learners should know, understand, and be able to transfer and apply. (These are examined further in Chapter Three.)
- Flexible groupings and respectful tasks that provide rigorous and engaging learning that challenges but also complements learner needs
- Diverse engagements in which learners have opportunities to demonstrate their understanding in a variety of ways
- Multifaceted evidence of understanding that is made visible in the learning environment and acts as a collaborative place for shared understanding

Differentiation and continuous assessment work hand in hand, which is why we strongly believe that continuous assessment is the most effective way to differentiate the learning. When continuously assessing, both the educator and learners are considering next steps in connection with learners' current understanding. Learners are at different stages and require a variety of learning strategies and tools to assist them in moving to the next stages of their learning. It is not a "one-size-fits-all" approach. Continuous assessment is about assessing, evaluating, and differentiating.

The Connection Between Continuous Assessment and Differentiation

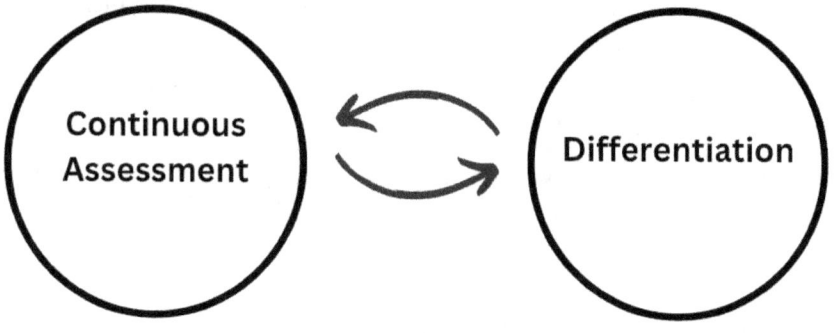

Continuously assess throughout the learning process.

Evaluate and use information from the assessment to differentiate the learning.

Continuous Assessment ⇄ Differentiation

It is continuous with each feeding into each other.

HINT! Differentiation does not require the development of different learning for each individual student. It is about looking for patterns and noticing similarities and differences within our learners and then continually grouping and regrouping them.

EDUCATOR'S VOICE

"[When using the Rubric of Understanding] I was able to immediately say which level a particular problem was connected to so I could differentiate the learning. I could easily explain why the problems were at different levels and refer to the rubric for how students could progress onto the higher levels."

— Lucy Allsopp, Math and Science Coach, KAUST School, Jeddah, Saudi Arabia

 Can you think of a time when you used assessment to inform next stages in the planning process and how that differentiated the learning?

MODEL FOR CONTINUOUS ASSESSMENT FOR CONCEPTUAL UNDERSTANDING

We have developed a process for continuous assessment that informs core approaches for assessing conceptual understanding. This process is key to ensuring that the learning taking place is responsive to the needs of all learners. The following chapters connect to and expand on this model and provide educators with examples and strategies for implementing this process. The most important thing to recognise is that this process is taking place continually (hence continuous assessment). It is used throughout the learning to build deep conceptual learning.

Reflect and Respond
Based on the evidence collated, regular and ongoing feedback is provided to learners during the learning process (peer, self, educator) which helps learners identify their strengths and areas for improvement in order to adjust the learning accordingly.

Design and Create
Develop understanding questions and identify concepts to design the criteria for the rubric for understanding. This can be co-created with learners.

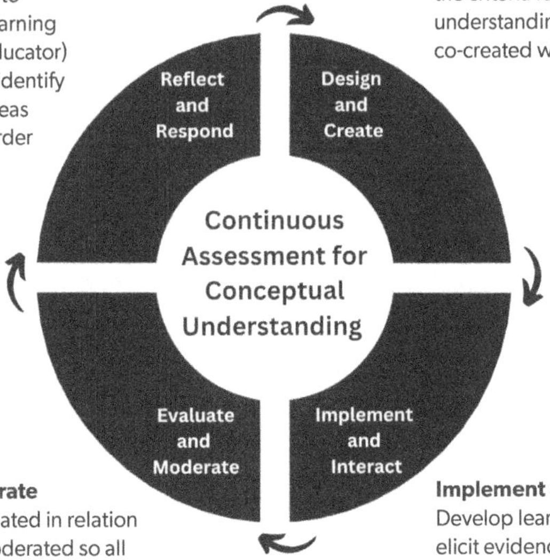

Continuous Assessment for Conceptual Understanding

Reflect and Respond — Design and Create — Evaluate and Moderate — Implement and Interact

Evaluate and Moderate
The evidence is evaluated in relation to the criteria. It is moderated so all have a clear understanding of next steps. The evaluation of terms is ongoing.

Implement and Interact
Develop learning engagements to elicit evidence of understanding that are varied and differentiated. Learners and educators collect evidence of learning around the criteria in the rubric for understanding.

A PROCESS MODEL FOR EDUCATORS AND LEARNERS IN ASSESSING UNDERSTANDING

This diagram represents stages and cyclical nature of continuous assessment. This is examined and explained in detail in the last chapter of the book.

CHAPTER THREE

Rubrics for Understanding

"Although nearly all teachers can report what they will 'cover' in a lesson or unit and what their students will do in the lesson or unit, few can specify precisely what students should know, understand, and be able to do as a result of participating in those segments of learning."

———— Carol Anne Tomlinson and Tonya Moon, ————
Assessment and Student Success

A Rubric for Understanding is an essential tool that aids educators and learners in continuous assessment while building deeper understanding over time. In this chapter, we examine the purpose and development of a Rubric for Understanding. We provide a step-by-step guide on creating effective rubrics *with* learners as they take an active role in their assessment process. Offering examples from various subject areas, we demonstrate how a rubric can serve both as a foundation to build on and a model that clearly outlines the criteria and expectations for each new level of understanding. As we delve into the design-and-create aspect of the learning cycle, we consider what kinds of questions best guide the progression of learning. Additionally, we offer insight on how to ensure consistency and fairness in evaluation and reporting by establishing clear guidelines for evidence of learning.

Designing for Conceptual Understanding

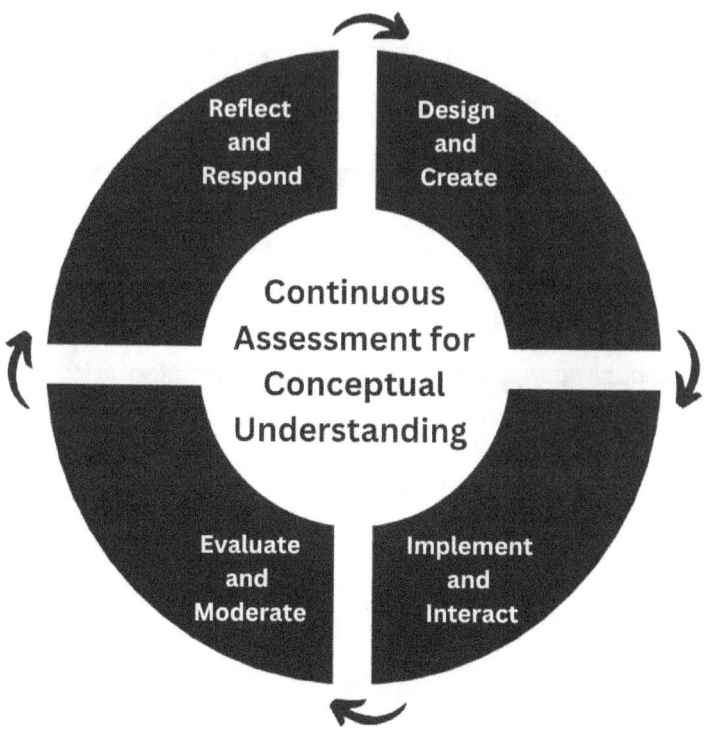

Design and Create
Develop understanding questions and identify concepts to design the criteria
for the Rubric for Understanding. This can be co-created with learners.

Throughout this book, we'll come back to the value of continuous assessment. One powerful tool that is beneficial, even essential, to the process is the Rubric for Understanding. This tool provides valuable insights into the learning process to both learners and educators by outlining how to check for understanding, what understanding looks like, and how to take learning to the next level.

Beyond assessment, the **rubric can be used as a planning tool to create engaging and challenging learning experiences.** By enabling educators to design learning experiences that promote higher-order thinking, deep learning, and authentic knowledge application, the rubric enhances learner achievement. Practising these skills is important because, as Paul Main states, rubrics allow students to "develop their capacity for critical thinking, problem-solving, and cognitive flexibility, all of which are essential skills for success in today's complex and rapidly changing world."

In contrast, we've found that without a rubric that clearly establishes progressive levels of understanding, learning tends to stall at the knowledge level rather than evolve into deeper conceptual understanding. For instance, educators may have learners describe an event or person. Further learning could include exploring that event's or person's impact or contribution. Taking the learning deeper still might entail developing theories related to that impact. With clearly established next steps, learners are challenged to think more deeply and to make connections across subject areas.

The Rubric for Understanding promotes . . .

- Continuous assessment
- The collection of evidence to check for understanding
- Effective and usable feedback
- Developing strategies that meet learners' needs
- Moving learners from knowledge to understanding
- Making connections for deeper learning
- Collaboration between learners and teachers

Getting to Know the Rubric for Understanding

The Basic Element of the Rubric for Understanding		
Visual Representation of the Levels	**Levels**	**Possible Command Terms for the Levels**
○ _____ ○ _____ ○ _____ ○ _____	**Level 1: Recalling** Learners recall and identify knowledge that relates to the conceptual questions.	Identify Recall Know Name Recognise Retell
	Level 2: Describing Learners describe in some detail information related to the conceptual questions. Learners begin to make inferences and interpret their understandings, making simple connections.	Describe Categorise Interpret Classify Define Distinguish Recount
	Level 3: Explaining and Connecting Learners make comparisons between existing knowledge and the concepts. They are able to explain in detail what they have learnt and the connections within it, with reasoning and evidence.	Connect Compare and Contrast Explain Reason Formulate Differentiate Reason Express
	Level 4: Analysing and Applying Learners analyse and evaluate through reasoning and application. Learners make new connections and justify their analysis using evidence and reason.	Evaluate Analyse Synthesise Critique Transfer Justify

ESSENTIALS OF THE RUBRIC FOR UNDERSTANDING

We explore the concepts introduced below more thoroughly in the coming chapters, but to ensure understanding as we explore the rubric, we wanted to offer a brief overview of some essential vocabulary. Some of these terms can be used in multiple ways, and we want to ensure that for the purposes of this book, we are all on the same page, so to speak.

Moderation

"One of the most profoundly important elements in designing for inquiry learning is the dialogue we have around the 'planning table' about the concepts and big ideas that lie at the heart of any inquiry journey. If the journey is exploring the way living things adapt to changing environments, it is not enough simply to find a few resources and develop some activities. We need to interrogate our own thinking about this big idea. What do we really understand about adaptation? What background knowledge do we bring to this?"

— Kath Murdoch, *Planning for Inquiry*

Moderation refers to the process of reviewing, understanding, and assessing learning. This practice involves educators and learners actively participating in the evaluation process. Educators and learners play a crucial role by reviewing evidence on an ongoing basis to ensure consistency of learning in connection with established criteria. This collaborative approach to moderation fosters a supportive learning environment, encourages continuous improvement, and promotes a deeper understanding of expectations.

Bringing multiple perspectives on the learning during the moderation process reveals insights that an educator may miss because of personal bias.

"[The rubric] makes sure that as a team we are on the same page as to what the main hitting points are. It doesn't tell us exactly how and when to teach parts of the unit but gives us the what. We can all put our individual spins on it and use it in our class based on our students."

— Ashley Sims, Grade 1, The International School, Ho Chi Minh City, Vietnam

Command Terms

To moderate learning consistently and fairly, educators and learners must understand the command terms used in the rubric. Having learners unpack what each command term means ensures that the expectations are clear for everyone. We suggest that command terms (and other elements of the rubric) be shared amongst all educators teaching the same subject and year level. Adopting a common language creates a stronger connection to the Rubric for Understanding for everyone and ensures consistency in moderation.

Command terms can include words such as *recall, know, name, describe, define, classify, connect, formulate, differentiate, evaluate, justify,* and *critique.* You'll find additional examples in the sample rubric on page 40. We invite you to also choose your own relevant command terms as you and your learners develop your rubric together.

"All who will be using the rubric need to have a voice in it—teachers and students alike. That way there is a common understanding and clarity as to what is expected."

— Louise McQuade, Grade 5, St Joseph's Institution International, Singapore

Levels of Conceptual Understanding

"There is no single, universally accepted and absolutely correct learning progression."

—————————————— W. James Popham, "All About Accountability"

Learners have different abilities and interests; as such, they may take the learning in different directions. The Rubric for Understanding allows for differentiated learning by empowering learners to demonstrate their understanding in a variety of ways. The key is defining the understanding level. The rubric is a powerful tool that provides educators with a common language and command terms for discussing and clarifying levels of cognitive complexity. It informs the design of instructional learning and is a tool for evaluating learner progress. To reinforce that, assessing for conceptual understanding is a collaboration between learner and educator, teaching teams, learner and learners, and it can take on many different forms.

The levels of conceptual understanding provide an opportunity for learners to personalise their own pace and progression for learning. It recognizes that individuals learn and acquire knowledge at different rates and in different ways. By developing the Rubric for Understanding, we are recognizing and respecting the varied pace and progression of learners that is essential in creating inclusive and effective learning environments. By doing so, educators can support each individual's growth, foster a love for learning, and maximise their potential for success.

The criteria in the rubric need to be clear and specific. The Rubric for Understanding and the criteria have been developed and adapted from Norman Webb's (2005) Depth of Knowledge (DOK). Schools may currently use Bloom's Taxonomy or Solo Taxonomy or Webb's Depth of Knowledge (DOK). All are frameworks that support teaching, learning, and assessment, but they differ in their focus and application. Bloom's Taxonomy centers on the type of cognitive skills students develop, progressing from lower-order skills to higher-order skills. SOLO Taxonomy emphasizes the depth and progression of understanding, moving from fragmented knowledge to integrated and abstract thinking. Webb's DOK focuses on the complexity of tasks and the depth of engagement required to complete them.

Unlike Bloom's and SOLO, DOK can be directly tied to task design and used to collect evidence of learning by analyzing the level of complexity at which students are working. It allows educators to measure how deeply students are reasoning, analyzing, and applying their knowledge through observable actions. This task-based focus makes DOK particularly valuable for assessing what students know and how they apply that knowledge in varied and complex contexts.

The key purpose of the Rubric for Understanding is that it provides *criteria for assessing how well learners demonstrate understanding*. It is organised using four levels for the purpose of informing continual assessment where evidence of learning is assessed against descriptors explaining what each level of understanding looks like.

Notice how they move from a surface level of knowledge to a deep level of understanding to an ability to transfer understanding to other areas. By clearly defining levels of understanding, educators and learners alike can monitor progress throughout the unit because everyone is aware of what success looks like.

The levels of understanding are as follows:

Level 1: Recalling—Learners recall and identify knowledge that relates to the conceptual questions.

Level 2: Describing—Learners describe in some detail information related to the conceptual questions. Learners begin to make inferences and interpret their understandings, making simple connections.

Level 3: Explaining and Connecting—Learners make comparisons between existing knowledge and the concepts. They can explain in detail what they have learnt and the connections within it, with reasoning and evidence.

Level 4: Analysing and Applying—Learners analyse and evaluate through reasoning and application. Learners make new connections and justify their analysis using evidence and reason.

"[The rubric] has ensured we have a greater level of depth in our teaching and that we are encouraging our students to think and reflect at a deeper level on their learning."

Laura Matchett, Year 1, St John Vianney's Primary School

Evidence

Evidence is how learners demonstrate understanding. Evidence should be collected, evaluated, and then discussed by educators as well as learners.

Throughout this book, we discussed the importance and value of collaborating with learners to develop the assessment. The same approach applies to evidence. Involve learners in the process of determining what effective evidence of understanding looks like. As Hattie and Donoghue (2016) state, "Students who can articulate or are taught these success criteria are more likely to be strategic in their choice of learning strategies, more likely to enjoy the thrill of success in learning, and more likely to reinvest in attaining even more success criteria."

"Multiple forms of evidence give students a chance to express themselves in a way that works for them, giving them opportunities to show they know more, can use skills and grasp concepts from numerous forms of assessments. E.g., EAL learners are not going to be writing, and some students express themselves either verbally or in writing better but not always both."

Susan Bartley, Grade 5, The International School, Ho Chi Minh City, Vietnam

HOW DO YOU KNOW?

When creating any assessment, asking the right questions is essential. We must be clear about what we want our learners to understand as well as what that understanding looks like.

Before you can create a rubric, you'll need to consider two sides of the same question:

1. How do you know your learners have attained the desired level of understanding?

2. How do your learners know they have attained the desired level of understanding?

Use the following questions or prompts to find the answers you need:

1. Who has understood fully? How do you know?

2. How do you know whether the learner understood the questions?

3. Who needs further scaffolding to build understanding? How do you know?

4. When you evaluate learners' thinking, are you clear about their level of understanding? How do you know?

5. What does the evidence tell you about what the learner understands? How do you know?

6. Are you challenging and engaging learners to engage in higher order thinking? How do you know?

Complexity of Understanding

Each of the four levels in the rubric requires greater complexity of understanding. Building complexity of understanding refers to a continuous and gradual process where learners move from foundational conceptual understanding to more nuanced, interconnected, and abstract ideas. Deep understanding doesn't happen in a moment, rather it evolves as learners engage in progressively more challenging tasks, make connections across different ideas, and apply their understanding in various contexts.

Understanding Questions

Before designing the rubric, educators will develop "understanding questions." These questions define the goals for the learning. In other curriculums and educational settings, *understanding questions* may be referred to as Lines of Inquiry, Conceptual Questions, Essential Questions, Understanding Goals, Understandings, or Big Ideas. We build each level of the rubric using these questions as the starting point.

Criteria for Understanding Questions

When crafting your understanding questions, keep the following guidelines in mind.

> **Understanding questions should be broadly written so as to not be too specific.**

The questions should not be factually based. Instead, they should be written so that there is not a simple answer. Questions should be broadly written to ensure they can be examined conceptually and not only through a factual lens.

> **Understanding questions should provide scope for learners' own inquiries.**

The questions need to be broad enough to encompass learners' interests and further inquiries. Leave room for learners wonder and curiosity!

> **Understanding questions should have concepts embedded within them.**

Conceptual understanding is the focus of the learning. With this in mind, connect the questions to concepts that will develop meaning and relevant learning.

> **Understanding questions should promote depth of understanding and transfer.**

The questions should encourage learners to make connections, build complexity of understanding over time, and then be able to transfer that understanding to other areas.

Understanding Question	Not an Understanding Question
How do people develop technique in individual pursuits?	How can I use a tennis racquet?
How are the interdependent parts of systems connected?	What are the systems of government?
How and why is our world represented?	How do we use maps?
How does community promote a sense of belonging?	What is a community?
How does historical evidence provide insight into the past?	What are the pyramids?
How does context influence the way people communicate?	How do we use language to order food?

How can I interpret and respond to artworks?	How does this artwork make you feel?
How does exploring tools and materials promote creativity?	What can people do with clay?

Using Supporting Questions for Conceptual Connections

When developing understanding questions, because they are broad and transferable, educators can define the parameters of these questions through supporting questions. They support the conceptual nature of the learning. The supporting questions can change and are supplemented by learners' questions that are encouraged throughout the unit.

Understanding Question	Supporting Question (Defining Curriculum Parameters)
How and why is our world represented?	How do we use maps? How do artists represent the world? How do mathematicians represent the world? How do scientists represent the world?
How does exploring tools and materials promote creativity?	Clay: What can I do with clay? How does clay behave? What tools can I use with clay? What effects do the tools make? Wire: What can I do with the wire? How does the wire behave? What tools can I use with wire? What effects do the tools make?
How do quantities help us to understand spaces?	How can I use surface area and volume to solve problems? How can I use trigonometry to find missing side lengths and angles?

6 STEPS TO DEVELOP THE RUBRIC FOR UNDERSTANDING

With this foundation of terms, let's look at exactly how to develop the Rubric for Understanding for a unit in your classroom. Here's a quick overview of the steps:

1   Insert your understanding questions.

2   Start developing the rubric, beginning at Level 3. Use the command terms to assist you.

3   Brainstorm possible evidence of understanding using the Brainstorm Map and other planning tools.

4   Decide on the criteria for Level 2 that will be effective to scaffold thinking toward the level of understanding expected in Level 3.

5   Use Level 2 criteria to guide what will be effective in Level 1 to scaffold thinking toward the level of understanding expected in Level 2.

6   Consider how learners will demonstrate their conceptual understanding through analysing and applying.

For educators who teach IBMYP, we recommend (where possible) that you develop conceptual questions (understanding questions) in connection to the criteria provided by the IB. From there you can develop the Rubric for Understanding using the command terms provided and follow the steps below to move to continuous assessment.

Now, let's take a closer look at each of the steps.

STEP 1: Insert your understanding questions.

Before inserting the questions, consider the effectiveness of the questions for conceptual depth and focus. How do these questions invite conceptual inquiry? If possible, collaborate with other educators to ensure your understanding questions meet the essential criteria.

What an understanding question is...	What an understanding question is not...
What contributes to people's identity?	What do people look like?
How do cultures (past/present) express their beliefs and values?	What do (religious groups) believe in?
How can I express my identity?	What are my characteristics?

TRANSFER & APPLY

Transfer and Apply your Understanding: Use the chart below to examine and reflect on your understanding questions.

Criteria for Understanding Questions	How you know?
The understanding question is broadly written and is not too specific	
The understanding question provides scope for learners' own inquiries and wonderings	
There is a concept embedded in the understanding question	
The understanding question promotes depth of understanding and transfer	

HINT! When developing understanding questions, ask: *How can this question provide scope conceptually so it can be investigated and represented in a variety of ways?*

Once you have reviewed your understanding questions, place them in the rubric.

Level 1: Recalling	Level 2: Describing
Learners recall and identify knowledge that relates to the conceptual questions.	Learners describe in some detail information related to the conceptual questions. Learners begin to make inferences and interpret their understandings.

Understanding Question: What contributes to people's identity?

Understanding Question: How do cultures (past/present) express their beliefs and values?

Understanding Question: How can I express my identity?

Level 3: Explaining and Connecting	Level 4: Analysing and Applying
Learners make comparisons between existing knowledge and the concepts. They are able to explain in detail what they have learnt and the connections within it, with reasoning and evidence.	Learners analyse and evaluate through reasoning and application. Learners make new connections and justify their analysis using evidence and reason.

STEP 2: Brainstorm Possible Evidence of Understanding

Using the brainstorming map or another planning tool, list out what evidence of understanding could look like at each of the four levels.

The process for deciding on criteria for the Rubric for Understanding requires clarity of the conceptual nature of the understanding questions being assessed and clear expectations as to what and how this might develop in terms of evidence of understanding.

In developing a Rubric for Understanding, ask:

- How will I know learners have understood the understanding questions?
- What evidence will I be looking for?
- What will learners be saying and demonstrating to show they understand?

In preparation for Step 2, we recommend discussing what command terms might be the most effective for assessing the concepts you are seeking evidence of within the understanding question. Also ensure that there is a collective understanding of the meaning of the concepts in the context of the unit or learning.

We recommend reviewing the brainstorming template before involving the learners, to ensure a consistent understanding of the concepts driving the learning and where the learning is heading.

> "For students truly to be able to take responsibility for their learning, both teacher and students need to be very clear about what is being learnt, and how they should go about it. When learning and the path toward it are clear, research shows that there are a number of important shifts for students. Their motivation improves, they stay on-task, their behaviour improves, and they are able to take more responsibility for their learning."
>
> — Absolum, M., *Clarity in the Classroom*

Brainstorm Map For Evidence of Understanding

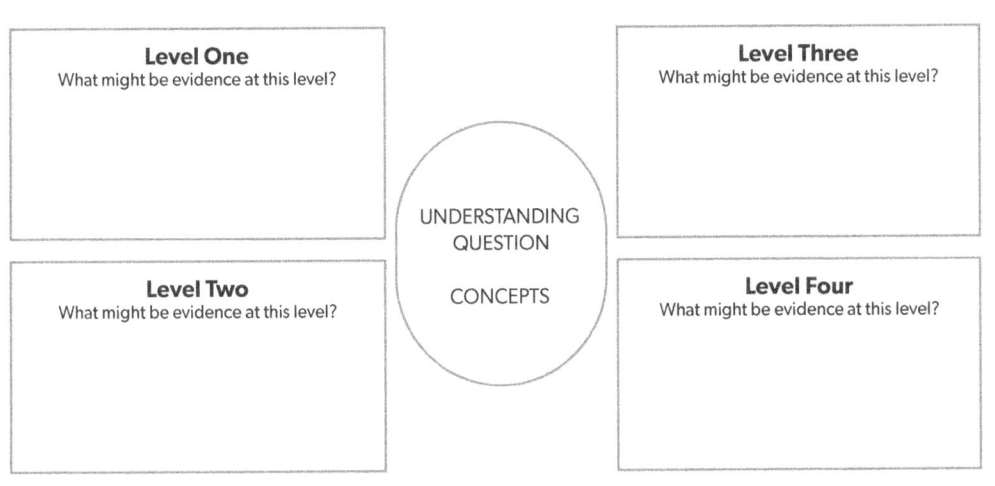

Level One	Level Three
What might be evidence at this level?	What might be evidence at this level?

UNDERSTANDING QUESTION

CONCEPTS

Level Two	Level Four
What might be evidence at this level?	What might be evidence at this level?

Brainstorming Examples

Brainstorm Map For Evidence of Understanding

Level One
What might be evidence at this level?

- Identify different types of identity.
- Name what identity is.
- Recall examples of identity.
- Recognise aspects of identity.

WHAT CONTRIBUTES TO PEOPLE'S IDENTITY?

IDENTITY

Level Two
What might be evidence at this level?

- Describe what identity is.
- Describe different types of identity.
- Categorise different aspects of identity.

Level Three
What might be evidence at this level?

- Explain aspects of identity and how they contribute to people's identity.
- Compare and contrast aspects of identity noticing similarities and differences.
- Explain how factors come together to contribute to someone's identity.

Level Four
What might be evidence at this level?

- Analyse people's identity.
- Evaluate what has the biggest impact on people's identity with reason.
- Synthesise what impacts identity with reason.

Brainstorm Map For Evidence of Understanding

Level One
What might be evidence at this level?

- Recognise how cultures express their beliefs and values.
- Identify past and present beliefs and values in cultures.
- Identify what beliefs and values are.

Level Three
What might be evidence at this level?

- Interpret and explain how beliefs and values define cultures.
- Compare and contrast various beliefs and values of cultures noticing similarities and differences.
- Explain connections that may be reflected in the beliefs and values across cultures.

HOW DO CULTURES (PAST/ PRESENT) EXPRESS THEIR BELIEFS AND VALUES?

BELIEFS/VALUES

Level Two
What might be evidence at this level?

- Describe different ways in which beliefs and values are expressed
- Define past and present beliefs and values in cultures.
- Categorize past and present beliefs and values in cultures.

Level Four
What might be evidence at this level?

- Analyse using evidence for how beliefs and values are expressions of culture.
- Evaluate different cultures and provide evidence as to the reasons there are connections

Brainstorm Map For Evidence of Understanding

Level One
What might be evidence at this level?

- Identify how I express my identity.
- Recognise the different ways I express my identity.

Level Three
What might be evidence at this level?

- Explain how the way I express my identity contributes to my overall identity.
- Compare and contrast how I express my identity noticing similarities and differences.
- Connect how I express my identity to the way I want others to perceive me.

HOW CAN I EXPRESS MY IDENTITY?

EXPRESSION

Level Two
What might be evidence at this level?

- Describe why I express my identity the way I do.
- Describe the different ways I express my identity.
- Define the ways I express my identity.

Level Four
What might be evidence at this level?

- Analyse why I express my identity the way I do.
- Evaluate how others may perceive my identity through the way I express myself with justification.
- Critique how I express myself in connection to how I see my identity.

STEP 3: Start developing the rubric.

Beginning at Level 3, the middle point of understanding, tends to guide what the thinking might look like before and after Level 3.

At Level 3, consider what evidence would enable you to know learners understand the questions.

What might this evidence look like for the learners in your classroom?

Decide on criteria, e.g., "Learners compare and contrast" as highlighted in the example below. This is not a task; it is a level of understanding. *Compare and contrast* can be demonstrated using a variety of strategies and tools. This is why we do not have a specific task, such as "create a Venn diagram" or "use a graphic organiser" at any of the levels—we want to ensure learners are provided with options to demonstrate their understanding.

> *If I am not a good writer, but if I can explain in detail what I understand about the understanding question, I should be able to demonstrate that understanding in ways beyond writing.*

Level 1: Recalling	Level 2: Describing
Learners recall and identify knowledge that relates to the conceptual questions.	Learners describe in some detail information related to the conceptual questions. Learners begin to make inferences and interpret their understandings.

Understanding Question: What contributes to people's identity?

Understanding Question: How do cultures (past/present) express their beliefs and values?

Understanding Question: How can I express my identity?

Level 3: Explaining and Connecting	Level 4: Analysing and Applying
Learners make comparisons between existing knowledge and the concepts. They are able to explain in detail what they have learnt and the connections within it, with reasoning and evidence.	Learners analyse and evaluate through reasoning and application. Learners make new connections and justify their analysis using evidence and reason.
Learners **compare and contrast** factors that contribute to people's identity and **explain** how those factors come together to develop a person's identity.	
Learners **compare and contrast** the ways in which cultures express their beliefs and values. Using **reasoning**, **explain** why some beliefs and values still exist and others do not.	
Learners express their identity and **explain** how their expression **connects** to who they are, their beliefs and values, and the perception they would like others to form in connection to their expression.	

STEP 4: Decide on the success criteria for Level 2 and command terms that will be effective to scaffold the thinking toward the level of understanding expected at Level 3.

Level 1: Recalling	Level 2: Describing
Learners recall and identify knowledge that relates to the conceptual questions.	Learners describe in some detail information related to the conceptual questions. Learners begin to make inferences and interpret their understandings.

Understanding Question: What contributes to people's identity?

	Learners **categorise** factors that contribute to a person's identity and **describe** different factors of people's identity.

Understanding Question: How do cultures (past/present) express their beliefs and values?

	Learners **describe** how cultures express their beliefs and values, which beliefs and values have changed, and which have not.

Understanding Question: How can I express my identity?

	Learners **express** their identity and **describe** how their expression is connected to identity.

Level 3: Explaining and Connecting	Level 4: Analysing and Applying
Learners make comparisons between existing knowledge and the concepts. They are able to explain in detail what they have learnt and the connections within it, with reasoning and evidence.	Learners analyse and evaluate through reasoning and application. Learners make new connections and justify their analysis using evidence and reason.
Learners **compare and contrast** factors that contribute to people's identity and **explain** how those factors com Learners **compare and contrast** factors that contribute to people's identity and **explain** how those factors come together to develop a person's identity.	
Learners **compare and contrast** the ways in which cultures express their beliefs and values. Using **reasoning, explain** why some beliefs and values still exist and others do not.	
Learners express their identity and **explain** how their expression **connects** to who they are, their beliefs and values, and the perception they would like others to form in connection to their expression.	

STEP 5: Decide on the criteria for Level 1 and command terms that will be effective to scaffold the thinking toward the level of understanding expected at Level 2.

Level 1: Recalling	Level 2: Describing
Learners recall and identify knowledge that relates to the conceptual questions.	Learners describe in some detail information related to the conceptual questions. Learners begin to make inferences and interpret their understandings.

Understanding Question: What contributes to people's identity?

Learners **identify** factors that contribute to a person's identity.	Learners **categorise** factors that contribute to a person's identity and **describe** different factors of people's identity.

Understanding Question: How do cultures (past/present) express their beliefs and values?

Learners **identify** the ways cultures express their beliefs and values.	Learners **describe** how cultures express their beliefs and values, which beliefs and values have changed, and which have not.

Understanding Question: How can I express my identity?

Learners **identify** when they are expressing their identity.	Learners **express** their identity and **describe** how their expression is connected to identity.

Level 3: Explaining and Connecting	Level 4: Analysing and Applying
Learners make comparisons between existing knowledge and the concepts. They are able to explain in detail what they have learnt and the connections within it, with reasoning and evidence.	Learners analyse and evaluate through reasoning and application. Learners make new connections and justify their analysis using evidence and reason.
Learners **compare and contrast** factors that contribute to people's identity and **explain** how those factors com Learners **compare and contrast** factors that contribute to people's identity and **explain** how those factors come together to develop a person's identity.	
Learners **compare and contrast** the ways in which cultures express their beliefs and values. Using **reasoning, explain** why some beliefs and values still exist and others do not.	
Learners express their identity and **explain** how their expression **connects** to who they are, their beliefs and values, and the perception they would like others to form in connection to their expression.	

STEP 6: Consider how learners will demonstrate their conceptual understanding through analysing and applying.

Level 1: Recalling	Level 2: Describing
Learners recall and identify knowledge that relates to the conceptual questions.	Learners describe in some detail information related to the conceptual questions. Learners begin to make inferences and interpret their understandings.

Understanding Question: What contributes to people's identity?

Learners **identify** factors that contribute to a person's identity.	Learners **categorise** factors that contribute to a person's identity and **describe** different factors of people's identity.

Understanding Question: How do cultures (past/present) express their beliefs and values?

Learners **identify** the ways cultures express their beliefs and values.	Learners **describe** how cultures express their beliefs and values, which beliefs and values have changed, and which have not.

Understanding Question: How can I express my identity?

Learners **identify** when they are expressing their identity.	Learners **express** their identity and **describe** how their expression is connected to identity.

This level is an evaluative process in which learners apply, analyse, evaluate, and transfer their deeper learning.

Level 3: Explaining and Connecting	Level 4: Analysing and Applying
Learners make comparisons between existing knowledge and the concepts. They are able to explain in detail what they have learnt and the connections within it, with reasoning and evidence.	Learners analyse and evaluate through reasoning and application. Learners make new connections and justify their analysis using evidence and reason.
Learners **compare and contrast** factors that contribute to people's identity and **explain** how those factors com Learners **compare and contrast** factors that contribute to people's identity and **explain** how those factors come together to develop a person's identity.	Learners **evaluate** which factors have the greatest impact on a person's identity and which factors can lead to perceived ideas about people's identity, with **reasoning.**
Learners **compare and contrast** the ways in which cultures express their beliefs and values. Using **reasoning, explain** why some beliefs and values still exist and others do not.	Learners **evaluate** how cultures express their beliefs and values, the impact this has on cultures, and others' perception of that culture, with **reasoning.**
Learners express their identity and **explain** how their expression **connects** to who they are, their beliefs and values, and the perception they would like others to form in connection to their expression.	Learners **analyse** their and others' expression of beliefs and values and **evaluate** which expressions are the most connected to perceived ideas of a person's identity.

"For me personally, rubrics make it very clear what students should be achieving and when they aren't achieving at a level. Also, when they need extending and further challenge. When you create a rubric, the teacher is very clear on the target—where you are trying to get the student to—but it also means consideration is given to what might be the next step in achievement for those students who need extending."

— Catherine Doig, Year 5 and 6, Holy Spirit Nicholls, Canberra, Australia

CONSIDERATIONS WHEN DEVELOPING THE RUBRIC FOR UNDERSTANDING

Developmental—Some learners may have prior knowledge and experience that puts their starting point beyond Level 1. This will not become evident until the learning is in process. Similarly, some learners may demonstrate an understanding at a Level 3 but revisit Level 1 to gather more knowledge with which to provide evidence for their thinking and understanding. It is about knowing your learners and responding to where their understanding is.

Not an Activity—As mentioned above, it is key to understanding that the levels are written not as activities, but rather as levels of understanding. Learners should have the opportunity to demonstrate each level of understanding in ways that are meaningful to them. Allowing for a variety of options for demonstrating understanding addresses the diverse needs within the learning community, promoting differentiation.

Planning Emerges from the Levels—The rubric is used as an assessment and planning tool. As the unit progresses, educators and learners are considering where they are in connection to the rubric and what next steps might be. This ensures that the conceptual focus of the learning is at the forefront and that educators and learners are planning specifically for deep understanding and transfer.

No Negative Language—With a focus on building levels of understanding, you will notice the absence of negative language. We do not use terms such as *with support* or *cannot* or *limited* (e.g., "cannot as yet identify geometrical shapes in their environment"). Instead, build the expectations of the levels so the difference between them, in terms of rigour and expectation, is clear.

No Quantities—In the rubrics we have purposefully avoided including quantities. We have not suggested learners have an amount they need to do, because more does not necessarily equate to understanding. I may be able to describe many ideas; however, it is my explanation, which may focus on fewer ideas and providing more detail, that indicates my developing understanding. The complexity is in the level of understanding.

Merging Questions or Levels—Because of how conceptually integrated units can be, it may be logical to combine more than one understanding question in a single continuum. Understanding questions can be merged to make the assessment more authentic and efficient.

It looks like there's an extra line or increased leading between paragraphs here. also can be done for levels, where there is no clear distinction. Educators may merge levels together to ensure a flow in the development of understanding. It is important that each level builds on the previous level and the difference between the levels is understood by all.

See more examples of Rubrics for Understanding in the Appendix.

ADDITIONAL TIPS FOR SUCCESSFULLY USING RUBRICS FOR UNDERSTANDING

Establishing Common Language and Shared Expectations—We strongly suggest collaboration when developing the Rubric for Understanding. Using a common language and establishing clear expectations across the grade level or subject area promotes moderation and clear pathways for learning.

Planning with *Your* Learners' Needs in Mind—When planning, your first consideration must be your learners. What learning has already occurred in your classroom? What have your learners understood? What do they know? Plan from there. Other educators may be facilitating the same unit; however, the needs of your learners should determine how the unit unfolds in your classroom.

Although it is mutually beneficial for educators within a school setting to have a shared understanding of the purpose and concepts driving the learning, every educator or learner does not need to follow the same path. Learning can and should look different in each class based on the needs, understanding level, and interests of the learners.

Planning *with* Your Learners—See the examples of Rubrics for Understanding and how to develop them. We have decided to include these to guide educators on clarifying how the Rubrics for Understanding can be developed. However, we strongly advocate for learner involvement when developing Rubrics for Understanding, to ensure that learners are aware of the levels so they can become self-adjusters of their learning. This also promotes learners taking more responsibility for their learning.

1-Point Rubric for Understanding

Clearly, we advocate using a Rubric for Understanding that focuses on developing complexity of understanding over time. The four levels in the rubric we've outlined show clear progress toward this goal and allow all to see where learners are on the continuum.

We also know that for various reasons some educators opt to use a 1-Point Rubric for Understanding rather than the full rubric with all four levels of understanding. These 1-point rubrics can be adapted for tasks and disciplines, making them a versatile tool for assessment in learning. Educators might choose to use a 1-point rubric for several reasons.

Simplicity and Clarity—One-point rubrics provide one entry point for learners and educators and therefore are more straightforward. They focus on describing the desired outcome or performance level without the complexity of multiple levels of proficiency.

Efficiency in Assessment—Because there is only one performance level to assess, using a 1-point rubric can be more efficient for educators and learners. It allows for focused feedback on areas in which learners have met the criteria and areas for improvement.

Promotion of Self-Assessment—One-point rubrics encourage learners to reflect on their own work and assess their performance against the criteria provided. This promotes metacognitive skills and empowers learners to take ownership of their learning.

A 1-Point Rubric for Understanding assessment tool, however, does not focus on the development of understanding over time; instead, it provides educators and learners with evidence on a single level. With that in mind, we suggest making that single point the equivalent of Level 3: Explaining and Connecting. At this level, learners make comparisons between existing knowledge and the concepts. They can explain what they have learnt and the connections within the concepts, with reasoning and evidence.

We still encourage educators to collaborate in considering what the understanding would look like and, where possible, to involve learners in the process. Use command terms and descriptors from level 3. As the learning takes place, evaluate the evidence with your learners to determine whether their learning has met or exceeded that level of understanding.

Below are examples of 1-Point Rubrics for Understanding.

Understanding Questions	Evidence of Understanding
How and why is measuring with accuracy important?	Learners • Select the tool to measure and explain why they have selected that tool. • Demonstrate how to accurately measure and explain why accuracy is key in measurement. • Record their measurements using correct terminology and symbols and explain the measurement to the nearest 0.5 with accuracy.

Understanding Questions	Evidence of Understanding
How do symbols carry meaning?	Learners • Compare and contrast symbols (numbers and mathematical symbols, letters and grammatical symbols, map symbols, symbols in our community, Chinese symbols, musical symbols). • Explain how symbols are similar and why, (including: what the radical is and why it is the same in each character). • Explain the differences between symbols connected to their purpose, including characters and how that changes the meaning of the word. • Explain the connection between the symbol and its meaning.

Understanding Questions	Evidence of Understanding
Why and how are cultural beliefs and values expressed?	Learners • Investigate and differentiate, using a range of resources as to how beliefs and values are expressed (symbols, artifacts, music, art, traditions, celebrations). • Compare and contrast how diverse cultural beliefs and values are expressed. • Explain the connections between beliefs and values and how they are expressed.

Understanding Questions	Evidence of Understanding
How and where are forces applied in our world?	Learners • Compare and contrast objects in the world that use force. • Demonstrate how people use the objects and explain how the types of forces are similar and different in the way they move, supporting their thinking with evidence.

Understanding Questions	Evidence of Understanding
How is the use and purpose of different forms of digital media decided?	Learners • Compare and contrast different forms of media and explain how they are similar or different in connection to their use. • Make connections between what people want to share and why they chose that media tool. • Distinguish between the different media in terms of target audience and effectiveness of the media.

Understanding Questions	Evidence of Understanding
Is globalisation a good thing or not and why?	Learners • Explain globalisation and distinguish what it looks like in different countries, with evidence. • Compare, contrast, and explain the impact of globalisation in different countries (positive or negative), with evidence. • Evaluate the impact of globalisation and use claims make an argument as to whether globalisation is good or bad.

EMPOWERING STUDENTS TO BE ASSESSMENT-CAPABLE LEARNERS

Frey, Fisher, and Hattie (2018) describe an "assessment-capable learner" as a student who

- Is aware of their current level of understanding in a learning area.
- Understands their learning path and is confident enough to take on the challenge.
- Can select tools and resources to guide their learning.
- Seeks feedback and recognizes that errors are opportunities to learn.
- Monitors their own progress and adjusts course as needed.

When learners are involved in their assessment, they take ownership and responsibility for their learning. They learn to become self-regulators and adjusters of the process. Thus, to support learner agency, we strongly suggest developing the Rubrics for Understanding with your learners, using their language. Doing so helps them understand what success looks like at each of the levels and how to get there.

As you develop your rubric with your learners, one way to ensure they understand the expectations is to have them create *I can* statements.

Using their own words, learners can clarify what the criteria looks like at each level.

Learner Success Criteria Examples

Level 1: Recalling—Learners recall and identify knowledge that relates to the understanding questions.
Learner Criteria: I can **identify** aspects of the concept.

Level 2: Describing—Learners describe in some detail information related to the conceptual questions. Learners begin to make inferences and interpret their understandings.
Learner Criteria: I can **describe** or **categorise** ideas connected to the understanding question.

Level 3: Explaining and Connecting—Learners make comparisons between existing knowledge and the concepts. They are able to explain in detail what they have learnt and the connections within it, with reasoning and evidence.
Learner Criteria: I can make **connections** with the understanding question and **explain** the connections with **reasoning.**

Level 4: Analysing and Applying—Learners analyse and evaluate through reasoning and application. Learners make new connections and justify their analysis using evidence and reason.
Learner Criteria: I can **analyse** the understanding question and **evaluate** the effectiveness of my response with **evidence** or **reasoning**.

You can also connect *I can* statements directly to specific understanding questions.

In the following examples, the learner criteria connect directly to the understanding questions. The specificity of the criteria that are written in the learners' language empowers them to be involved in monitoring their progress and clearly outlines the expectations at each level in the Rubric for Understanding.

Understanding Innovation

Developed with the Grade 5 team at KAUST School, Saudia Arabia

This rubric was developed with the specific intention of involving learners in the continuous assessment process. First, educators developed the Rubric for Understanding and clarified the criteria for each level. Then they formulated and clarified what evidence of understanding would entail by developing *I can* statements that learners can access.

Level 1: Recalling	Level 2: Describing
Learners recall and identify knowledge that relates to the conceptual questions.	Learners describe in some detail information related to the conceptual questions. Learners begin to make inferences and interpret their understandings.
Understanding Question: Why do we have innovations?	
I can **name** some innovations over time.	I can **describe** innovations over time. I can **list** reasons why people have innovated.
Understanding Question: What innovations and creativity exist in our community, and what is the impact of this now and for the future?	
I can **name** some of the innovations and creative solutions in our community. I can **name** some of the impacts of innovations in our community.	I can **describe** innovations and creative solutions in our community.
Understanding Question: How can we innovate and create for our community?	
I can **plan** and innovate or create for our community.	I can **plan,** innovate, or create, and **determine** how my innovation will help our community.

Level 3: Explaining and Connecting	Level 4: Analysing and Applying
Learners make comparisons between existing knowledge and the concepts. They are able to explain in detail what they have learnt and the connections within it, with reasoning and evidence.	Learners analyse and evaluate through reasoning and application. Learners make new connections and justify their analysis using evidence and reason.
I can **compare and contrast** different innovations over time. I can **explain** why and how people go about designing innovations.	I can **analyse** innovations over time and **evaluate** their impact using evidence.
I can **compare and contrast** innovations and creative solutions within our community. I can **explain** which of these innovations will have the greatest impact now and in the future, with **reasoning.**	I can **analyse** innovations over time and **evaluate** their impact using evidence.
I can **plan,** innovate, or create, and **explain** how my innovation will help our community now and in the future with **reasoning.**	I can **analyse** my own innovations or creations and **evaluate** their effectiveness. I can **analyse** the innovations or creations of others and offer feedback on how they could be improved, with **reasoning.**

Understanding Identity

Developed with the Grade 4 Team at Dresden International School, Dresden, Germany

Level 1: Recalling	Level 2: Describing
Learners recall and identify knowledge that relates to the conceptual questions.	Learners describe in some detail information related to the conceptual questions. Learners begin to make inferences and interpret their understandings.
Understanding Question: How do beliefs and values contribute to identity?	
I can **identify** my beliefs and values. I can **identify** others' beliefs and values.	I can **describe** my and others' beliefs and values. I can **describe** how beliefs and values contribute to people's actions and identity.
Understanding Question: What factors contribute to the development of identity?	
I can identify invisible factors that contribute to identity. I can identify visible factors that contribute to identity.	I can **describe** my and others' visible and invisible factors. I can **describe** how these contribute to the development of people's identity.
Understanding Question: What factors contribute to the development of identity?	
I can **explore** the ways people express themselves. I can **list** how people express themselves.	I can **describe** how people express themselves. I can **describe** the connection between the expression and their identity.

Level 3: Explaining and Connecting	Level 4: Analysing and Applying
Learners make comparisons between existing knowledge and the concepts. They are able to explain in detail what they have learnt and the connections within it, with reasoning and evidence.	Learners analyse and evaluate through reasoning and application. Learners make new connections and justify their analysis using evidence and reason.
I can **compare and contrast** beliefs and values of myself and others. I can **explain similarities and differences** between beliefs and values. I can **explain** how these contribute to people's actions and identity.	I can **analyse** factors that contribute to people's identity. I can **analyse** which factors have the biggest impact on identity and actions and why (justification).
I can compare and contrast visible and invisible factors and explain similarities and differences between visible and invisible factors. I can **explain** how these factors connect to and impact the development of people's identity and actions.	*Please note that the two understanding questions at this level have been merged to transfer their understanding of beliefs and values to analyse the impact they have.
I can **explore and explain** the connection between how people express themselves and their identity. I can **explain** why they chose to express themselves that way.	I can **evaluate** people's expression in connection to their identity and whether the expression displayed connects to their identity or not and give justification for my reason.

Understanding Structure and Function

Developed with the Science and Math Team Grade 6 at KAUST School

How was this developed? In this example, two subject teams collaborated on a key understanding question that addressed the concepts structure and function. The question was broad in design and offered opportunities for both authentic mathematical and science investigation. To guide this, the educators then designed a rubric that transcended both subjects. To ensure the subject lens, the learner success criteria are specific to the subject in the *I can* statements.

Level 1: Recalling Learners recall and identify knowledge that relates to the conceptual questions.	**Level 2: Describing** Learners describe in some detail information related to the conceptual questions. Learners begin to make inferences and interpret their understandings.
Understanding Question: How is structure connected to function? (Science Connection)	
I can **identify** the structure and function of cell types.	I can **describe** the **connection** between the structure and function of cell types.
Understanding Question: How is structure connected to function? (Math Connection)	
Given the **exact formula,** I can **apply** it to solve geometric problems.	Given the **formulas,** I can **select** and **apply** the correct one to solve geometric problems.

Level 3: Explaining and Connecting	Level 4: Analysing and Applying
Learners make comparisons between existing knowledge and the concepts. They are able to explain in detail what they have learnt and the connections within it, with reasoning and evidence.	Learners analyse and evaluate through reasoning and application. Learners make new connections and justify their analysis using evidence and reason.
I can **compare and contrast** the **connection** between the structure and function of cell types. I can **explain differences and similarities** using claim evidence and reasoning.	I can find my **own examples** of cell structure and analyse the function. I can **create** my own cell type or organism and **explain** how its cell structure **connects** to its function.
I can **effectively choose** the right equation to solve geometric problems. I can give **reasons** for my choices.	I can **design** a functional space by **analysing** the structures within it (e.g., size, perimeter).

Understanding Math Knowledge and Strategies
Year 9 Math Unit

The Year 9 team at KAUST School included their factual questions to assist them in ensuring the knowledge supported the conceptual questions. This assisted them in developing the levels of understanding.

Level 1: Recalling	Level 2: Describing
Students recall and select **mathematical knowledge** to solve simple problems by generally selecting and applying **mathematical strategies** successfully.	Students describe in some detail **mathematical knowledge** to solve familiar problems by selecting and applying **mathematical strategies**, generally, successfully.
Understanding Question: How do quantities help us to understand how spaces are used? **Factual Questions:** How can I use surface area and volume to solve problems? How can I use trigonometry to find missing side lengths and angles?	
Students **identify** the mathematical knowledge that shows how quantities allow them to understand how different spaces are used.	Students describe, using mathematical knowledge, how quantities allow them to understand how different spaces are used.
Student Criteria Given the exact formula, I can **apply** it to solve geometrical problems connected to quantities and space.	**Student Criteria** Given the formulas, I can **select and apply** the correct one to solve geometrical problems connected to quantities and space.

EDUCATOR'S VOICE

"The rubric was firstly a great planning tool. It helped me to understand the progression of the knowledge and understanding in the topic so that students could be provided with opportunities at each of these levels as appropriate. I feel like this was one of the first times that the progression of the unit was crystal clear from the very beginning. As I was now clearer on the planning, I was able to build in more opportunities for students to show their understanding and be less reliant on a single summative assessment."

— Lucy Allsopp, Secondary Coach, KAUST School, Saudi Arabia

Level 3: Explaining and Connecting	Level 4: Analysing and Applying
Students explain and connect **mathematical knowledge** to solve challenging problems in familiar situations by selecting and applying **mathematical strategies** successfully.	Students analyse and apply their **mathematical knowledge** to solve problems in unfamiliar situations by selecting and applying **mathematical strategies** successfully.
Students explain and connect mathematical knowledge to show how quantities allow them to understand how different spaces are used.	Students analyse and apply mathematical knowledge to show how quantities allow them to understand how different spaces are used.
Student Criteria I can **effectively choose** the right formula to solve geometrical problems connected to quantities and space. I can **give reasons** for my choices.	**Student Criteria** I can **effectively choose** the right formula to solve geometrical problems connected to quantities and space and **transfer** my knowledge to unfamiliar problems. I can **give reasons** for my choices.

Level 1: Recalling	Level 2: Describing
Understanding Question: How and why do relationships between quantities exist? **Factual Questions:** What is the relationship between surface area and volume? What relationships exist between sides of a right-angled triangle?	
Students **identify** relationships between quantities.	Students **describe** relationships between quantities and comment on why they exist.
Student Criteria I can **identify** maximum and minimum problems and given the exact formula, I can **apply** it to solve the problem. I can **identify** the trigonometric ratios of a right-angled triangle.	**Student Criteria** I can **describe** maximum and minimum problems and given the formulas, **select and apply** the correct ones to solve the problem. I can **describe** and use the trigonometric ratios of a right-angled triangle.
Understanding Question: How and why do relationships affect quantities and space? **Factual Question:** How can we use our ability to apply geometric knowledge to design spaces?	
Students **state** how their design of the use of space is affected by the relationship between the quantities they have calculated. **Student Criteria** I can use my knowledge of maximum and minimum problems to **design** a space. I can **state** my choices with reasons.	Students **describe** how their design of the use of space is affected by the relationship between the quantities they have calculated. **Student Criteria** I can use my knowledge of maximum and minimum problems to **design a functional space** for a desired quantity. I can **describe** my choices with reasons.

Level 3: Explaining and Connecting	Level 4: Analysing and Applying
Students **explain** relationships between quantities and why these connections exist.	Students **analyse** and **evaluate** relationships between quantities and prove why these connections exist.
Student Criteria I can **explain** maximum and minimum problems and connect the correct formulas to the problems and solve them. I can **give reasons** for my choices. I can **effectively choose** the correct trigonometric ratios of a right-angled triangle to solve problems. I can **give reasons** for my choices.	**Student Criteria** I can **analyse** maximum and minimum problems and apply the correct formulas to unfamiliar problems and solve them. I can **logically prove** my choices. I can **effectively choos**e the correct trigonometric ratios of a right-angled triangle to **solve problems** and **transfe**r my knowledge to unfamiliar problems. I can **logically prove** my choices.
Students **explain** how their design of a space is affected by the relationship between the quantities they have calculated.	Students **analyse** how and why their design of a space is affected by the relationship between the quantities they have calculated.
Student Criteria I can use my knowledge of maximum and minimum problems to **design a functional space for a desired** quantity. I can **compare and contrast** my design choices and how these affect the accuracy of my design with **reasons.**	**Student Criteria** I can use my knowledge of maximum and minimum problems to **design a functional space for a desired quantity**. I can **evaluate** my design choices and how these affect the accuracy of my design with **reasons.**

Examples of Rubrics for Understanding with Learner Criteria I Can Statements

Developed with the Grade 1 Team at KAUST School

With a focus on evidence and discoveries, this rubric can be used across subject areas. When focusing learning across subject areas, be intentional about making connections amongst and between learning explicit for learners.

Level 1: Recalling	Level 2: Describing
Learners recall and identify knowledge that relates to the conceptual questions.	Learners describe in some detail information related to the conceptual questions. Learners begin to make inferences and interpret their understandings.
Understanding Question: How do we explore what evidence is?	
I can **name** different types of evidence.	I can **sort** evidence into different **categories.** I can **tell** how they are connected.
Understanding Question: How does the discovery of evidence lead to new understandings?	
I can **say** what I understand when looking at evidence.	I can **describe** what I have learned after looking at evidence.
Understanding Question: How do we curate evidence to tell a story?	
I can **display** different forms of evidence. I can **curate** evidence.	I can **display** different kinds of evidence and **describe** what they show. I can **curate** evidence and **describe** the story it tells.

Level 3: Explaining and Connecting	Level 4: Analysing and Applying
Learners make comparisons between existing knowledge and the concepts. They are able to explain in detail what they have learnt and the connections within it, with reasoning and evidence.	Learners analyse and evaluate through reasoning and application. Learners make new connections and justify their analysis using evidence and reason.
I can **explain** how the different types of evidence I collected are **similar**. I can **explain** the **differences** between the different types of evidence.	I can **analyse** a curation and **evaluate** how effectively the section tells a story of the past with **reasoning.** *This part of the rubric remains the same at each level as it is the transfer and apply stage. Once students have gone through levels 1–3, the next thing for them to do is to transfer and apply what they have learnt in the other 3 levels.*
I can make **connections** between evidence and the things I've learned. I can **explain** why my thinking has changed.	
I can **curate** evidence and **explain how** the pieces in my collection **tell the story** I want others to see or hear.	

Integrated Arts

The rubric is for both visual and performing arts; where it states "the arts" or "artworks," it is referring to both performing and visual arts. There are many opportunities to have rubrics across subject areas so that learners can make further connections as they build their understanding over time.

Level 1: Recalling	Level 2: Describing
Learners recall and identify knowledge that relates to the conceptual questions.	Learners describe in some detail information related to the conceptual questions. Learners begin to make inferences and interpret their understandings.
Understanding Question: How and why are the elements of art/music used in the arts?	
I can **recall** the elements used in the arts.	I can **distinguish** the elements used in the arts. I can **predict** why artists may have used them.

Level 3: Explaining and Connecting	Level 4: Analysing and Applying
Learners make comparisons between existing knowledge and the concepts. They are able to explain in detail what they have learnt and the connections within it, with reasoning and evidence.	Learners analyse and evaluate through reasoning and application. Learners make new connections and justify their analysis using evidence and reason.
I can **notice patterns** and **connections** between the elements used in the arts. I can **explain** why artists have chosen to use those elements, with **reasoning.**	I can **transfer** my understanding of the elements to my own artwork/music. I can **justify** why I have used the elements I have. I can **evaluate** how these elements contribute to the overall artwork/music with **reasoning.**

Whilst the rubric may be completed, it is important to note it may change. It is not set in stone and may need to be adapted or changed based on learners' individual understanding. It would be okay for learners to have rubrics that connect directly to their own learning.

 Develop a Rubric for Understanding that focuses on empowering learners to become self-adjusters and take responsibility for their learning.

Level 1: Recalling Learners recall and identify knowledge that relates to the conceptual questions.	**Level 2: Describing** Learners describe in some detail information related to the conceptual questions. Learners begin to make inferences and interpret their understandings.
Understanding Question:	
Understanding Question:	
Understanding Question:	

Level 3: Explaining and Connecting	Level 4: Analysing and Applying
Learners make comparisons between existing knowledge and the concepts. They are able to explain in detail what they have learnt and the connections within it, with reasoning and evidence.	Learners analyse and evaluate through reasoning and application. Learners make new connections and justify their analysis using evidence and reason.

"They (learners) are using (the rubric) to know where they are going, when to move on with my direction and assistance, checking to see if they are understanding it."

Susan Bartley, Grade 5, The International School
Ho Chi Minh City, Vietnam

Brainstorming Template

Brainstorm Map For Evidence of Understanding

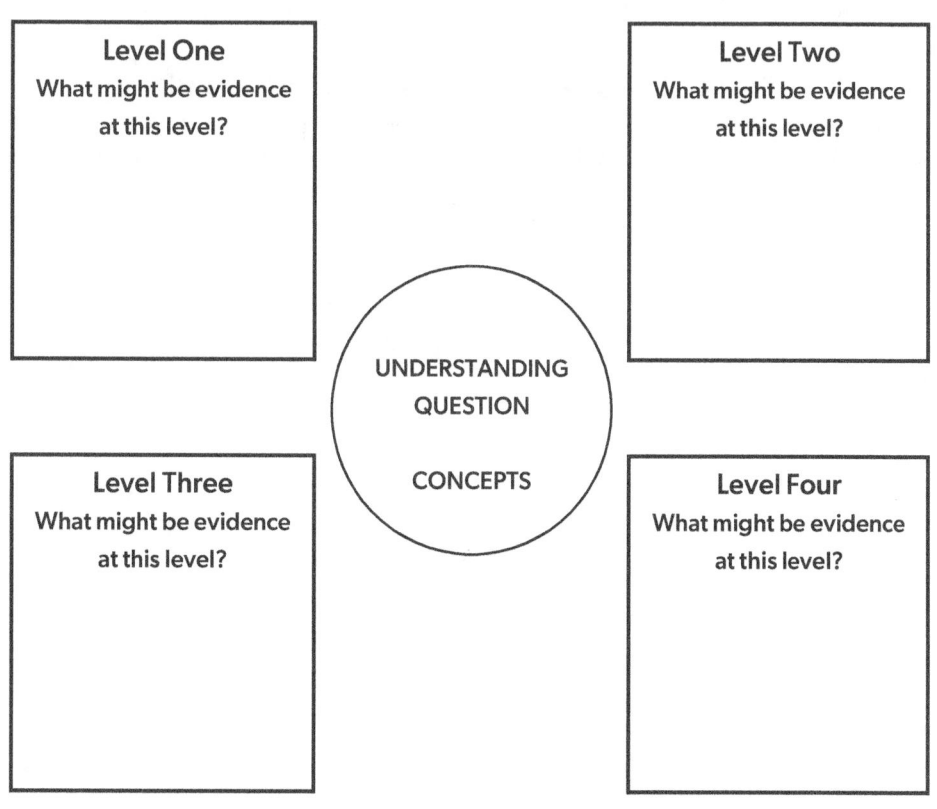

Level One	**Level Two**
What might be evidence at this level?	What might be evidence at this level?

UNDERSTANDING
QUESTION

CONCEPTS

Level Three	**Level Four**
What might be evidence at this level?	What might be evidence at this level?

THE RUBRIC FOR UNDERSTANDING: A TOOL FOR AUTHENTIC CONTINUOUS ASSESSMENT

As a continuous assessment tool, the Rubric for Understanding aids educators and learners at every stage of the learning process, from knowing what evidence to collect, to evaluating when and how learners are progressing. The evidence then serves as feedback that directs the next steps in the learning journey.

In summary, the Rubric for Understanding (or a similar model) offers significant value by providing structure and a comprehensive framework for assessing learning and performance through the lens of understanding. Here are a few of the key benefits of the Rubric for Understanding:

- Clarity of expectations
- Consistency in assessment
- A framework for feedback and improvement
- Differentiation in learning, as it can be adapted for varying levels of complexity
- The development of critical thinking and self-assessment skills

The Rubric for Understanding offers an authentic measure for understanding through continuous assessment. It promotes transparency, consistency, feedback, and learner engagement, all of which support more effective and authentic assessment of the learning.

LEVELS OF UNDERSTANDING IN ACTION: LEARNERS AS ASSESSMENT CAPABLE

The examples below provide ideas and strategies for how to involve learners to become assessment capable when using the Rubric for Understanding.

In Jamie House's class at KAUST School, he uses the anchor charts below to emphasise the developing levels.

EDUCATOR'S VOICE

"I start the year by asking students what thinking looks like to them. Can they explain it to someone who cannot think? They come with general ideas, and I list some of the verbs that come through the discussion. We come up with levels-of-understanding verbs."

— Jamie House, Grade 4, KAUST SCHOOL, Jeddah, Saudi Arabia

Jamie assists his learners in fully understanding the command terms by discussing this with them and providing examples of what the levels could look like. Once learners understand this, as in the example below, they are able to co-construct the rubric together.

Levels of Understanding

1	2	3	4
RECALL	DESCRIBE	COMPARE & CONTRAST	ANALYSE

Jamie discusses the levels with learners and provides examples of what it might look like. The examples are not necessarily connected to the learning that they are embarking on but instead give clarity to the type of understanding the levels are focused on.

⦿ U.O.I   Levels of thinking and understanding

1 To show understanding, we think and *recall* examples of a topic.

2 To show understanding, we *describe* the features of a topic, example or item with lots of detail.

3 To show understanding, we think by *comparing and contrasting* the features of two or more items or situations.

4 To show our understanding, we think by *analyzing* the features of items or situations by interpreting and inferring based on the information we have.

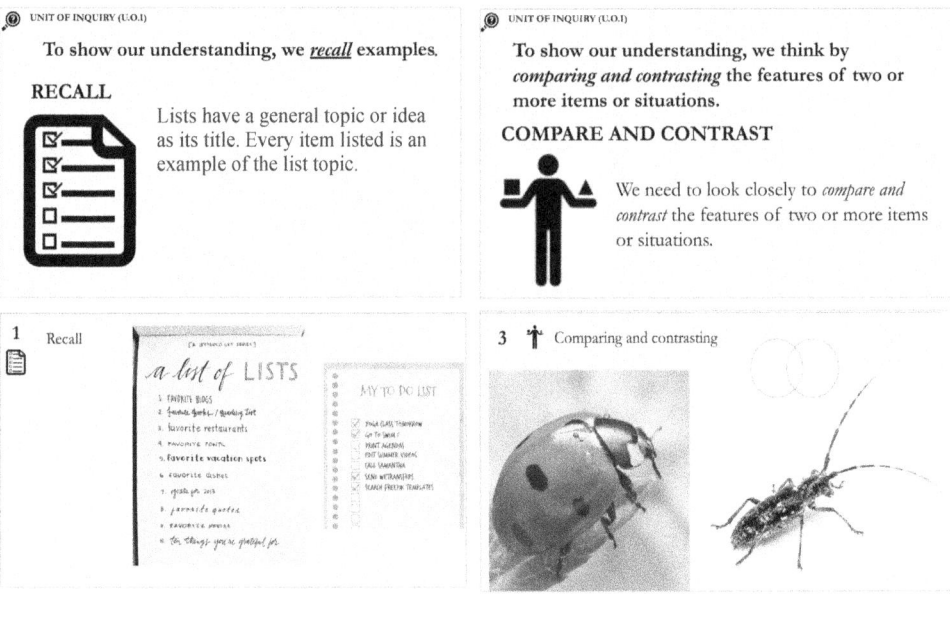

RECALL   COMPARE AND CONTRAST

⦿ UNIT OF INQUIRY (U.O.I)

To show our understanding, we *recall* examples.

RECALL

Lists have a general topic or idea as its title. Every item listed is an example of the list topic.

⦿ UNIT OF INQUIRY (U.O.I)

To show our understanding, we think by *comparing and contrasting* the features of two or more items or situations.

COMPARE AND CONTRAST

We need to look closely to *compare and contrast* the features of two or more items or situations.

1 Recall

3 Comparing and contrasting

The levels around the understanding questions are co-constructed using the anchor charts above and made visible in the learning environment. He refers to the levels of understanding with learners throughout the learning process. As the learning takes place, learners consider the engagements they are involved in and how they are demonstrating their learning. They use the levels that are visible in their environment to consider where they are in the learning process. This provides an opportunity for collection of evidence (discussed in detail in Chapter 4) and for peer, self, and educator feedback. It promotes self-regulation and the development of new goals and next steps in the learning process to ensure all are developing further in their understanding, regardless of where they currently are (discussed in more detail in Chapter 5).

Co-Constructing Criteria with Learners:
Jamie House KAUST SCHOOL

Understanding Earth's Processes Enables People to Respond and Design Solutions

How the World Works	1 RECALL	2 DESCRIBE	3 COMPARE & CONTRAST	4 ANALYZE
CHANGE — How and why the Earth continues to change	Can list ways the Earth is changing	I can describe at least one event using a model and a detailed written explanation	·I compare how one event is the same or different to another. ·I identify similarities and differences between my model and explanation and another student's (scientist)	
CAUSATION — Impact of Earth's changing processes	List ways changes in the Earth impact life on Earth	I describe the impact on people, groups, towns, cities using adjectives, relative pronouns, adverbs	I compare and contrast how different events impact people, groups, etc.	
RESPONSIBILITY — Human response to changes in the Earth.	A list of ways humans respond		I compare how humans respond emotionally to how we respond through action.	

	1 RECALL	2 DESCRIBE	3 COMPARE & CONTRAST	4 ANALYZE
PERSPECTIVE — What are beliefs and values?	I can list my own beliefs and or values	I can also describe my beliefs or values in details		Am I living my values?
CAUSATION — Experiences ... influence belief and values		Describe why I have my values?		
RESPONSIBILITY — Community members take action to support each other				How am I upholding our class values?

Nature can inspire artistic expression

	1	2	3	4
Connect — Perspective — How artists use their inspiration from nature	Make art inspired by nature	Describe how nature inspired my art	Compare my inspirations and art pieces to others	Analyze how an art piece may be inspired by nature
Form — How artists use different elements to create	Identify elements used in an art piece	Describe what knowledge, skills, and elements are used in the piece	Compare and contrast the elements, skills and knowledge between two pieces	Interpret and evaluate art based on skills, knowledge, and elements
Perspective — How artists engage in a creative process	Retells the steps in an art making process	Has a meaningful and purposeful goal and identified steps	Makes goal and documents their steps along the way	Evaluates how their steps and reflections allow goal achievement

Craig Dwyer, a Grade Five teacher from The International School of Ho Chi Minh City, assists his learners in understanding how the rubric is used by breaking down the meaning of the levels and having a shared space for documentation. Learners can see how they are progressing through learning and building their understanding over time. Learners make decisions on where they think they are in connection to the levels and consider whether their evidence meets the level and why or why not. They use different colours to indicate at different times where they think their evidence of understanding connects along the rubric. It also promotes moderation of the learning, as the thinking is made visible.

Levels for Understanding: Craig Dwyer

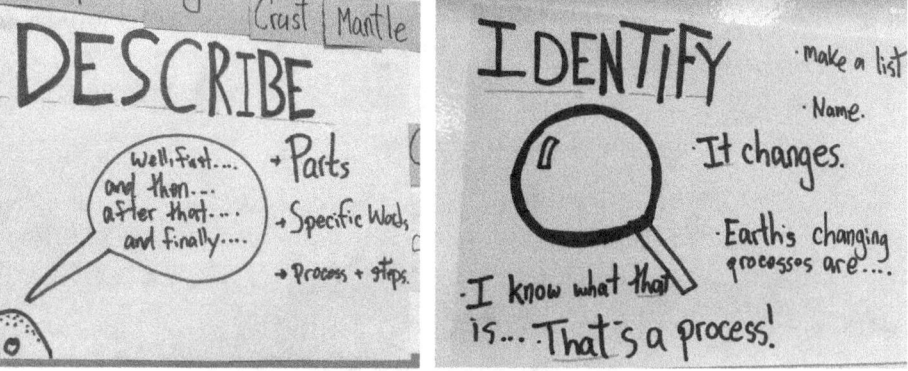

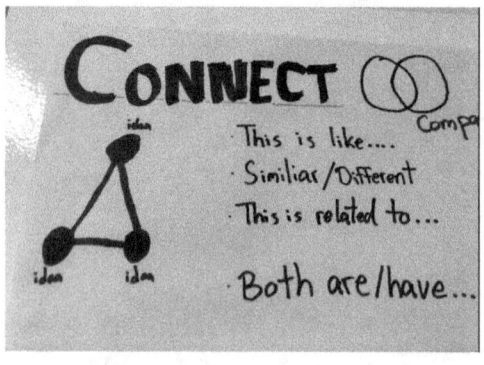

Craig Dwyer's Class: Learners Evaluating Themselves in Connection
to the Rubric for Understanding

I can identify Earth's changing processes.	I can describe Earth's changing processes. I can describe the cause and effect relationships.	I can compare the Earth's changing processes. I can explain similarities and difference changing processes. I can explain the cause and effect relationship within and between Earth's changing processes.
I can identify impacts of Earth's changing processes.	I can categorise the impacts of Earth's changing processes. I can describe the long-term and short-term impact of Earth's changing processes.	I can compare and contrast the impact Earth's changing processes. I can explain similarities and difference the impact of Earth's changing processe I can explain short term and long term impacts of Earth's changing with justific
I can identify how people respond to Earth's changing processes.	I can describe how people have responded to Earth's changing processes (local and global). I can formulate a solution to a changing process.	I can explain how and why people have responded to Earth's changing processe (local and global). I can formulate a solution to a changing process in my world and beyond and exp why my solution will work.

Anchor Charts to Assist in Learners Building Their Levels of Understanding

The anchor charts below can be used by both learners and educators to assist in co-constructing the rubric to develop *I can* statements around the levels. They can also be used for learners and educators to consider where they are in their learning, recognizing their current level of understanding and reflecting on this to consider next steps, developing a relationship between educators and learners.

Identify	Identify
_____ _____ _____ _____	Recall Know Name Recognise
Describe	Describe Categorise Interpret Classify Define
Explain	Connect Transfer Compare and Contrast Explain Reason
Analyse	Evaluate Analyse Synthesise Critique Transfer and Apply

Sentence Stems to Use in Your Classroom to Support Understanding of the Rubric for Understanding

Educators can develop sentence stems with learners as prompts for how they might recognise evidence at the different levels. These can be co-constructed and placed in the learning environment as the learning process takes place for learners to refer to. In terms of evidence of learning, using sentence stems helps learners connect ideas, explain their reasoning, and show understanding.

Identify	Recall examples of the learning: I know ____. Identify examples of the learning: I see ____ here. The parts of ____ are ____.
Describe	Describe details about the learning: This is what ____ is and/or looks like ____ I have categorised ____ and have make these groups that show ____.
Explain	Compare and contrast different examples and ideas, and explain those comparisons: This is how and why ____ is similar and/or different to ____. I know this because ____ Make connections between the learning: ____ is connected to ____ because ____ and that is important for ____. I know this because ____.
Analyse	Analyse ideas and examples connected to the learning and evaluate them with evidence or reasoning: When analysing ____, I can see that ____. I know this because of ____. When analysing ____, I evaluated that it could be improved by ____. this would assist in ____. When analysing ____, my evaluation is that ____ had the biggest impact. I think this because ____.

Learners Building Their Understanding

Learners can develop words that connect to the command terms to help them understand their meaning. They can then think about what they would be doing or saying if they were to fulfil the criteria of that command term. In doing this, there is moderation as a class. To ensure consistency, the criteria can also be shared with other educators who are teaching the same subject area.

Understanding Question

How does using elements in our artwork/performance contribute to its effectiveness?

Learners together discuss words that connect to the command term and then what this might look like in connection to the understanding questions. At each of the different levels, they develop words and sentence starters to enable them to take more responsibility for their learning and to consider what their next steps may be in the learning.

Explanation of the Level:	Words we may use at this level:	Sentences we may use at this level:
Recall Identifies elements in their artwork or performance.	Recall Notice Recognise Point out Show	I can notice ___ in my artwork or performance. I can identify ___ in my artwork or performance. I can see ___ in my artwork or performance.
Describe Outlines elements in their artwork or performance.	Outline Give a brief account or summary Main ideas Conclusion Succinct Concise	I can make conclusions about ___ in my artwork or performance. I can succinctly state ___ in my artwork or performance. I can give the main ideas about ___ in my artwork or performance.
Explain and connect Gives a detailed description of the elements in their artwork or performance.	Define Detail Connect Explain	I can make connections between ___ in my artwork or performance. I can describe the details of ___ in my artwork or performance. I can explain how ___ connects to my artwork or performance.

| Analyse and evaluate Explain connections and relationship between the elements and the artwork or performance. | Examine Relate Interpret Evaluate | I can examine ___ in my artwork or performance and how it connects to the overall piece. I can interpret my artwork or performance in connection to ___ and how effective it is in contributing to the artwork. I can relate the individual parts connected to ___ in my artwork or performance and how they come together in my artwork. |

Providing Examples and Models at Each Level

Provide learners with examples of what the levels look like. Offer generic examples so they can understand what success at the different levels looks like.

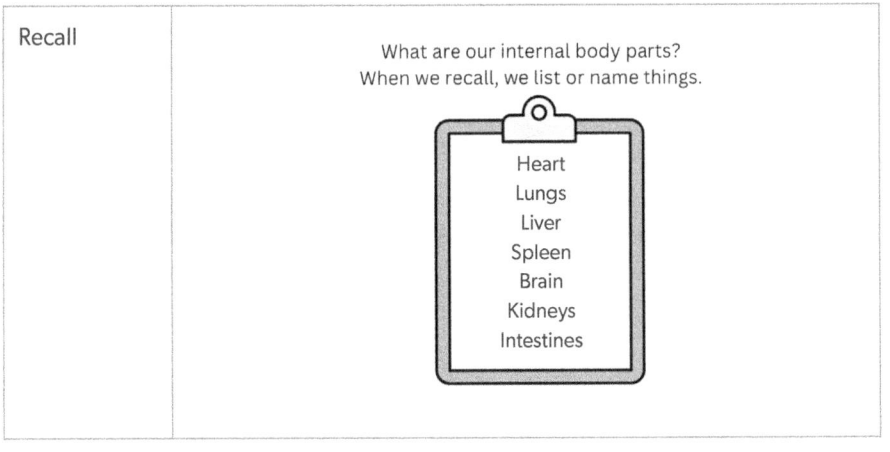

| Recall | What are our internal body parts? When we recall, we list or name things. Heart Lungs Liver Spleen Brain Kidneys Intestines |

Describe and Categorise	**When we categorise and describe, we put things into categories and describe why those things all belong in that category.**
	These are examples unicellular organisms because they consist of a single cell. / *These are examples of multicellular organisms because they are composed of multiple cells that work together.*
	Bacteria / Humans Algae / Plants Yeast / Animals Plankton / Fungi
Compare, Contrast, and Explain	**When we compare and contrast we explain differences and similarities.** 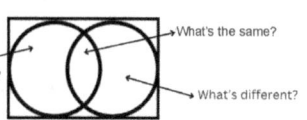 What's the same? / What's different? / What's different?
	Unicellular organisms are made up of a single cell that performs all the functions necessary for life. / Multicellular organisms are made up of multiple cells organized into tissues, organs, and organ systems. The functioning of multicellular organisms is more complex than that of unicellular organisms due to the specialization and coordination of different cell types.
	Unicellular organisms can adapt to changes in their environment over time. Unicellular organisms obtain nutrients from their environment. Unicellular organisms reproduce to create new individuals. Within the single cell, metabolic processes take place to convert nutrients into energy. Unicellular organisms grow by increasing the size of their single cell. Unicellular organisms maintain internal stability, or homeostasis, by regulating their internal environment. Waste products generated during metabolic processes need to be eliminated. / Multicellular organisms regulate their internal environment to maintain homeostasis. In multicellular organisms, cells undergo differentiation, where they become specialized for specific functions. Cells with similar functions group together to form tissues. Multicellular organisms have complex communication systems to coordinate activities among different cells, tissues, and organs. Specialized cells and tissues are responsible for the absorption and transport of nutrients. Multicellular organisms can adapt to their environments through evolutionary processes. Multicellular organisms grow by increasing the number of cells and/or the size of cells.
Transfer and Apply	**Transfer and Apply: When we transfer and apply our understanding we are taking what we have learnt and transferring it and applying it to our world and understanding the impact it has.**
	Using your understanding of multicellular organisms, transfer and apply your understanding of how studying them has had an impact on one of the following.
	Evolution Medical Research Food Production Cell Biology Biotechnology

It is important to understand that involving learners in their assessment can be a journey, and you need to develop the skills of them being assessment capable as Frey, Fisher, and Hattie (2018) state, "Assessment-capable learners are cultivated by teachers and school leaders who intentionally foster these skills."

It is a journey.

Providing Examples at Each Level

Another way to actively involve learners is to give them samples of learning and have them consider where they think they fit along the rubric and why. Learners can consider why one piece of learning connects to the analysing level and why they think this, and which piece connects to the describing level and why they think this. This interrogation of the learning samples by learners promotes a shared understanding and dialogue around the learning and levels.

EDUCATOR'S VOICE

"[When using the Rubric for Understanding] for the students, they had much better clarity on what we were doing in class and the purpose. I think that there is still work to be done on getting them to a better place with their conceptual understanding, but this is a journey for them, and we have just started."

— Roxanne Hankinson Previous Grade 3 Teacher
St Joseph's Institution International, Singapore

HINT! Provide time and create learning that promotes learners developing the skills to become self-adjusters.

CHAPTER FOUR

Evidence of Understanding

"An important part of effective professional practice is collecting evidence that provides the basis for ongoing feedback, reflection, and further development. The complex work of teaching generates a rich and varied range of evidence that can inform meaningful evaluations of practice . . ."

———————— AITSL: Australian Teacher and Performance ————————
Development Framework

The Rubric for Understanding provides a framework to plan meaningful learning. As noted in the previous chapter, the evidence collected at each level answers the question of whether learners truly understand the material and are able to move beyond knowledge to making connections with their learning on a broader scale.

In this chapter, we examine *evidence*, what it is, why it is valuable as we work toward continuous assessment, and how and when to collect it. Being *evidence-driven* educators (or *data-driven educators*, depending on the terminology used in your school setting) means that what we and our learners observe and collect informs every step of the learning process. It is this evidence that enables us to keep our learners' needs at the forefront and to adjust the engagements as necessary to ensure learners grasp the connections we and they intend for them to make.

Effective, ongoing evidence collection lets us know where to go next—and where to begin. Moving forward in the Continuous Assessment for Conceptual Understanding Model, from Design and Create, we move into the Implement and Interact phase. This chapter offers a wealth of examples, tools, and strategies you can use throughout the learning process.

THE CONNECTION BETWEEN EVIDENCE AND CONCEPTUAL UNDERSTANDING

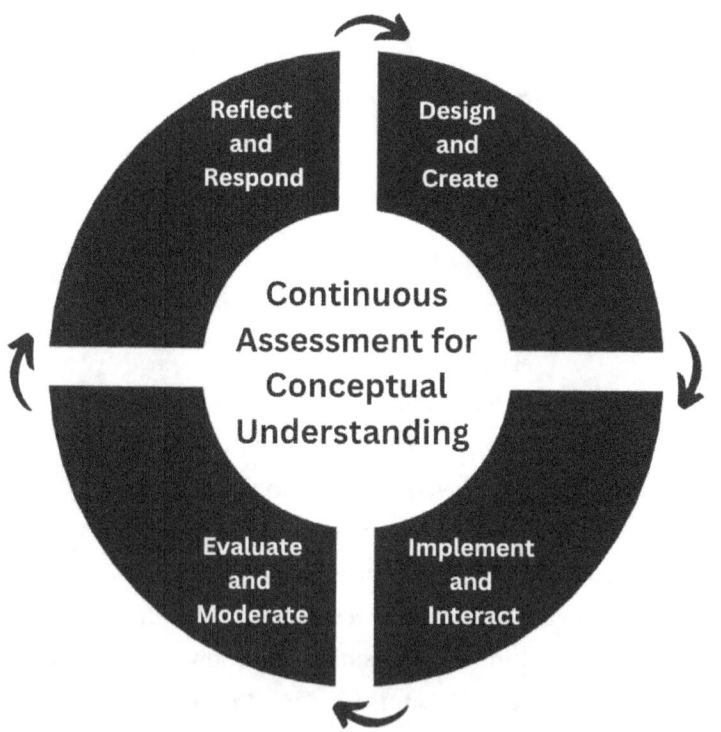

Implement and Interact
Develop learning engagements to elicit evidence of understanding that are varied and differentiated. Learners and educators collect evidence of learning around the levels in the Rubric for Understanding.

EDUCATOR'S VOICE

"Students can see that learning is a process. It's important that they view 'grades' as levels. Often, they just see the number and decide if it's good or bad. They don't always connect that the number reflects where they are in the learning process."

Claire Margaret Cotton, Head of Arts, Middle Years Drama and English A, Stonehill International School, Bangalore, India

As noted previously, the purpose of collecting evidence is not to create projects or tasks; it is to draw out understanding. We must design learning engagements with that purpose in mind. It is not enough to simply gather evidence. Educators and learners need to analyse the effectiveness of the evidence in terms of learners' understanding to be able to plan for the next steps in the learning process.

Every aspect of learning is an opportunity for assessment. In continuous assessment, it is not one piece of work; it is the understanding that assessment can take place at all times and takes on different forms.

HINT!

Evidence can be a conversation, a question answered, a piece of work, or observation. The key is documenting the evidence as data to inform next steps.

COLLECTING EVIDENCE OF UNDERSTANDING

Assessment should be designed to elicit evidence that aligns with desired learning outcomes—the understanding questions. Using a range of approaches is helpful in working to establish your learners' progress and depth of understanding. To that end, we've provided numerous tools and strategies to equip you to gather evidence throughout the learning process, as well as insights into prior knowledge and misconceptions.

When linking assessment to the Rubric for Understanding, the evidence collected corresponds to levels 3 and 4 in which we are asking learners to make connections and analyse concepts related to the understanding questions. Levels 1 and 2 build the context toward that learning. As learners progress through the levels, they develop more complex understanding.

The following section outlines several types of understanding and **what learners might be cognitively processing at levels 3 and 4**. Additionally, we've provided questions to consider to help you determine whether a learner has reached that level of understanding.

Understanding: Making Connections

When learners make connections, they can link new learning to what they already know, creating a deeper understanding and improving their retention.

Evidence of Conceptual Understanding Connected to Levels 3 and 4 in Rubric for Understanding

- **Relate and apply new information to prior knowledge:** Learners make connections and see patterns by relating and applying new learning to something they already know.
- **Synthesize information:** Learners make connections by synthesizing concepts and seeing patterns from multiple sources.
- **Compare and contrast:** Learners make connections and notice patterns by comparing and contrasting or classifying.

Possible Understanding Questions for Each Type of Understanding

- How is ___ connected to ____?
- What connections are there between _____ and ____?

- How is/are ___ similar and different?
- How are you connected to_____?

Understanding: Seeing Patterns

 When learners notice patterns, they see connections including similarities and differences within and across contexts. They can analyse patterns and make predictions based on this.

Evidence of Conceptual Understanding Connected to Levels 3 and 4 in Rubric for Understanding

- **Ask questions:** Learners make connections, and they ask questions to further their understanding and to make sense of patterns they see.
- **Identify key features:** Learners make connections and notice patterns by identifying key features or characteristics of concepts that are common across different examples.
- **Make predictions:** Learners notice patterns by making predictions based on previous examples or experiences.

Possible Understanding Questions for Each Type of Understanding

- How are patterns evident in our world?
- What patterns emerge when examining _____?
- How do patterns enable people to make predictions about ____?

Understanding: Seeing Perspectives

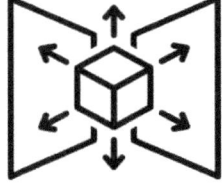 When learners observe different perspectives, they can gain a more comprehensive and nuanced understanding of a concept or idea.

Evidence of Conceptual Understanding Connected to Levels 3 and 4 in Rubric for Understanding

- **Consider different viewpoints:** Learners see different perspectives and consider the viewpoints of others.
- **Analyse multiple sources:** Learners see perspectives by analysing information from multiple sources.
- **Reflect on personal bias:** Learners see perspectives by reflecting on their own biases and assumptions.
- **Engage in dialogue:** Learners see perspectives by engaging in dialogue with others who have different viewpoints.
- **Synthesise viewpoints:** Learners hear and see different perspectives; they may synthesise the viewpoints to form a more nuanced understanding.

Possible Understanding Questions for Each Type of Understanding

- Why do people have different perspectives on ____?
- What influences people's perspectives about ____?
- How is ___ different to ____ and why?
- How do our perspectives influence our actions/beliefs?
- What leads to bias, and what is the impact of this?
- How does exploring multiple sources build perspective?

Understanding: Reason

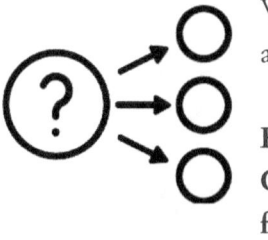 When learners reason, they can think critically and logically about concepts.

Evidence of Conceptual Understanding Connected to Levels 3 and 4 in Rubric for Understanding

- **Analyse information:** Learners reason by analysing information and identifying patterns or relationships conceptually.

- **Make connections:** Learners reason by making connections between concepts and contexts.
- **Evaluate arguments:** Learners reason by evaluating arguments and evidence to determine their validity.
- **Solve problems:** Learners reason by using logical thinking to solve problems and apply concepts.
- **Reflect and revise:** Learners reason by reflecting on their learning and revising their thinking or approach as needed

Possible Understanding Questions for Each Type of Understanding

- How and why are _____ the way they are?
- How can we develop solutions for_____?
- How can we evaluate ____ to determine_____?

Understanding: Transfer

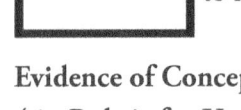

When learners transfer their learning, they are able to apply knowledge, skills, and concepts in one context to new and different situations.

Evidence of Conceptual Understanding Connected to Levels 3 and 4 in Rubric for Understanding

- **Identify similarities and differences:** Learners transfer their learning by identifying similarities and differences between the original learning context and the new context.
- **Apply prior knowledge:** Learners transfer their understanding of concepts by applying prior knowledge to new situations.
- **Use analogies:** Learners transfer their learning by using analogies to connect the original context to the new context.
- **Generalise concepts:** Learners transfer their learning by developing their own generalisations of concepts across situations.

- **Reflect on learning:** Learners transfer their learning; they reflect on their prior learning experiences and apply that knowledge of concepts to new situations.

Possible Understanding Questions for Each Type of Understanding

- Where do we see_____ in our world and what does this mean for me, others, and society?
- How can we use our understanding of_____ to _____?
- How would you develop a generalisation about_____?

Understanding: Explain

 When learners explain, they are able to communicate their understanding of a concept, idea, or process in a clear and concise manner.

Evidence of Conceptual Understanding Connected to Levels 3 and 4 in Rubric for Understanding

- **Use appropriate language:** Learners use appropriate language when explaining their understanding (including specialised subject language).
- **Provide examples:** Learners provide examples to help clarify their explanation.
- **Use visuals:** Learners use visuals, such as diagrams or charts, to help illustrate their explanation.
- **Connect ideas:** Learners connect different ideas together to help explain their understanding of a concept.
- **Check for understanding:** Learners explain their understanding of a concept; they also check for understanding from their audience. They ask questions, check for comprehension, or encourage feedback to ensure that their explanation is clear and understandable.

Possible Understanding Questions for Each Type of Understanding

- How can we explain our understanding of____?
- How do the parts of____ function or come together?
- How can I explain my understanding of_____to others?

Understanding: Theorise

When learners theorise, they are able to think abstractly and conceptually to develop hypotheses, models, or explanations for a phenomenon or idea.

Evidence of Conceptual Understanding Connected to Levels 3 and 4 in Rubric for Understanding

- **Formulate hypotheses:** Learners theorise by formulating hypotheses connected to the concepts.
- **Develop models:** Learners theorise by developing models that are representations of complex phenomena or systems.
- **Synthesise information:** Learners theorise by synthesising concepts from different sources to develop new insights or perspectives.
- **Identify relationships:** Learners theorise by identifying relationships between different concepts.
- **Test ideas:** Learners theorise, through testing their conceptual ideas or understanding through research, experimentation, or analysis.
- **Refine theories:** Learners refine their theories based on new information or evidence.

Possible Understanding Questions for Each Type of Understanding

- What theories do we have about____?
- How can we investigate to test our theories about____?
- How can we create a model to demonstrate our theories about ____?

- What new theories have we discovered based on evidence about _____?

"Using multiple ways to show evidence of understanding and learning allows us to check in with our students and for them to show us their understanding through their lens (not our predetermined 'answer')"

Ashley Sims, Grade 1, The International School, Ho Chi Minh City, Vietnam

When designing any unit of learning, the understanding questions guide the goals for learning. With those questions in mind, we consider what types of evidence we are seeking, for example, the learners' ability to reason or explain. From there, we must determine how to elicit that evidence. In other words, we must ask ourselves, **what am I expecting learners to demonstrate in terms of their understanding and therefore, how can I go about eliciting that evidence?**

The beauty of continuous assessment is that it offers multiple opportunities to gather evidence. The ongoing reflection on learners' progress results in a more accurate understanding as well as a more effective and personalised approach to instruction.

"'Evidence-based' teaching uses evidence about where students are in their learning to guide and personalise teaching. The objective is to develop a good understanding of where a student is in their learning so that they can be provided with appropriately targeted teaching and learning opportunities."

— Geoff Masters, "The Role of Evidence in Teaching and Learning"

"You get a much more rounded picture of where the learner is at and are more informed about what they need to do and where they need to go for improvement and success. Providing a variety of ways for learners to show their growth and development allows for the learner to show their growth and development in a way that works for them, therefore making them be and feel more successful in their learning."

— Louise McQuade, Grade 5, St Joseph's Institution International, Singapore

Evidence collection should take place at every level of understanding and involve both the learner and the educator. It is important to recognise that **collecting evidence does not require everyone doing the same learning at the same time or demonstrating learning the same way.** If you have learners who struggle to write, for example, requiring them to write about the connection between their learning and the understanding question will not be the most effective way for them to demonstrate their understanding. They may be better able to show their understanding by making a short video presentation or creating a piece of art.

As Geoff Master states in his research, "In evidence-based teaching, assessments are undertaken to gather evidence and draw conclusions about where students are in their learning. The objective is to use **observations** of student performances and work to draw inferences about their current levels of attainment."

Observation can provide many insights into learners' understanding. Evidence of learning can be visible, tangible, or audible. Observe your learners as they are engaged in the learning process:

- What are they doing with that picture?
- Why do they keep going back to it?
- How are they playing with the material/tool?
- What am I noticing?

- What are they saying?
- What are they doing?
- What are they thinking?

With ongoing assessment and a variety of options available to learners throughout the learning process, you achieve the most important goal: ensuring that learners have the opportunity to demonstrate their understanding.

EDUCATOR'S VOICE

"The advantage to seeing teachers use various forms of evidence demonstrates a deeper level of depth of understanding students. Walking into classrooms, I can see on the walls, in students' books, conversations, and in the work they do that they are using the vocabulary and building on the command terms to develop understanding around concepts. The more pieces of data or evidence from a shared range of engagements or experiences, the more students discuss their learning."

— Daniel Baker, PYP Coordinator, The International School, Ho Chi Minh City, Vietnam

A strategy is what we use to gather information about a learners understanding. Such as:

- Observation
- Conferencing
- Questioning
- Learning Samples
- Recordings (video/audio)
- Photographs
- Tests
- Artistic Endeavours

A tool is what we use to record evidence; it acts as an ongoing record of the learning. Such as:

- Anecdotal notes
- Checklists
- Continuums
- Rubrics

STRATEGIES AND TOOLS FOR GATHERING EVIDENCE

TRANSFER & APPLY

What strategies do you use to gather evidence of understanding?

What tools do you use to document and evaluate the evidence of understanding?

What might you need to do more or less of?

When considering tools for gathering evidence, remember that assessment is a collaborative process. This process as well as the tools you choose should involve interaction between you and your learners, among your learners, and potentially between you and your peers.

Collecting Evidence Tool
Educator / Learner

The following tool can be used by educators or learners to gather evidence of learning around the levels of understanding. As the unit progresses, you or your learners can gather evidence to indicate how they have developed in their understanding at each level.

Dated observations can be anecdotal notes, links to digitally captured learning samples, or other examples of evidence that demonstrate the individual learner's understanding. The evidence collected throughout the learning can be used for reporting and other evaluative processes, such as learner conferences. The document also serves to ensure moderation of the conceptual elements when shared with other educators teaching the same unit.

Student Name:		Date:	
Understanding Question:			
Level 1: Recalling Evidence of Learning	**Level 2: Describing Evidence of Learning**	**Level 3: Explaining and Connecting Evidence of Learning**	**Level 4: Analysing and Applying Evidence of Learning**
Learners **identify** factors that contribute to a person's identity.	Learners **categorise** factors that contribute to a person's identity and **describe** different factors of people's identity.	Learners **compare and contrast** factors that contribute to people's identity and **explain** how those factors come together to develop a person's identity.	Learners **evaluate** which factors have the greatest impact on a person's identity and which factors can lead to perceived ideas about people's identity, with **reasoning.**

"Sharing with students a rubric has had tremendous impact. It communicates with students exactly what you are looking for and gives them every opportunity to achieve at a high standard—they see the target and are therefore more likely to hit it. Using work examples has also been a powerful tool to support student achievement. It allows students to self-assess and see areas where they might focus to improve."

— Catherine Doig, Upper Primary, Holy Spirit Nicholls

Peer-Assessment and Continuous Assessment Tool
Learner/Learner | Critique Groups of Three

The following tool can be used by learners to gather evidence for one another. Place students in groups of three. As the unit progresses, the group members exchange and discuss ideas and then use the prompts to record their evidence of understanding.

The peer group discussions assist with moderation and consistency of the learning. Additionally, the robust dialogue around the understanding questions deepens the students' understanding.

Criteria (developed with the secondary math team at KAUST School) **Understanding Question:** How and why do relationships affect quantities and space?	What does this look like?	How do you know you have achieved this?
I can use my knowledge of maximum and minimum problems to design a space. I can state my choices, with reasons.		

I can use my knowledge of maximum and minimum problems to design a functional space for a desired quantity. I can describe my choices, with reasons.		
I can use my knowledge of maximum and minimum problems to design a functional space for a desired quantity. I can compare and contrast my design choices and how these affect the accuracy of my design, with reasons.		
I can use my knowledge of maximum and minimum problems to design a functional space for a desired quantity. I can evaluate my design choices by and how these affect the accuracy of my design, with reasons.		

Self-Assessment Tool
Learner/Learner/Educator | One to One

This tool is used by the learner to collect evidence of their own understanding. Before placing the evidence in the tool, the learner checks with one other peer that the evidence meets the criteria. Once that peer agrees that the evidence meets the criteria, they then check with the educator. This greatly assists with moderation of the learning.

Criteria How do writers use literary forms and devices as a form of expression?	Students **identify** literary forms and devices in literature.	Students **describe** literary forms and devices and how the device and form add to the expression of the literature.	Students **compare and contrast** different literary forms and devices and **explain** how the device and form add to the expression of the literature and its effectiveness, with **justification.**	Students **evaluate** how devices and forms are being used in literature and **analyse** the effectiveness of how they add to the expressions. They make suggestions for how it could be improved, with **evidence.**
Evidence I have understood this:				

Collaborative Tool
Learner/Learner/Educator | Critique Groups of Three

This tool is used by learners to collect evidence and data of learning. Learners are placed in critique groups of three. Each time they feel they have evidence that connects to the level, they exchange and discuss their understanding with their critique group. From there, the group discusses their next steps for learning. This reflection of understanding and consideration on how to further their learning encourages learner agency.

Understanding Question: How am I evaluating the elements of art in my artwork?	Evidence That I have Achieved This	Next Steps in My Learning
Identify Recognise and state briefly a distinguishing fact or feature.		
Outline Give a brief account or summary.		
Describe Give a detailed account or picture of a situation, event, pattern, or process.		
Analyse Break it down to bring out the essential elements or structure.		

Making Learning Visible at Every Level
Learner/Learner/Educator | Whole Class

Making learning visible for all to see is another way for learner to share their understanding. Designate a space in the learning environment, either on a wall in the classroom or in a shared online space, where learners can display their evidence of understanding. Throughout the unit, learners can post their learning when they believe they have reached a new level of understanding. This visibility also ensures moderation because the classroom community can review the evidence, learn from one another, and develop expectations of evidence for each level.

I can identify physical traits of a character.

Evidence I can do this:

I can describe different traits of a character.

Evidence I can do this:

I can explain and give examples of
the character displaying those traits.

Evidence I can do this:

I can give examples of the character displaying traits,
evaluate these, and make inferences about them.

Evidence I can do this:

CONCEPTS IN ACTION
Equipping Learners to Self-Assess

> *"Teachers collect information about students' understanding almost continuously and make adjustments to their teaching on the basis of their interpretation of that information. They observe . . . formulate hypotheses . . . question students to test their hypotheses, interpret students' responses, and adjust their teaching plans."*
>
> —————————— National Research Council

At St. Joseph's Institution International School, the Grade 4 team plans for each of the four levels of the Rubric for Understanding. To ensure learners are clear about expectations, educators connect supporting questions to each level's understanding question.[1] Students consider those questions and the specified criteria to make judgements about their learning and determine whether they have met the different levels of understanding.

---

1 In this example, the term lines of inquiry is equivalent to the understanding questions, and the guiding questions are supporting questions.

Rubric for this unit of work (part 1)

What a Wonderful World - Learning Rubric				
Lines of inquiry	Level 1: Recalling	Level 2: Describing	Level 3: Explaining and connecting	Level 4: Analysing and applying
How and why is the earth continuously changing?	Identify the changes in the earth -continents -landforms	Describe how and why the earth is changing over time -movement of plates -forces -pressure	Explain similarities and differences in how the earth has changed over time (eg slow processes and fast processes)	Hypothesise how these changes can impact future generations
Guiding Questions	How were the continents formed? What are tectonic plates? What are earth's processes? What are slow and fast processes? What is the difference between natural and manmade changes? Why are there no natural disasters in Singapore?			

Rubric for this unit of work (part 1)

What a Wonderful World - Learning Rubric				
Lines of inquiry	Level 1: Recalling	Level 2: Describing	Level 3: Explaining and connecting	Level 4: Analysing and applying
How and why is the earth continuously changing?	Identify the changes in the earth -continents -landforms	Describe how and why the earth is changing over time -movement of plates -forces -pressure	Explain similarities and differences in how the earth has changed over time (eg slow processes and fast processes)	Hypothesise how these changes can impact future generations
Guiding Questions	How were the continents formed? What are tectonic plates? What are earth's processes? What are slow and fast processes? What is the difference between natural and manmade changes? Why are there no natural disasters in Singapore?			

Rubric for this unit of work (part 1)

What a Wonderful World - Learning Rubric				
Lines of Inquiry	Level 2: Recalling	Level 3: Describing	Level 3: Explaining and Connecting	Level 4: Analysing and Applying
How and why is the earth continuously changing?	Identify the changes in the earth -continents -landforms	Describe how and why the earth is changing over time -movement of plates -forces -pressure	Explain similarities and differences in how the earth has changed over time (eg slow processes and fast processes)	Hypothesise how these changes can impact future generations
Guiding Questions	How were the continents formed? What are tectonic plates? What are earth's processes? What are slow and fast processes? What is the difference between natural and manmade changes? Why are there no natural disasters in Singapore?			

Rubric for this unit of work (part 1)

What a Wonderful World - Learning Rubric				
Lines of Inquiry	Level 2: Recalling	Level 3: Describing	Level 3: Explaining and Connecting	Level 4: Analysing and Applying
How and why is the earth continuously changing?	Identify the changes in the earth -continents -landforms	Describe how and why the earth is changing over time -movement of plates -forces -pressure	Explain similarities and differences in how the earth has changed over time (eg slow processes and fast processes)	Hypothesise how these changes can impact future generations
Guiding Questions	How were the continents formed? What are tectonic plates? What are earth's processes? What are slow and fast processes? What is the difference between natural and manmade changes? Why are there no natural disasters in Singapore?			

Here is an example of a learner reflecting on their understanding and assessing their progress based on the rubric.

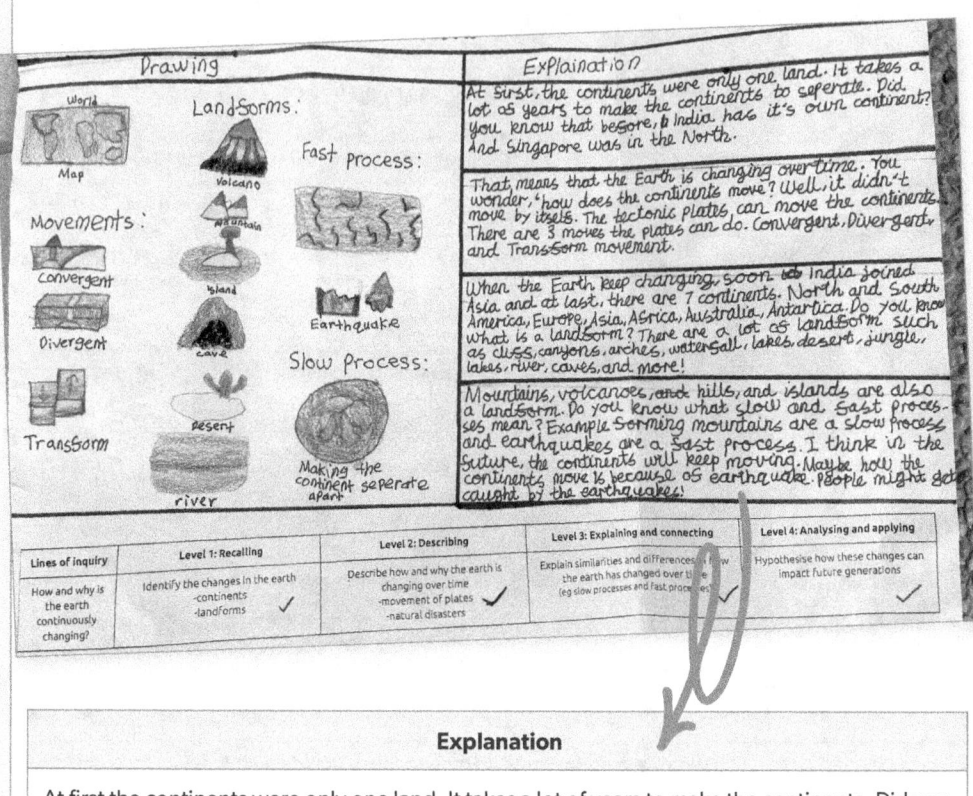

Explanation

At first the continents were only one land. It takes a lot of years to make the continents. Did you know that before India has its own continent and Singapore was in the North.

That means that the earth is changing over time. You wonder, "how does the continents move?" Well, it didn't move by itself. The tectonic plates can move the continents. There are three moves the plates can do. Convergent, divergent and transform movement.

When the earth keep changing, soon India joined Asia and at last there are seven continents. North and South American, Europe, Asia, Africa, Australia, and Antarctica. Do you know what is a land form, there are a lot of landforms such as cliffs, canyons, arches, waterfall, lakes, desert, jungle, river, caves and more!

Mountains, volcanoes, hills and islands are also landforms. Do you know what slow and fast processes mean? Examples forming mountains are a slow process, and Earthquakes are a fast process. I think in the future the continents will keep moving. Maybe how the continents move is because of earthquake. People might get caught by the Earthquakes!

"Students reflecting and marking themselves on the rubric provides for agency and constant self-reflection—particularly if you don't just pull it out at the end of the unit. It (the rubric) should be used regularly by students to see how they are progressing. Students should be asking themselves, 'where am I now and what are the steps I need to take to move myself on this rubric?'"

Maureen Sackmaster Carpenter, PYP Coordinator at BBIS
Berlin Brandenburg International School, Germany

CONSIDERATIONS WHEN COLLECTING EVIDENCE
(ADAPTED FROM AITSL 2020)

1. Start collecting the evidence as soon as it is appropriate. Once you've developed the Rubric for Understanding and made sure the expectations are clear, it's time to collect evidence.

Consider developing invitations (provocations) as a way to collect evidence of prior knowledge and begin to ascertain learners' conceptual baseline in connection to the Rubric for Understanding. An invitation (provocation) is a display of materials or objects or carefully selected resources that are arranged to draw learners' attention and engage them in a world of wonder, exploration, and discovery where they tap into their prior knowledge.

2. Collect evidence throughout the learning process. Remember that you and your learners can and should regularly be collecting evidence of understanding. Allow your learner the opportunity to connect with what they consider evidence of the levels and self-regulate as they advance through the learning process.

The rubric is a *continuous* assessment tool, which means we collect evidence in connection to the levels of understanding in the learning process. As you interact with learners throughout the day, be mindful of what evidence you observe (see questions on page 130). Evidence can take many forms and does not always require a completed piece of learning.

3. Take time to moderate and evaluate the evidence. Collecting the evidence is important; however, to ensure quality moderation and consistency of learning, it is vital that the evidence is analysed. Thus, moderation also takes place throughout the learning process. As you and your learners collect evidence, examine it to determine whether and why (or why not) it meets the criteria for the level. This evaluation can be done individually, as a class, with peers, and with other educators.

Moderation builds understanding and clarity of the levels throughout the process. This intentional reflection also allows you to plan the next steps in the learning process with the needs of learners in mind.

4. Consider how much evidence you require to evaluate learners' understanding. It is not necessary to collect extensive amounts of evidence. Collecting too much evidence, particularly without a plan for evaluation and moderation, can lead to you and your learners feeling overwhelmed. Set clear expectations from the onset regarding what is needed at each level; for example, you may decide that two or three pieces of evidence and a conferencing/feedback session with you or a peer are sufficient.

Decide together, as you are co-constructing the rubric, what an efficient selection of evidence would entail. The purpose—the connection to the level—should also be part of your discussion.

QUESTIONS TO GUIDE COLLECTING EVIDENCE OF UNDERSTANDING

The following tool offers additional consideration that you can use as you and your learners deliberate the guidelines for collecting evidence for a particular unit. We've included questions that you can use to elicit understanding around the levels of understanding as well as possible strategies that you could use to elicit evidence of that level. This list is not exhaustive. Use it as a starting point to consider the type of understanding you are looking for and therefore what engagements will elicit that evidence.

Level of Understanding
Recalling

Generic Sample Questions

What do you know about the concept?

Can you identify the concept?

What are examples of the concept?

What characteristics does the concept have?

Can you identify key knowledge about the understanding question?

Possible Ideas to Elicit Evidence

- List
- Label
- Create illustrations
- Answer knowledge questions
- Spider map
- Concept walk and photos

Level of Understanding
Describing

Generic Sample Questions

Can you define the concept?

Can you tell why this concept might be important to understand?

Can you describe the understanding question/concept using examples?

Can you categorise aspects of the understanding question/concept?

Can you describe different features of the understanding question/concept?

Can you describe the different points of view or perspectives on the understanding question/concept?

Can you break down the understanding question/concept into smaller parts or sub-concepts?

Possible Ideas to Elicit Evidence

- Categorisation
- Writing or drawing descriptions
- Write/draw

- Describe points of view
- Models
- Frayer model (See continuous assessment tools for an example.)
- Visual representations

Level of Understanding
Explaining and Connecting

Generic Sample Questions

How would you explain the understanding questions/concept?

What do you notice in terms of similarities and differences around the understanding question/concept and why?

What trends or patterns are you noticing in connection to the understanding question/concept?

Why are there varying perspectives about the understanding question/concept?

What is the cause/effect relationship in connection to the understanding question/concept and why does this exist?

What is the significance of the understanding question/concept in the context of the subject or disciplines? What connections are you noticing?

How would you explain this understanding question/concept to someone who is not familiar with it?

Possible Ideas to Elicit Evidence

- Concept mapping
- Venn diagrams
- Points of view (Visible Thinking Routine)
- Cause/Effect charts
- Debates
- Diamond ranking
- Models and explanations
- Agree/Disagree

- Graphic organisers
- Case studies
- Developing experiments and investigations to test theories

Level of Understanding
Analysing and Applying

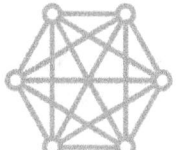

Generic Sample Questions

How would you analyse the understanding question, and what suggestions might you make about it?

What has had the greatest impact on the understanding question and why?

How can you transfer and apply your knowledge and understanding of the understanding question? How might it be applied in different situations or contexts?

What are some of the potential implications or consequences of understanding this question? How do you know?

How might different interpretations or understandings of this understanding question influence the way it is applied or used?

Can you explain how this understanding question might be used to solve a particular problem or challenge?

Can you identify any assumptions or biases that might be underlying this understanding question?

Possible Ideas to Elicit Evidence

- Analyse and evaluate solutions and ideas.
- Justify and provide evidence for conclusions.
- Develop generalizations with evidence and justification.
- Develop further ideas and solutions.
- Extend research/inquiry projects, e.g., photographic exhibition.

THE ROLE OF PRIOR KNOWLEDGE
IN CONTINUOUS ASSESSMENT

> *"If I had to reduce all of educational psychology to just one principle, I would say this: The most important single factor influencing learning is what the learner already knows. Ascertain this and teach him [her/them] accordingly."*
>
> — David Ausubel, *Educational Psychology*

Conceptual understanding occurs over time as learners add new understanding to their existing knowledge. Consider the following benefits of accessing and assessing learners' prior knowledge:

Differentiating Instruction

When you are aware of learners' existing knowledge and conceptual understanding, you can adjust the instruction accordingly for each learner.

Building Connections

Prior knowledge provides the starting point for new learning. By tapping into learners' existing understanding, you can work together to make connections between what they already know and the new concepts being introduced. Building on the foundation of their prior understanding helps learners grasp and make connections with the new information. At the same time, returning to or recalling what they have learned in the past reinforces that understanding and promotes deeper learning.

Addressing Misconceptions

Learners may hold misconceptions or incomplete understandings of certain concepts and knowledge. Ascertaining prior knowledge allows educators to identify and address misconceptions relevant to the unit's content and concepts. Armed with this insight about your learners, you will be able to plan learning engagements that provide them with the opportunity to discover their misconceptions. With experience, you will become aware of common misconceptions. By targeting and clarifying these early on, you may also be able to prevent misunderstandings.

Engaging Learners

Acknowledging and building on learners' prior knowledge enhances learner engagement. When we recognise their existing knowledge and understanding, learners feel empowered and more motivated to take ownership of and actively participate in the learning process. Gathering this knowledge in a visible space in your classroom is one way to assess and celebrate what your learners already know

Scaffolding Learning

Assessing learners' knowledge helps you determine the appropriate level of support and scaffolding they need. When you understand their starting points, you are better able to provide guidance, resources, and learning engagements that will gradually lead learners to develop their conceptual understanding. We encourage educators to make explicit to learners how they have adapted the learning and how this takes into consideration their individual needs.

Planning and Curriculum Design

Educators can use information about learners' prior knowledge to inform the planning and teaching design. Aligning instruction means that you ensure a proper sequence of new material and concepts by building on what your learners already know and understand.

Encouraging Metacognition

Assessing prior knowledge prompts learners to reflect on their understanding and articulate what they know. This metacognitive process supports learners in becoming aware of their own thinking and learning processes. It also encourages them to monitor their progress and take responsibility for their learning. (We discuss self-assessment more in Chapter 5.)

 Consider the purposes for assessing learners' prior knowledge. Have you used prior knowledge for any of those purposes? If so, what did it look like and how did you do it?

Differentiating instruction	
Building connections	
Addressing misconceptions	
Engaging learners	
Scaffolding learning	
Planning and curriculum design	
Encouraging metacognition	

Gathering and Assessing Prior Knowledge

Knowing *why* you want to assess and gathering prior knowledge will equip you to determine the most effective way to do so. With this in mind, begin by reviewing your Rubrics for Understanding questions, then plan learning that will elicit evidence of what your learners already know and understand in connection to those questions.

In organising and planning for assessing prior knowledge, we suggest the following steps:

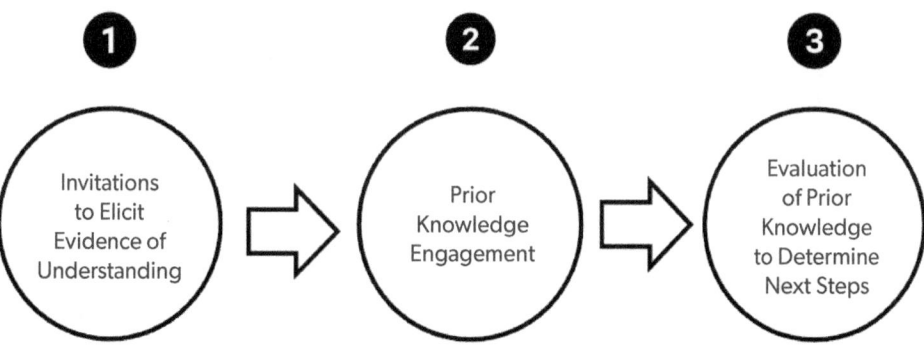

1. **Invitations to Elicit Evidence of Understanding**—Set up invitations connected to the concept and understanding questions. Use prompts and questions to intentionally promote inquiry, collaboration, and the construction of meaning in connection to any prior knowledge your students may have about the concept or topic.

2. **Prior Knowledge Engagement**—Following the invitations, develop prior knowledge engagements that allow learners to share what they understood about the invitation.

3. **Evaluation of the Prior Knowledge to Determine Next Steps**— Evaluate the evidence of prior knowledge in connection to the Rubric for Understanding and understanding questions to inform next steps in the learning process.

WHAT IS AN INVITATION TO LEARNING?

An invitation to learning gets learners to start thinking about the concept or understanding questions you are going to explore together. A synonymous educational term for invitation is *provocation*. Regardless of the term used in your setting, the purpose is the same.

Characteristics of Effective Invitations to Learning

- Promote curiosity and interest around the learning
- Use authentic resources (when possible) to connect concepts
- Connect to the desired evidence of understanding
- Build on prior knowledge
- Promote thinking
- Promote the co-construction of meaning
- Allow for multiple entry points into learning
- Invite inquiry by being open-ended and having multiple possibilities

Invitations require educator intent. To be effective, first consider what kind of evidence you are looking for in connection to prior knowledge. In addition to engaging learner interest, invitations provide a learning context for learners to wonder, collaborate, discuss, and co-construct meaning about a concept. The opportunity for dialogue allows them to consider other perspectives and learn from each other.

Invitations are organised around one (or more) of the understanding questions in your rubric as well as evidence that is to be elicited at the different levels. With each invitation, learners have the opportunity to discuss and connect previous knowledge to new understanding. By providing invitations throughout the learning, rather than only at the beginning of the unit, you empower your learners to tap into what they already know and understand about the purpose for the learning. You also give them the valuable time to co-construct their learning and engage in the concepts before gathering evidence. This space for processing and reflecting ensures the evidence of understanding is elicited.

Ideas for Invitations

An invitation could be one or more of the following:

- Artifacts
- Loose parts

- Quotations
- Photographs and Images
- Newspaper headings
- Media: videos and podcasts
- Books
- Problems to solve
- Learning samples
- Excursions
- Guest speakers
- Infographics
- Experiments and investigations
- Concept walks (school and beyond)
- Small world play

What ideas would you add to this list?

Please note the following are examples. There are many other ways that invitations can be organised and used.

Artifacts

Example provided by Anglo American School Moscow

Understanding Question: Why and how do people innovate?

Learners explored artifacts from the past.

Prompt: What do you see, think, and wonder? (Visible Thinking Routine)

After allowing time for discussion, the teacher introduces modern versions of each artifact. Learners match the new items to the old artifacts.

Prompt: What changed? How did it change? Why did it change?

Loose Parts

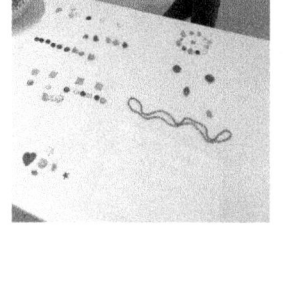

Example provided by International School of Berne, Gümligen, Switzerland

Understanding Question: What contributes to identity?

Prompt: Use the loose parts to tell the story of your identity. Use a sticky note to explain your thinking.

Example provided by International School of Berne, Gümligen, Switzerland

Understanding Question: How is our world connected?

Prompt: Can you tell a story of connection? Use a sticky note to explain your thinking.

Example provided by Radford College, Canberra

Understanding Question: How and why are systems evident in our world?

Prompt: Can you use the materials to create a system? Explain your system using a sticky note.

Quotations

"Peace cannot be kept by force; it can only be achieved by understanding."

———————————— Albert Einstein ————————————

"It isn't enough to talk about peace. One must believe in it. And it isn't enough to believe in it. One must work at it."

———————————— Eleanor Roosevelt ————————————

"It is not enough to say, 'We must not wage war.' It is necessary to love peace and sacrifice for it. We must concentrate not merely on the negative expulsion of war, but the positive affirmation of peace."

———————————— Dr. Martin Luther King ————————————

"You may encounter many defeats, but you must not be defeated."

———————————— Maya Angelou ————————————

"I do not want the peace which passeth understanding; I want the understanding which bringeth peace."

———————————— Helen Keller ————————————

"Peace is not merely the absence of visible conflict."

———————————— Barack Obama ————————————

Understanding Question: How can understanding peace impact people's ideas of conflict?

Prompt: What do these quotations make you think of? Do you agree or disagree with them? Why?

Photographs/Images

Photographs by Tania Lattanzio

Understanding Question: How do characteristics and environment connect to the survival of living things?

Prompt: As you look through the photos, record your ideas connected to the following questions:

- What does the environment look like?
- What characteristics do animals have?
- How are they behaving?

Photographs by Andrea Müller and Tania Lattanzio

Understanding Question: How is math represented in nature?

Prompt: What mathematical ideas or principles do you see in the images?

Newspaper Headings

"Australia's rich getting richer while the poor get poorer"
Source: ABC Radio National, Lisa Needham, 16 January 2023

"Income inequality surges as richest group gets more than 90
per cent of the gains, Australia Institute finds"
Source: ABC News, Daniel Ziffer, 12 April 2023

"66 Australian Millionaires Paid No Tax Last Year: ATO"
Source: 9 News, Nick Pearson, 10 June 2023

Understanding Question: How does wealth impact nations?

Prompt:

- What do you think these quotations mean in connection to fairness?
- What do these quotations mean in connection to the economy?
- What do you want to understand or know more about?

Problems to Solve

Can your group solve the following:

- You are at the shops, and there are 3 lines.
  - 1st line: 3 people: first person has 10 items; the second person has 15 items, and the third person has 12 items.
  - 2nd line: 2 people: first person has 23 items, and the second person has 17 items.
  - 3rd line: 5 people: first person has 2 items, second person has 3 items, third person has 4 items, fifth person has 4 items.
- Which line do you go to and why?

Understanding Question: How can we use logic to solve mathematical problems?

Prompt: Did you solve the question? What steps and thinking did you use? Record your process.

Infographics/Graphs

Food Waste Is Becoming A Billion Tonne Problem

Estimated annual global food waste by sector (million tonnes)

569

244

118

Household

Food service

Retail

Source: UNEP Food Waste Index

Source : Statista
https://www.statista.com/chart/24349/estimated-annual-global-food-waste-by-sector/

Understanding Question: How do people's actions impact sustainability? (positive/negative)

Prompt: What do you think causes this? Why?
What do you think the impact of this will be? Why?

Concept Walks (school and beyond)

Diversity Concept Walk

Understanding Question: What impact does diversity have on communities (people, living things)?

Activity: Learners go on a concept walk at home or at school to collect evidence of where they see diversity in their world.

Prompts: Collect evidence (photos, writing, sketches) of where you see diversity in our community.

Share your photos with each other and consider these questions:

- How is that diversity?
- What is diversity?

Combining Invitations, Living Things, Artifacts, and Books

Example from Australian International School, Singapore

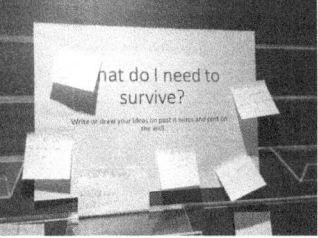 

Understanding Question: What contributes to the growth and survival of living things?

Students observe a turtle in an aquarium or bin of water and look through books about how turtles live and grow.

Prompt: What do I need to survive?

Using Invitations to Gather Prior Knowledge

The following examples show you how to use invitations specifically to assess prior knowledge.

Understanding Question:	Why do people explore?
Invitations	Set up a variety of stations around the room. Use different types of invitations connected to exploration. Invitations could include the following: • Videos • Images • Quotations • Books • Images of famous explorers **Prompt:** What do you see, think, wonder? (Visible Thinking Routine) Learners explore the invitations and record their thoughts as they visit the different stations.

Prior Knowledge Engagement	**Concept Map** Learners brainstorm what they have learnt from the invitation.
	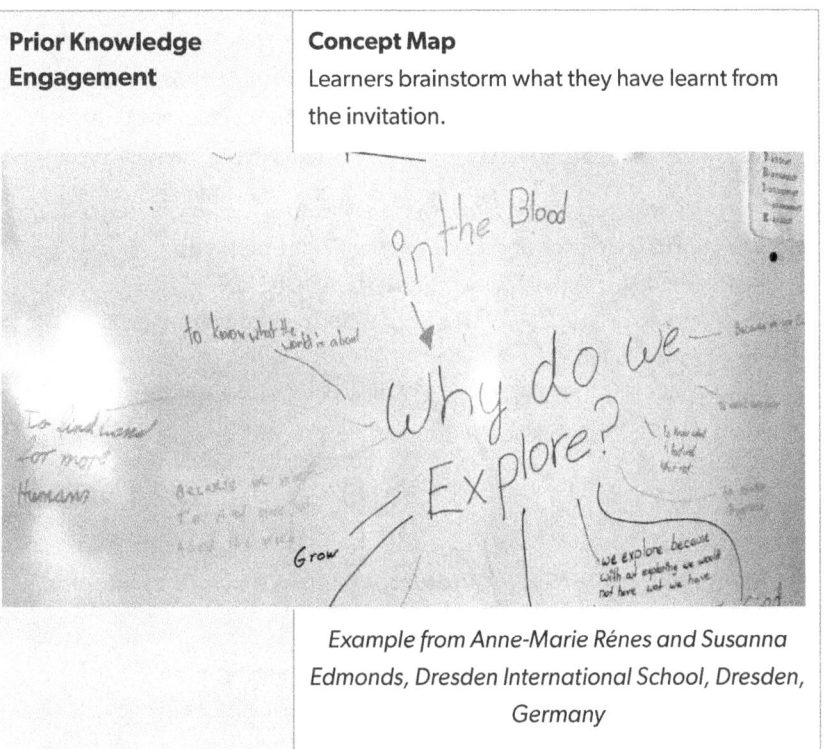
	Example from Anne-Marie Rénes and Susanna Edmonds, Dresden International School, Dresden, Germany

How to Gather Evidence and Evaluate the Prior Knowledge

- Evaluate the concept map to identify misconceptions and knowledge gaps where the concept needs further exploration. Use the insights to plan the next teaching steps.
- Have learners explore the invitations on their own and answer the question, *Why do people explore?* Consider where learners are in connection to the Rubric for Understanding.

Understanding Question:	**How and why do we measure things?**
Invitation	**Challenging Task** In pairs, learners are asked to measure the length of one of them, using any object in the room.

Prior Knowledge Engagement	Educator takes photos, observe, and take notes about how learners are going about measuring each other, whether they understand what is meant by length, and whether they can use nonstandard tools of measurement accurately.

How to Gather Evidence and Evaluate the Prior Knowledge

- Review the notes to determine the next steps in the learning process. The observations will help reveal who understands the concept and who may need further scaffolding.
- Consider what the observations indicate about where learners are in connection to the Rubric for Understanding.

Understanding Question	**What happens when materials interact and why?**
Invitations	**Experiment and Investigation** Students work in small groups of two or three. The educator provides them with the following materials to investigate: • A sphere of ice (frozen in a balloon) • Food colouring • Salt • Torches • Water • Toothpicks

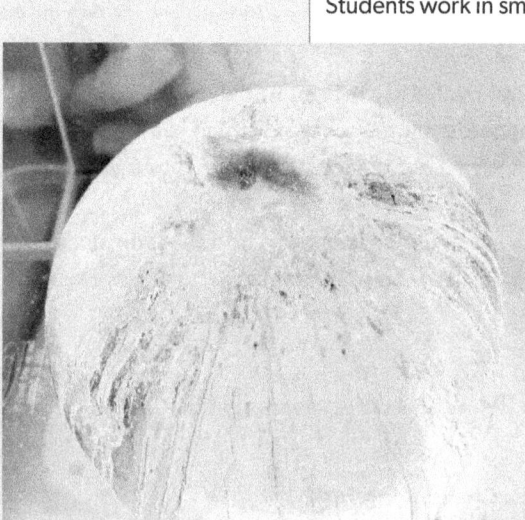

Prior Knowledge Engagement	**Documenting the Investigation** Educators and learners take photos and make observations. Educators intentionally observe and take notes about what learners are saying and doing as well as the questions they are asking. **Creating a Graffiti Board** Following the investigation, the small groups record everything they understood and learnt from the investigation. Learners capture their findings and previous knowledge on a Graffiti Board, a piece of paper or poster, by drawing, writing notes, labelling images, etc.

How to Gather Evidence and Evaluate the Prior Knowledge
- Review the notes, photos, and graffiti board to determine what misconceptions existed and where learners are in their understanding.
- Plan next steps in connection to these findings and students' understanding related to the Rubric of Understanding.

Develop an invitation and prior knowledge engagement for your understanding question.

Understanding Question	
Invitation	
Prior Knowledge Engagement	
How to Gather Evidence and Evaluate the Prior Knowledge	

Moderation Exercise: How Deep is Your Understanding

Grade Five Team (Daniel Larrosa, Kate Ross, Cameron Gensemer,
Amber Nelsen, Craig Dwyer, Ashley Lai), The International School,
Ho Chi Minh City, Vietnam

How deep is your understanding?

This question promotes moderation and collective understanding as learners consider where they believe they are in relation to the levels of the Rubric for Understanding. The rubric is posted in the classroom, and after collecting evidence, learners place their name or photo and explain why they feel they are at that level. The graphics symbolise connections: where there is one idea, many ideas, related ideas, and extended ideas. These assist learners in considering where they think their current understanding is.

Example 1

Level of Understanding	How deep is your learning?	Connections
Recalling	I can **recall** and **identify.**	**One idea**
Describing	I can **describe.**	**Many ideas**
Explaining and Connecting	I can **explain** and **connect.**	**Related ideas**
Analysing and Applying	I can **analyse** and **apply.**	**Extended ideas**

"Performances of understanding help learners build and demonstrate their understanding. They give both you and your learners a chance to see their understanding develop in new and challenging situations over time."

———————————— Tina Blythe, Teaching for Understanding Guide

STRATEGIES FOR GATHERING EVIDENCE OF PRIOR KNOWLEDGE AND CONCEPTUAL UNDERSTANDING

Note from all of the examples provided that these strategies for gathering prior knowledge can be revisited throughout the learning as part of your continuous assessment practice. These assessment tools provide evidence of understanding around the understanding questions. They connect to the evidence of understanding defined at the levels of the understanding, enabling learners and educators to see the development of conceptual understanding over time.

It may be appropriate to have the assessment focused just on the concept or the understanding question. Below are examples of both.

Questions to Consider When Developing Learning Engagements for Gathering Evidence of Conceptual Understanding

The following questions are important because they promote educators thinking about the purpose for the learning engagements. We intentionally use the phrase *learning engagements* because we want learners engaged in their learning. It also promotes the idea that an engagement is purposeful, active, and connected to the learning. When educators consider the following questions, they are interrogating their engagements to ensure they have purpose and add meaning to the learning.

Adapted from Blythe and Associates, *Teaching for Understanding Guide*
Do the learning engagements require learners to demonstrate understanding and concepts identified in your understanding questions?
Do the learning engagements allow learners to build and demonstrate understanding?
Are the learning engagements sequenced so that learners can engage in them throughout the unit, from beginning to end?
Do the learning engagements allow learners to demonstrate their understanding in a variety of ways (written, orally, artistic endeavours, and so on)?
Are the learning engagements clearly mapped to your understanding questions?
Do the learning engagements provide you and the learner with clear evidence of understanding indicated in the rubric for understanding?

*Please note the ideas suggested are not an exhaustive list; they are simply some ideas that can be used.

Learning Engagements as Continuous Assessment Tools
Frayer Model: A Continuous Assessment Tool

The Frayer Model was designed by Dorothy Frayer (1969) and her colleagues at the University of Wisconsin. It is a great tool to unpack concepts or understanding questions. The concept being focused on or the question is placed in the middle, and learners fill in each section. This tool can be used throughout the learning, with learners adding their understanding at different points of the learning. We encourage learners to fill it in with different colours each time so it is easy to see how they are developing in their understanding.

Definition: Define the concept.
Characteristics: What characteristics make up the concept?
Examples: Give examples of the concept.
Non-Examples: These are what the concept is not.

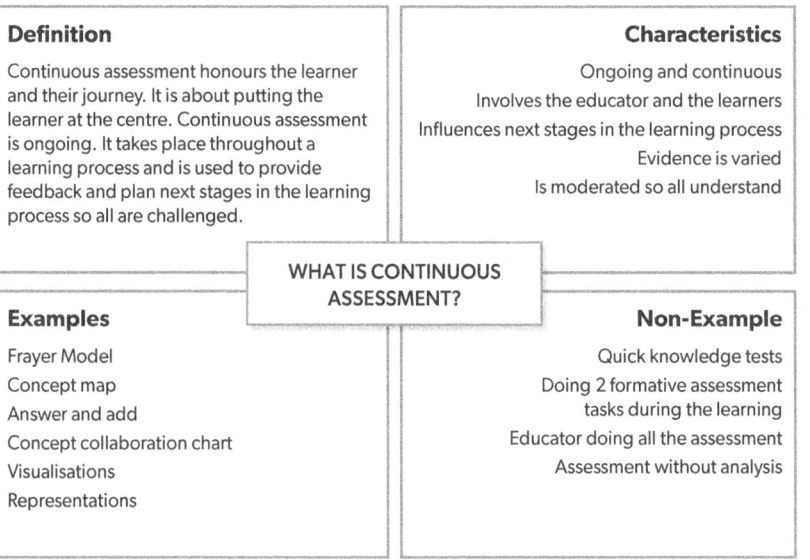

Definition

Continuous assessment honours the learner and their journey. It is about putting the learner at the centre. Continuous assessment is ongoing. It takes place throughout a learning process and is used to provide feedback and plan next stages in the learning process so all are challenged.

Characteristics

Ongoing and continuous
Involves the educator and the learners
Influences next stages in the learning process
Evidence is varied
Is moderated so all understand

WHAT IS CONTINUOUS ASSESSMENT?

Examples

Frayer Model
Concept map
Answer and add
Concept collaboration chart
Visualisations
Representations

Non-Example

Quick knowledge tests
Doing 2 formative assessment tasks during the learning
Educator doing all the assessment
Assessment without analysis

Frayer Model Template

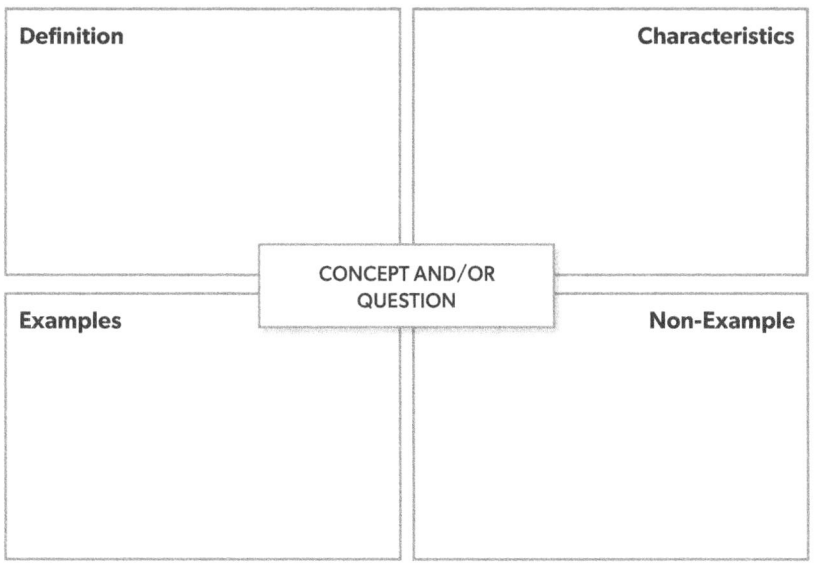

Definition

Characteristics

CONCEPT AND/OR QUESTION

Examples

Non-Example

Placemat: A Continuous Assessment Tool

Individually, in the four corners of the page, learners record their responses to the understanding question/concept. They then share what they wrote and collaboratively in the centre, decide and record what they feel are the most important ideas to consider.

It is important that we provide learners with time to think. This thinking time allows them to consider their own point of view before listening to other perspectives. It benefits learners who may be reluctant to talk in groups and our ELL (English Language Learning), who need time to think. It is also important that they can demonstrate their learning beyond just writing, especially if this is something they struggle with. The purpose of this engagement is to unpack learners' understanding of a concept, question, or idea; how they do that can differ. Learners also have to defend their point of view if they feel their idea belongs in the middle section. This can lead to learners realising they need a deeper understanding to defend that point of view.

Placemat Template

OUR
IMPORTANT
IDEAS ARE

Roll the Dice: Continuous Assessment Tool

Prepare six questions on a die connected to the learning. As learners respond, they take notes on what others are saying. This is used throughout the learning.

Please note, the questions can change based on the learning.

Conflict Questions

- Explain what conflict is.
- How does conflict work?
- Where do you see conflict in your world?
- What is conflict connected to?
- Is conflict always the same or does it change in different situations?
- What is the most important thing to understand about conflict? Why?

Generic Questions to Adapt Based on the Concept

- Explain what the _____ means.
- How does the _____ work?
- Where is the _____ evident in our world?
- How is the _____ connected to other ideas/things?
- Does the _____ change in different situations? Why? Why not?
- What is the most important thing to understand about the concept? why?

Record your new understandings.

Die Template

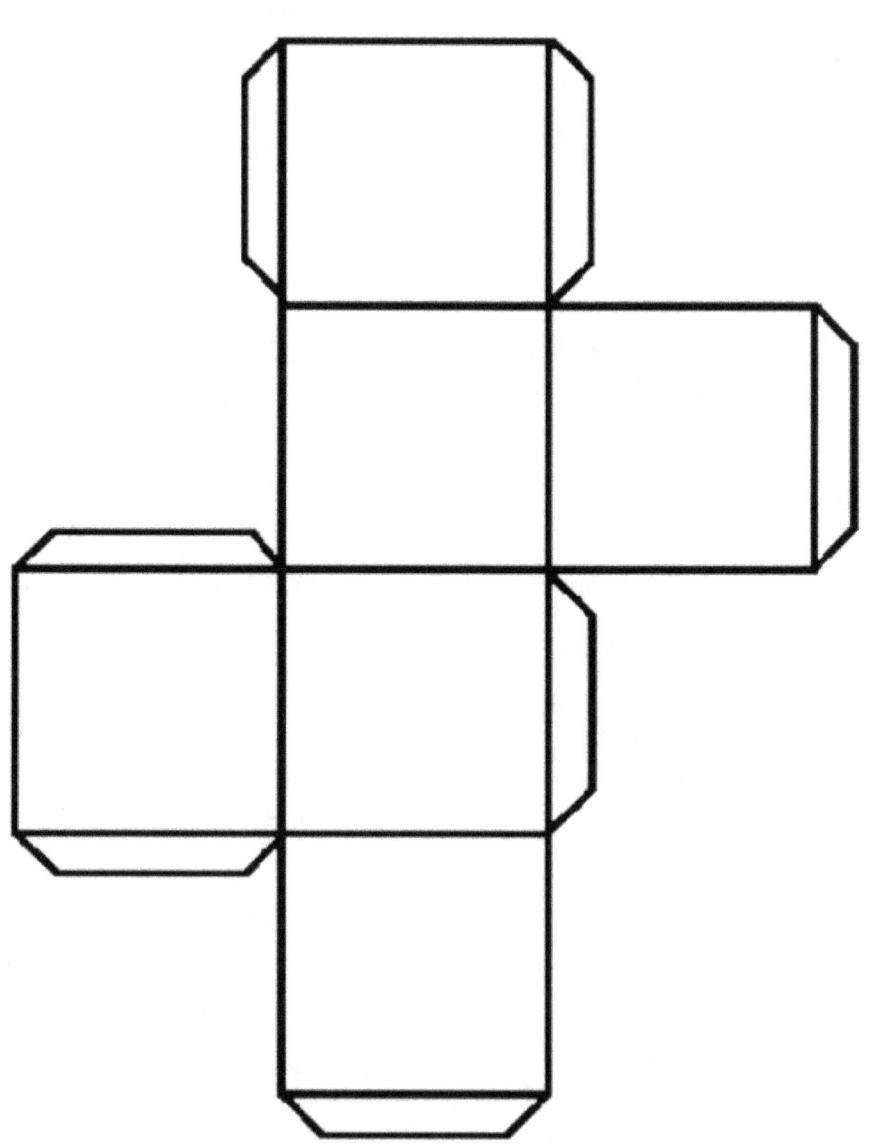

Concept Collaboration Chart: A Continuous Assessment Tool

Learners revisit the chart throughout the unit, adding their understanding each time they revisit it in a different colour. The questions can be adapted to directly connect to the learning taking place.

What are examples of the concept?	What do you now understand about the concept?
What questions do you have about the concept? What do you still want to know?	**What generalisations can you make about the concept?**

Concept Collaboration Chart Template

Visualisation: A Continuous Assessment Tool

Throughout the learning, ask learners to create a visualisation of the concept.

- Have learners explain their visualisation and make this visible so they and others can revisit it.
- Have learners do this several times throughout the learning so they can see how their understanding has developed.

Community: in a community everyone is different
but they come together to make sure everything goes
well and everyone is happy.

Answer and Add: A Continuous Assessment Tool

The understanding questions are written in an online space (e.g., Google Docs, Padlet). Throughout the learning, learners add what they have understood about the questions. We stop or pause throughout the learning to give learners the opportunity to add to their initial ideas. This is a useful tool for building understanding over time.

Conceptual Representation: A Continuous Assessment Tool

Throughout the learning, ask learners to use materiality (e.g., loose parts, tin foil, paper) to represent their understanding of the concept.

Take a photo of their representation, and have learners explain how it is connected to the concept. This evidence is made visible so learners can collaborate to learn from each other and see their understanding develop over time. The examples can be placed into an online place throughout the unit (e.g., Padlet) and become a **"Gallery of Understanding."**

Have learners do this several times throughout the learning.

Handwritten note:
Concept: Interdependence
Title: Interconnected Machine
Explanation:
All the parts of this machine
are connected in one or more
ways. For it to work they
all need to work. If one part
breaks it stops. The parts are
interdependent.

Concept Wall: A Continuous Assessment Tool

The concept or understanding question is placed on the wall in the classroom. As learners understand more, they add their learning to the wall. This can be done on sticky notes. As more ideas are added, the learners are asked:

- What patterns do you notice?
- What connections do you notice?

Learners then look for connections and patterns, which they organise on the concept wall to show their understanding. The connections can be reorganised as learners make and add new understandings.

As learners begin to unpack the understanding question, they add their ideas collectively to the concept wall.

1. Provide learners with a blank space and an understanding question or concept.
2. Have learners add their ideas to the space as the learning takes place.
3. Have learners see what connections they can make to the ideas in the space.
4. Have learners see what patterns they can see in connection to the ideas in the space.

Concept Wall
What factors contribute to people's identity?

Celebrations   Experiences   **Beliefs**   **Values**   Appearance   **Age**   Characteristics

Peer Pressure   **Education**   **Clothes**   Relationships   **Likes**   Nationality

Accessibility   **Social Class**   **Friends**   **Dislikes**   Interests

Culture

Background   Language   **Where we live**   **Family**

As learners add their ideas, they notice connections and start to group the ideas presented to notice similarities and differences.

Concept Wall
What factors contribute to people's identity?

This continues throughout the learning as learners see new connections or patterns and add their ideas. The concept wall is referred to throughout the learning to enable sharing and learning from each other as a class.

Concept Wall
What factors contribute to people's identity?

Concept Museum: A Continuous Assessment Tool

Use an online space where photos, videos, headlines, and articles can be collected (e.g., Padlet). Learners and educators contribute to the "Concept Museum." Resources are collected and added to the museum on an ongoing basis. Each time an idea is added to it, whoever adds it must explain how it connects to the understanding question or concepts and how they feel it will assist others in deepening their understanding. This becomes a resource space that learners can access to build on their current understanding. Throughout the learning, we stop and pause to look at what has been added to the museum and why.

Building Understanding: A Continuous Assessment Tool

We can develop specific continuous assessment tools that directly connect to the levels of understanding in our rubric. This enables both the learner and the educator to consider where they are in the different levels.

This chart gets filled in collaboratively as the unit takes place. Each time learners understand more, they add their thinking in a different colour. Throughout the unit, we provide opportunities for learners to look at others' charts to compare and contrast their learning with that of others as a way to deepen their own.

Identify factors that contribute to a person's identity.	Categorise factors that contribute to a person's identity and describe different factors of people's identity.	Compare and contrast factors that contribute to people's identity and explain how those factors come together to develop a person's identity.	Evaluate which factors have the greatest impact on a person's identity and which factors can lead to perceived ideas about people's identity, with reasoning.
What are factors that contribute to people's identity?	What are the categories you would use in connection with people's identity? Why?	How do factors come together to contribute to someone's identity? How does this make people similar or different?	Which factors have the biggest impact on people's identity and why? Which factors lead to people having perceptions about others? Why?

Diversity in Our Community

Hexagonal Thinking: Developed by Betsy Potash: A Continuous Assessment Tool

Developed by curriculum designer Betsy Potash, hexagonal thinking is an activity designed to get learners thinking critically, making novel connections, debating, and providing evidence to support their reasoning—by visually connecting a series of ideas written on paper or digital hexagons around a theme.

To find more about this tool and how to use it, go to: https://www.edutopia.org/video/using-hexagons-build -critical-thinking-skills

Photographic Gallery: A Continuous Assessment Tool

Throughout the learning, learners take photos of where they see that concept in their world. They upload their photo to a shared online space and explain how the photo is a representation of that concept. Learners are given time to reflect on others' photographs in connection to the concept and to share their own thoughts.

Diversity in Our Community

CONSIDERATIONS FOR EVALUATING EVIDENCE: QUESTIONS TO CONSIDER WHEN EVALUATING EVIDENCE

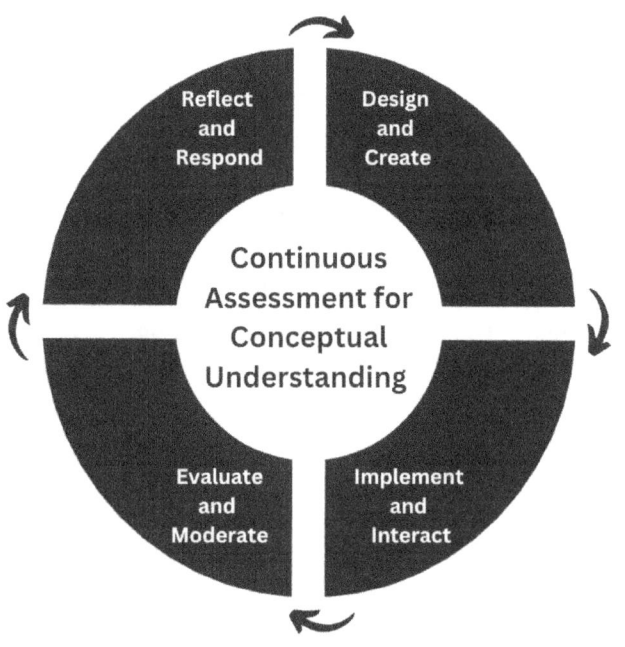

Continuous Assessment for Conceptual Understanding

Evaluate and Moderate

The evidence is evaluated and measured in terms of whether it meets the criteria for moderation (Rubric for Understanding) so that all have a clear understanding of next steps. Key to this is that the analysis of evidence collected is ongoing.

As mentioned previously, it is not enough to collect the evidence of learning; educators and learners need to evaluate the evidence in connection to the understanding questions to determine next steps in the learning process.

When evaluating evidence of understanding, educators and learners are making judgements about the levels of understanding and connecting this to the Rubric for Understanding. It is important that the evaluation takes place, because it is through the interrogation of the evidence that everyone gains an understanding of where the learner's current understanding is. The dialogue around the evidence also provides multiple perspectives on the learning, therefore ensuring the opportunity for learners to revisit their understanding. This can be in connection to others' ideas as well as reflecting on their previous misconceptions or understanding to enable them to see their own progress.

Questions to Consider When Evaluating Understanding

These questions can also be used by educators and learners to assist in the development of the Rubric for Understanding.

Please note that questions will vary depending on the understanding questions and levels indicated in your Rubric for Understanding. These are some suggestions.

Building Evidence of Understanding	Questions to Evaluate Evidence for Understanding
Level 1: Recalling Learners recall and identify knowledge that relates to the conceptual questions. ○ _____ ○ _____ ○ _____ ○ _____	• Have ideas connected to the concept been identified? • Is there recall of the main aspects of the concept/understanding question? • Has the concept been identified in a variety of situations?

Level 2: Describing Learners describe in some detail information related to the conceptual questions. Learners begin to make inferences and interpret their understandings. 	• Is there a description of the understanding question? • Have categories been developed and do they connect to the understanding question? • Are the categories logical; have learners made sense of them and described them? • Have different perspectives been identified and described?
Level 3: Explaining and Connecting Learners make comparisons between existing knowledge and the concepts. They are able to explain in detail what they have learnt and the connections within it, with reasoning and evidence. 	• Have connections been made around the understanding question? • Is there a clear, detailed explanation of the understanding question? • Have similarities and differences been explained and are they valid? • Have varying perspectives been explained with evidence of why they are varied? • Have cause-and-effect relationships been established along with the impact of this?

Level 4: Analysing and Applying Learners analyse and evaluate through reasoning and application. Learners make new connections and justify their analysis using evidence and reason. 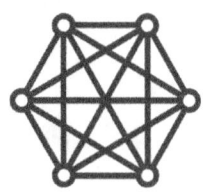	• Has the impact of the cause and effect been analysed, and does the evaluation of this come with justification or evidence? • Has the idea or solution been analysed, and in the evaluation are the suggestions for improvement backed up with justification or evidence? • Has the learner transferred and applied their learning and analysed the connections between what they learnt and how they transferred the understanding to different contexts? • Has the learner analysed different perspectives and evaluated which perspectives are justified with reasoning and evidence?

By asking these questions, educators and learners can assess the level of conceptual understanding demonstrated through the evidence provided. This evaluation helps identify the depth and quality of the learner's understanding, enabling educators and learners to provide targeted feedback, support, and further opportunities for development. This is discussed in detail in the next chapter.

PUTTING IT TOGETHER:

THE CONNECTION BETWEEN THE RUBRIC, PRIOR KNOWLEDGE, AND CONTINUOUS ASSESSMENT

The understanding levels in the Rubric for Understanding provide the context for the invitations and prior knowledge and continuous assessment engagements. We want to make sure that the engagements we are using to assess understanding also provide scope for learners to move along the Rubric for Understanding.

Developed with Grade 1 Team at American Community School, Amman

You will see in this example how the invitations and continuous assessment engagements directly connect back to the levels of understanding and criteria in each level. Based on learners' understanding, engagements are developed to meet the needs of learners at different levels.

Level 1: Recalling	Level 2: Describing
Learners recall and identify knowledge that relates to the conceptual questions.	Learners describe in some detail information related to the conceptual questions. Learners begin to make inferences and interpret their understandings.
Understanding Question: What contributes to an effective learning community?	
Students **name** factors in a learning community.	Students **describe** what makes a learning community and the factors that contribute to a learning community.
Understanding Question **Student Criteria:** What contributes to an effective learning community?	
I can name factors in a learning community.	I can describe what makes a learning community. I can describe factors that contribute to a learning community.

Level 3: Explaining and Connecting	Level 4: Analysing and Applying
Learners make comparisons between existing knowledge and the concepts. They are able to explain in detail what they have learnt and the connections within it, with reasoning and evidence.	Learners analyse and evaluate through reasoning and application. Learners make new connections and justify their analysis using evidence and reason.
Students **compare and contrast** the factors that contribute to an effective learning community, noting **similarities and differences** with **reasoning**.	Students **analyse** the factors that contribute to an effective learning community and **evaluate** which factors they think are the most important, with **reasoning**.
I can explain what an effective learning community is. I can explain the different factors that contribute to a learning community. I can explain how these factors make the learning community effective.	I can analyse the factors that contribute to an effective learning community. I can evaluate which factors I think are the most important, with reasoning.

Invitations	**Videos**
Set up stations for each of these invitations and allow students to rotate through them.	Videos of animal communities Videos of how animals work together in their community

Videos

Videos of animal communities

Videos of how animals work together in their community

Prompts

What do we notice?

How do they work together?

Why do they need to work together?

What is the benefit of them working together?

Literatures and Images

Books about people working together for their community

Prompts

- What do we notice?
- How do they work together?
- Why do they need to work together?
- What is the benefit of them working together?

Concept Walk

Going for a walk in their community and taking photos of when they see people working together to share with the class

Prompts

- What do we notice?
- How are they working together?
- What makes what they are doing work?
- What is a community?
- How do communities function?

Prior Knowledge and Continuous Assessment	**Definitions** Define what a learning community is (to be adapted and changed as the learning takes pace). Define what is effective (to be adapted and changed as the learning takes pace). **Concept Wall** What makes an effective learning community? <ul><li>As learners understand more about what makes an effective learning community, their ideas are added to the concept wall.</li><li>As ideas are added, learners will be encouraged to make connections moving along the Rubric for Understanding.</li><li>This is also used by educators to see what learners have not yet thought of, and further invitations are planned to ensure engagement with the areas not currently addressed.</li></ul> For example, if the educator notices that collaboration has not been placed on the concept wall, they would intentionally plan to elicit this understanding from learners through an invitation, such as photos of people collaborating in learning communities, or videos of living things collaborating in learning communities. **Prompt:** What do we notice?

Ongoing Continuous Assessment Tool: Concept Chart

Throughout the unit, individual learners will complete the concept chart (using sticky notes). The questions connect directly back to the levels in the Rubric for Understanding. The concept chart will be shared with peers and the educator to ascertain learners' understanding.

What makes an effective learning community?	Similarities and differences between the factors? Highlight any you notice.	Which factors have the biggest impact and why?

Level 1: Recalling	**Level 2: Describing**
Learners recall and identify knowledge that relates to the conceptual questions.	Learners describe in some detail information related to the conceptual questions. Learners begin to make inferences and interpret their understandings.

Understanding Question: What contributes to an effective learning community?

Students name factors in a learning community.	Students describe what makes a learning community and the factors that contribute to a learning community.

Learning Engagements

Educators develop engagements that focus on the different levels of understanding and are based on where students are in their understanding. Before the learning, educators may like to consider a few possibilities around each level, with the understanding that it may change in connection to learners and their individual needs and interests.

Possible Engagements at Different Levels:

Photographic Evidence

Photos of the classroom are taken by the teacher and used by students to consider what factors contribute to their learning community.

Concept Walk

Students go on a concept walk to look for evidence of factors that contribute to the learning community; they share these photos with each other and identify the factors.

Definition

Develop a definition about what a learning community is as a class. (This may change as the students learn more.)

Agreements

Develop agreements

Information Piece

Using photos or images, create an information piece about what makes an effective learning community, describing the factors (e.g., verbally, written, podcast, book, infographic).

Interviews

Interview educators or students and ask them to describe what contributes to making their class a learning community.

My Contributions

Have students individually record how they contribute to their learning community.

Level 3: Explaining and Connecting	Level 4: Analysing and Applying
Learners make comparisons between existing knowledge and the concepts. They are able to explain in detail what they have learnt and the connections within it, with reasoning and evidence.	Learners analyse and evaluate through reasoning and application. Learners make new connections and justify their analysis using evidence and reason.
Students compare and contrast the factors that contribute to an effective learning community, noting similarities and differences, with reasoning.	Students analyse the factors that contribute to an effective learning community and evaluate which factors they think are the most important, with reasoning.

Categorizing and Connecting

Using photos/images connected to the factors that contribute to a learning community, students categorise them and explain their categories. They record their thinking.

Once the factors have been identified and described, students may categorise them; e.g., being kind, helping each other, sharing, listening to each other is *collaboration*.

Making Connections

Students use photos, images, and words connected to factors that make up a learning community, place them on paper, and make connections between them, explaining the connections.

Tug of War

(Visible Thinking Routine)

Different ideas connected to what makes an effective learning community are given to students, and they have to decide which are more important and why.

Diamond Ranking

Students are given nine ideas about factors that contribute to an effective learning community. They must arrange them in order from what they feel is the most important to least, in the form of a diamond: one on top, two in the next row, three in the next, then two, then one, with the last one being what they feel is the least important. They must explain their reasoning for their ranking.

They share their ranking with another group to hear other perspectives.

At Kardinia International College in Geelong, Victoria, Australia, they place their continuous assessment strategy connected to their Rubric of Understanding. This allows educators to know what assessment tool they will use to gather evidence for levels in the Rubric for Understanding. This is a collaborative process where educators decide on what strategy would best work for evidence gathering.

Developed with the Grade 5 Team

Level 1: Recalling	Level 2: Describing
Learners recall and identify knowledge that relates to the conceptual questions.	Learners describe in some detail information related to the conceptual questions. Learners begin to make inferences and interpret their understandings.
Understanding Question: How do we explore tools, materials and techniques used in art?	
I can explore materials, tools and techniques and **identify** effects.	I can explore materials, tools, and techniques used in art and **describe** the different effects they make.

Continuous Assessment

Concept wall—Our exploration of materials and techniques. Photos and comments of how students are exploring and what they are discovering through their exploration.

Journal—Tools, materials, and effects (individual). Students reflect in their journal about the effects they notice the tools and materials make during their expiration. They note similarities and differences between tools, materials, and techniques.

Wondering Wall—students place any questions they have on the wondering wall, which will become their research questions for them to plan next steps.

Level 3: Explaining and Connecting	Level 4: Analysing and Applying
Learners make comparisons between existing knowledge and the concepts. They are able to explain in detail what they have learnt and the connections within it, with reasoning and evidence.	Learners analyse and evaluate through reasoning and application. Learners make new connections and justify their analysis using evidence and reason.
I can **compare and contrast** different materials, tools, and techniques used in art, **explaining** similarities and differences with evidence.	I can **analyse** my and others' artwork in connection to effects, artistic intent, and aesthetics and **evaluate** how effective the intent is and use feedback to make improvements using techniques.

Developed with the Grade 2 Team

Level 1: Recalling	Level 2: Describing
Learners recall and identify knowledge that relates to the conceptual questions.	Learners describe in some detail information related to the conceptual questions. Learners begin to make inferences and interpret their understandings.

Understanding Question: What is the impact of sustainable practices?

I can **identify** sustainable practices and their impact.	I can **describe** sustainable practises and connect this to their impact.

Collaborative Concept Chart:

In groups of three, students will have a collaborative concept chart. They will add to this throughout the unit and share collectively to see what each group is recording.

Level 3: Explaining and Connecting	Level 4: Analysing and Applying
Learners make comparisons between existing knowledge and the concepts. They are able to explain in detail what they have learnt and the connections within it, with reasoning and evidence.	Learners analyse and evaluate through reasoning and application. Learners make new connections and justify their analysis using evidence and reason.
I can **compare and contrast** the impact of sustainable practices and explain which are the most effective.	I can **analyse** sustainable practices in my community, evaluate their positives and, with reasoning, effectively plan for how we can be more sustainable.

They will record the following:

What is the sustainable practice?	What is the impact of the sustainable practice?	Is the sustainable practice positive or negative? How do you know?	Could the sustainable practice be more sustainable? How?

In this chapter, you've seen how evidence plays a crucial role in learning and assessment of understanding. Design invitations to elicit evidence of prior knowledge and ongoing learning; the evidence acts as a form of assessment. Additionally, the data collected by the educator and learners reveals progress as well as areas that need more focus.

If we pay attention to this feedback, we can enhance our learners' experiences in the classroom as well as their ability to retain and build on what they've learned. Remember: It is not sufficient to merely collect evidence; educators and learners must evaluate what the evidence reveals in terms of learners' understanding and then use those insights to plan next steps in the learning process. In the next chapter, we focus on designing learning engagements in response to evidence as we examine the role of feedback and reflection.

CHAPTER FIVE

Using Feedback and Reflection to Shape Learning

"Feedback should cause thinking. It should be focused; it should relate to the learning goals that have been shared with the students; and it should be more work for the recipient than the donor. Indeed, the whole purpose of feedback should be to increase the extent to which students are owners of their own learning."

—— Dylan Wiliam, *Embedded Formative Assessment* ——

In this chapter, we examine the role of feedback and reflection in continuous assessment. We look closely at the role of the educator in providing constructive and ongoing feedback to empower the learner in making adjustments to improve their learning. We explore how feedback is viewed as an ongoing dialogue between the learner and educator and how it is informed through the learners' self-reflection and peer assessment. We examine the importance of clear criteria to inform success and ensure meaningful, constructive feedback that is aimed at helping learners plan for next steps and deepen their understanding. Included in this chapter are techniques and strategies educators can use for learner reflection and evaluation, so through the continuous assessment process they are empowered as assessors of their own learning.

THE CONNECTION BETWEEN CONTINUOUS ASSESSMENT AND FEEDBACK

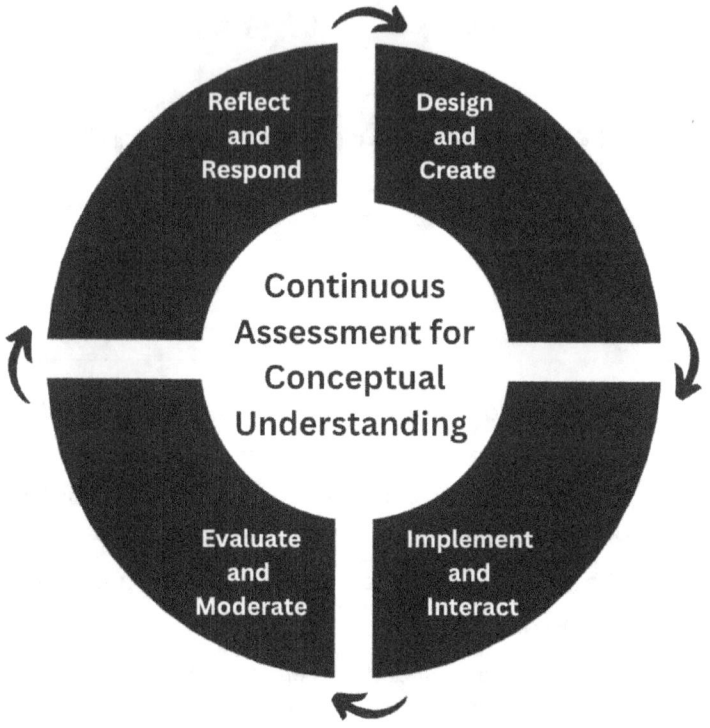

Design and Create + Feedback

An integral part of continuous assessment for conceptual understanding is that the criteria are well defined in the planning process, using the Rubric for Understanding. This is a collaborative approach within a teaching team or it can be developed by the learners in the context of their units of learning. For feedback to be effective and move the learner forward, it should be connected to specific goals and outcomes—understanding questions, concepts, and conceptual understanding.

Implement and Interact + Feedback

As part of being effective in continuous assessment practice, feedback is viewed as an ongoing dialogue between the learner and the educator. It is informed through the learners' self-reflection and peer assessment. What is important in this stage of continuous assessment is that both the educator and the student respond to the feedback by making adjustments.

Evaluate and Moderate + Feedback

Through careful and close moderation, educators tailor their feedback to address each learner's specific strengths, challenges, and goals. In the context of continuous assessment, feedback should be constructive and aimed at helping learners plan for next steps and deepen their understanding as they progress through the learning.

The process of interpreting evidence leads the educator to evaluate what the learner understands in relation to the learning goal. The educator then determines the next steps to increasing students' understanding of concepts.

Reflect and Respond + Feedback

Based on the continuous assessment using the evidence collected, regular and ongoing feedback is provided to learners during the learning process (peer, self, educator). The feedback helps learners identify their strengths and areas for improvement, just as the feedback equips educators to plan next steps for learning.

THE CONNECTION BETWEEN THE PROCESS FOR ASSESSING UNDERSTANDING, PROVIDING FEEDBACK, AND ENCOURAGING REFLECTION

Collaboration and assessment for understanding are interrelated in that they both promote deep learning and understanding. Continuous assessment involves collaboration between the educator and learners. Learners collaborate, sharing ideas and perspectives, and building on one another's understanding. Educators and learners work together to evaluate evidence of understanding and identify areas for further development.

WHAT ARE FEEDBACK AND REFLECTION?

Feedback is a process in which information about the learner's progress or performance is provided to that individual. This information is typically used to make adjustments, improvements, or corrections. Feedback serves as a mechanism for learning and growth.

Reflection is the process of thinking deeply or carefully about the learning, often with the intention of gaining insight or understanding from past experiences. It involves examining one's thoughts, emotions, actions, and experiences in a critical and introspective manner.

Although both feedback and reflection contribute to learning and growth, feedback is generally externally focused, action-oriented, and specific to performance evaluation. In contrast, reflection is more internally focused, is more holistic, and aims to promote deeper understanding, and personal development.

Effective Feedback Practices: What Is Happening? What Does It Look Like?

> "A simple clue that a student's work is not ready for feedback is that you can't find any legitimate success feedback to offer. When the work doesn't demonstrate any understanding, don't give feedback—reteach instead."
>
> — Hattie and Timperley, "The Power of Feedback"

To provide feedback that supports our learners, we must be astute to their level of conceptual understanding. If students have misunderstandings or are having trouble grasping concepts, we must first consider how to reframe the teaching of the concepts, using different approaches or resources to improve the learner's understanding. From there, we can provide clear feedback to direct their next steps.

Combining dialogue with carefully designed engagements regarding concepts and conceptual understanding increases effectiveness of feedback. Regularly checking in with their teacher and peers, and articulating their understanding, enhances student learning. Therefore, feedback from the educator, self-assessment, and peer assessment are all integral in informing the quality of the learning.

What Makes Feedback Meaningful and Effective?

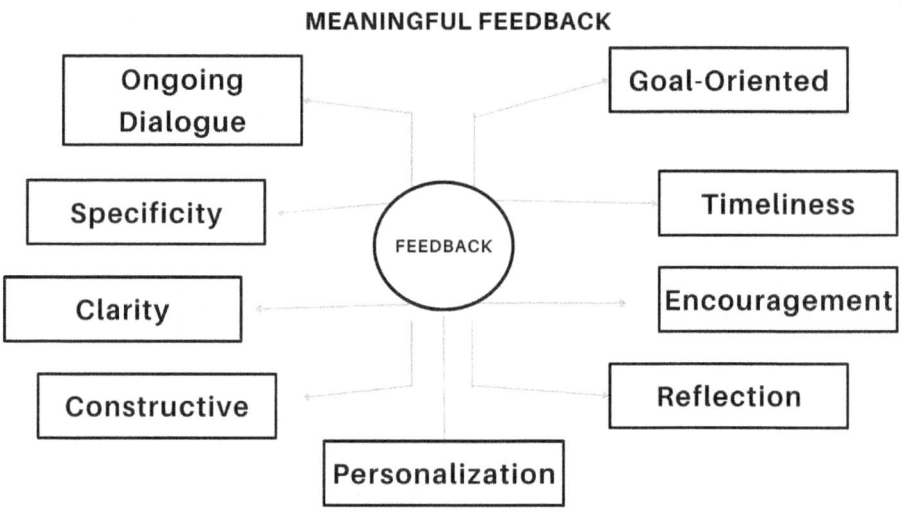

ELEMENTS FOR EFFECTIVE AND MEANINGFUL FEEDBACK

The elements of effective and meaningful feedback are also key to continuous assessment.

Meaningful and Effective Feedback

Timeliness—Providing feedback in a timely manner is essential. When the feedback occurs while the learning is still fresh in their minds, learners can make immediate connections and adjustments.

Specificity—Feedback should be specific and focused on the learning engagement or concept being addressed. Instead of using general statements like "Good job," provide specific feedback that encourages the learner to acknowledge their achievements and to reflect, think about, and identify areas for improvement.

Clarity—Feedback should be clear and easily understandable. Use concise language, avoid jargon, and provide examples or explanations to support your points. Learners should be able to grasp the feedback and know exactly what actions to take to deepen their level of understanding.

Constructive—Feedback should be constructive and aimed at helping learners deepen their understanding. Highlight both strengths and areas for improvement, and offer suggestions or strategies for growth.

Personalization—Recognise that learners have unique learning needs. Tailor your feedback to address each learner's specific strengths, challenges, and goals. Personalised feedback demonstrates that you understand and value each learner as an individual.

Goal-Oriented—Connect feedback to specific understanding questions or concepts. Clearly communicate how the feedback relates to the criteria, and guide learners on how to bridge the gap between their current understanding and the "big idea."

Encouragement—Effective feedback provides encouragement and motivation. Encouraging feedback helps build learners' confidence, fosters a positive learning environment, and promotes a growth mindset.

Reflection—Provide opportunities for learners to reflect on feedback and engage in self-reflection. Encourage them to consider their strengths and areas for growth, set goals, and develop strategies for improvement. Reflection fosters metacognitive skills and helps learners take ownership of their learning.

Ongoing Dialogue—Feedback is most effective when it is part of an ongoing dialogue between educators and learners. Engage in conversations with learners, listen to their perspectives, and provide follow-up feedback as they develop and deepen their understanding. This dialogue allows for clarification, deeper understanding, and continuous support.

Questions for Educators to Ask Themselves

In continuous assessment, it is critical to regularly review conceptual learning and provide feedback for learners. For educators, this process starts by reviewing the evidence and then asking questions of themselves to gain insights into their learners' progress, identify areas for improvement in conceptual understanding, and inform future instructional decisions. The following questions will help you ensure your feedback is connected to the learning goals:

- What is the understanding question; how can I ensure my feedback connects to this?
- What evidence will assist me in giving feedback? Are the opportunities for this to be elicited throughout the learning?
- How can I, together with the learners, plan next steps of the learning to meet their individual needs?
- Based on the feedback, how can I make adjustments to better support the diversity within the learning community?
- What evidence indicates that the learning experience aligns and connects with learners' interests and real-world relevance?

These questions will allow you to gain valuable insights into your learners' progress, identify areas of strength and growth, and make informed decisions to enhance the learning experience for learners.

HINT! When planning, carefully consider which questions will promote timely and meaningful feedback.

EDUCATOR'S VOICE

"Continuous assessment supports me as an educator by looking at the data and doing analysis or evaluation of where we are at and what steps to take further for learning. Having an ongoing check-in with progress allows for guided inquiry to really show authentic process-driven learning."

Daniel Baker, PYP Coordinator, The International School, Ho Chi Minh City, Vietnam

The Learner's Role

The key role of the learner in this process is to actively engage with the feedback provided and take appropriate actions to enhance their learning experience. Continuous assessment, when combined with a proactive and reflective approach from learners, can lead to better learning outcomes, deeper understanding, and increased success.

Actively Receiving Feedback—Learners should be open to the feedback they receive from educators, peers, or self-assessment tools. They need to focus on the feedback shared and understand where they excel and the areas that might require improvement.

Reflecting on Feedback—It's essential to give learners time to reflect on the feedback. They should consider how the feedback aligns with their learning goals, what specific areas it addresses, and how it can contribute to their overall growth and development. Part of the reflection process can include learners recording or journaling their thinking.

Embracing a Growth Mindset—Feedback can at times be constructive criticism, and learners need to develop a growth mindset to view such feedback as an opportunity for growth and not as a personal failure. Embracing challenges and seeing mistakes as learning opportunities can lead to significant progress.

Setting Goals and Determining Next Steps— Feedback in continuous assessment helps learners identify their strengths, which they can leverage to build on their existing knowledge, skills, and

understanding. Simultaneously, it highlights their areas for improvement, giving them a clear direction for further learning.

Seeking Clarification—If learners need clarification regarding the feedback they received, they should not hesitate to seek help from educators or mentors. Clarifying feedback ensures they understand what is expected of them and how they can improve.

Taking Initiative—Learners should ideally take the initiative to apply the feedback in their ongoing learning. They can use it to guide their learning approaches and overall engagement in the learning process.

Monitoring Progress—Continuous assessment involves ongoing monitoring of progress. Learners should keep track of their development, compare it with previous feedback, and determine whether they are making the desired improvements in terms of their understanding.

By implementing these effective feedback practices, learners can develop metacognitive skills, become active participants in their learning, and take meaningful steps toward achieving their learning goals and deepening their conceptual understanding.

In summary, effective feedback practices involve actively engaging learners in the feedback process and empowering them to take ownership of their learning. We can promote learner agency by observing, listening, and reaffirming how our learners are making connections and articulating their thinking. By accessing and using evidence both we and our learners have collected, we can then provide feedback that is focused on the understanding questions.

Feedback makes learners think. *Thinking is reflection.* As educators, we can promote reflection by providing feedback that helps them consider how they can move forward, rather than merely imposing direction. Giving learners the opportunity to revisit their learning invites them to think for themselves. The examples below demonstrate how a shift in feedback can encourage learners to engage in reflection and self-adjustment.

Feedback	Feedback That Causes Thinking
I do not like the images you have chosen for your presentation.	Consider your images; how do you think they enhance your presentation? How could they enhance it more?
Your paragraph does not make sense.	Look through your paragraph. The first sentence is written well, but read through the rest of it, and share it with someone else. Visit our criteria on what makes a good paragraph and see whether there is something that might need changing.
You are not working well together.	Why are you not working well together? Consider what it means to collaborate. What needs to change?
You are awesome.	I really like the way you did that; it shows you understand the problem. What do you think you need to do next?
That is not the correct answer to your math problem.	Have a look at your math problem and explain your thinking about the problem and how you solved it. What do you notice? Is there anything you would do differently?

USING EVIDENCE TO PROVIDE FEEDBACK

When it comes to informing feedback for learners' next steps in learning, evidence of understanding plays a crucial role. Below are processes and approaches that highlight how evidence can inform feedback for learners' next steps:

Assessment and Data Collection	Analysis and Interpretation	Identification of Next Steps
Educators gather evidence of understanding through various assessments, including observations, discussions, drawings, and self reflections. These assessments provide data and evidence about what learners understand, what they are thinking, and how they are making connections conceptually.	Educators analyse and interpret the collected evidence to gain insights into learning, strengths, weaknesses, and areas for improvement. The Rubric for Understanding provides clear criteria which is the basis for the analysis and, therefore, feedback. It also provides a progression of understanding that informs ongoing learning but also provides a level of differentiation to support access to the conceptual learning.	Based on the analysis of evidence, educators, with the learner, identify specific areas where there is need to improve or advance their learning. These next steps are tailored to address individual learning needs and may involve specific skills, concepts, or strategies

Feedback Provision	**Goal Setting and Action Planning**	**Ongoing Monitoring and Support**
Feedback is given to learners based on the identified next steps. The feedback should be specific, actionable, and focused on helping learners understand what they did well and how they can improve.	Collaboratively, educators and learners can set goals based on the identified next steps. Learners are involved in the process, helping them take ownership of their learning. Action plans might be created, outlining the steps learners will take to work toward their goals and address the identified areas for improvement.	Educators continuously monitor learning and progress, using ongoing feedback to provide additional support as needed. This allows for further adjustments to instruction and feedback to ensure learners are making progress toward their next steps in their conceptual understanding.

By using ongoing and varied evidence to inform feedback throughout the continuous assessment process, educators can provide targeted and personalized guidance to learners, supporting their continuous growth and improvement in their learning journey.

Using the Rubric for Understanding to Guide Feedback in Continuous Assessment

Level 1: Recalling	Level 2: Describing
Learners recall and identify knowledge that relates to the conceptual questions.	Learners describe in some detail information related to the conceptual questions. Learners begin to make inferences and interpret their understandings.
Understanding Question: What contributes to people's identity?	
Learners **identify** factors that contribute to a person's identity.	Learners **categorise** factors that contribute to a person's identity and **describe** different factors of people's identity.
Student Criteria: What contributes to people's identity?	
I can **identify** factors that contribute to a person's identity.	I can **describe** what makes identity. I can **describe** factors that contribute to identity.
Collection of Evidence	
A range of engagements concept map showing factors that define identity, illustration labelled with descriptions about identity	A range of graphic organisers to provide opportunities for learners to categorise the factors that contribute to people's identity.

Level 3: Explaining and Connecting	Level 4: Analysing and Applying
Learners make comparisons between existing knowledge and the concepts. They are able to explain in detail what they have learnt and the connections within it, with reasoning and evidence.	Learners analyse and evaluate through reasoning and application. Learners make new connections and justify their analysis using evidence and reason.
Learners **compare and contrast** factors that contribute to people's identity and **explain** how those factors come together to develop a person's identity.	Learners **evaluate** which factors have the greatest impact on a person's identity and which factors can lead to perceived ideas about people's identity, with **reasoning.**
Continuous Assessment	
I can **explain** connections between experiences and identity. I can **explain** the different factors that contribute to identity.	I can **analyse** the factors that contribute to people's identity. I can **evaluate** which factors I think are the most significant, using reasoning.
A range of Visible Thinking Routines to provide structures for learners to make connections. See, Think, Wonder See, Think, Me, We Same and Different	Opportunity for learners to share their thinking through a range of presentations. Viewing and listening to the diverse personal stories about what has contributed to their identity.

Level 1: Recalling	Level 2: Describing
Evaluation and Feedback Based on Evidence	
Through **observation and dialogue with learners**, it was evident that some learners still need further support in clarifying their understanding of the concept of what is identity.	Through **observation** and the referencing of the graphic **organisers**, and **dialogue** with learners, it was clear that many were still unsure of how to effectively categorise identity.
Identified Next Steps	
Next Steps Based on the feedback and dialogue, further opportunities using different invitations are provided for learners to make connections and make sense of the concept of identity.	**Next Steps** Further opportunities for learners to explain and categorise their ideas was decided. Scaffolding learners with other ways to categorise gave them new pathways.
Adapting and Adjusting the Learning	
Look at the images. What aspects do you think make up people's identity? Write a list or draw and label.	Looking at the ideas about what makes up people's identity, can you categorise them and describe why you think they belong in that category? Categorise, take a photo, and voice record your description of why.

Level 3: Explaining and Connecting	Level 4: Analysing and Applying
Through **dialogue, listening, and conferencing** with learners, it was apparent that some needed more time to compare and contrast factors that contribute to identity. Others were ready to shift to analysing and evaluating the Understanding Question.	**Peer assessment** as a tool for feedback was used. Individuals and groups of learners were interviewed about their understanding and how their evidence supported the Level 4 criteria. A useful tool for peer assessment is the Ladder of Feedback, which you can download here: 
Next Steps The teacher and learners discuss their current thinking and assess their level of understanding. For some, more time was allocated for compare-and-contrast factors that contribute to identity. Others moved toward Level 4.	**Next Steps** At this stage of the learning based on the feedback etc., it would be important for learners to reflect on and identify what they feel they learnt and what they might do differently, as well as further questions they might have.
Looking at the categories of what makes up people's identity, can you compare and contrast them and explain your thinking? Create a concept web that shows the connections you are making, take a photo, and explain your connections. Summarise how all of those factors contribute to the person's identity.	Looking at the case study of this person, what do you think had the biggest impact on their identity? Record your ideas and voice record yourself with your justifications.

Example

Level 1: Recalling	Level 2: Describing
Learners recall and identify knowledge that relates to the conceptual questions.	Learners describe in some detail information related to the conceptual questions. Learners begin to make inferences and interpret their understandings.

Understanding Question: How and why are the elements of art used in artworks?

Students recognise the elements used in artworks.	Students notice the elements used in artworks and connect to why artists may have used them.

Student Criteria: How and why are the elements of art used in artworks?

I can name the elements used in an artwork.	I can explain why I think the artist has used certain elements in the artwork. I can recognise how these elements have been used.

Collection of Evidence

Learners engaged in various invitations that showed a variety of ways in which the **elements of art (line, shape, colour, texture, form, space)** are represented in artworks. They grouped these and categorised them to show their understanding or identify the elements using a range of artworks.	Learners continue to engage in various invitations that showed a variety of ways in which the **elements of art (line, shape, colour, texture, form, space)** are represented in artworks. Now they are guided to look more closely and explain why the artist may have used certain elements. What do they see in the artwork? How do they think the artist created the artwork?

Level 3: Explaining and Connecting	Level 4: Analysing and Applying
Learners make comparisons between existing knowledge and the concepts. They are able to explain in detail what they have learnt and the connections within it, with reasoning and evidence.	Learners analyse and evaluate through reasoning and application. Learners make new connections and justify their analysis using evidence and reason.
Students compare and contrast the elements used in art works and explain why artists have chosen to use those elements, with reasoning.	Students analyse the elements in artwork in connection to why the artist chose to use them and evaluate the effectiveness of the artwork, making suggestions for how the elements could further be used to enhance the artwork.
I can compare and contrast the different ways the elements have been used in artworks. I can distinguish the different effects and explain how the elements can be identified.	I can apply and transfer the use of elements of art, showing various interpretations of how these elements can be applied.
Through continually engaging in the artworks, learners **experimented** with various art media to **compare and contrast** the different approaches. Observing, noting, and keeping a visual process journal provided evidence for ongoing feedback.	From their understanding of the elements of art (line, shape, colour, texture, form, space), learners **created and applied** their personal interpretations. Using their **visual process journal,** they reflected and analysed why and how they have interpreted the various elements.

continued…

Level 1: Recalling	Level 2: Describing
Evaluation and Feedback Based on Evidence: Because creating through visual arts is practical and tactile, evaluation and feedback are supported using **visual process journals** for artistic reflection and response.	
Through observation, documentation of thinking, and dialogue, learners' responses are gathered. The elements of art are concepts and are used to scaffold the learning and inform feedback.	Through referencing the learners' visual process journal, there was dialogue around the responses to how artists use the **elements of art (line, shape, colour, texture, form, space).**
Identified Next Steps: Next steps in learning refer to the actions or strategies that individuals or groups take after completing a particular phase or milestone in their learning journey.	
Next Steps **Clarification of Concepts**: For learners who are still grappling with the concepts, further explanations and examples of grouping and categorizing elements in artworks. Break down the process into smaller steps and use additional resources such as visuals to reinforce understanding. Those that understand shift to more complex engagements.	**Next Steps** Further support learners with learning engagements that show the context of artworks. Assist learner/s in understanding the historical, cultural, or artistic context in which the artwork was created. Discuss how these contextual factors might influence the artist's choice of elements and their meanings. Those that understand shift to more complex engagements.
Adapting and Adjusting the Learning	
Images of Artwork Record all the elements you see in the art piece.	**Images of the artwork** Record the elements used in the artwork. Record why you think the artist used them.

Level 3: Explaining and Connecting	Level 4: Analysing and Applying
Constructive feedback was provided on learners' comparisons and contrasts, highlighting strengths and areas for improvement. Learners were encouraged to reflect on their comparisons and revisions and revise their analyses based on feedback and further reflection.	**Peer and Self-Assessment:** Opportunities for peer and self-assessment were incorporated, where learners evaluated their own work and provided feedback to their peers based on established criteria and rubrics. This process promoted metacognitive awareness and reflective thinking.
Next Steps **Peer Collaboration**: Facilitate peer collaboration to deepen understanding in which learners work in pairs or small groups to compare and contrast artworks. Encourage learners to discuss their observations, share insights, and provide feedback to each other.	**Next Steps** **A reflective tool** could be used to guide students in their analysis of artworks created: • Look at the artwork or object for a moment. • What colours do you see? What shapes do you see? What lines do you see? • What do you think the artist has expressed? Another strategy could be **What Makes You Say That?** (Visible Thinking Routines https://pz.harvard.edu/thinking-routines) Looking closely at the artwork: • What's going on? • What do you see that makes you say that?
Two Different Artworks How are they the same or different? How have the artists used the elements? Why have they used them this way?	**Artworks** What do the elements tell you about this artwork? Why did the artist use them? Do they work? Do you think they could be used differently? How and why?

THE ROLE OF PEER ASSESSMENT

Peer assessment is a form of evaluation in which learners assess one another. Instead of being solely assessed by their teacher, learners participate in the continuous assessment process by evaluating the learning of their peers and providing feedback. Peer assessment can take various forms, depending on the nature of the task and the learning objectives.

To ensure that peer assessment provides effective feedback for conceptual understanding, educators should establish clear assessment criteria, provide guidance on how to give constructive feedback, and facilitate conversations to help learners interpret and use the feedback they receive. This way, peer assessment becomes a valuable tool for enhancing conceptual comprehension and promoting a deeper and more meaningful learning experience.

Peer assessment fosters a collaborative learning environment in which learners work together to improve their understanding. Learners learn from each other's strengths and challenges, which leads to a collective growth in conceptual understanding. Additionally, this practice promotes active learning and critical thinking.

The value of peer assessment for conceptual learning is:

Specificity and Detail	Effective peer feedback often includes specific and detailed comments. When learners provide specific feedback, it guides the recipient to focus on particular aspects of the concept, leading to a deeper exploration of those areas.
Promotes Metacognition	Peer assessment encourages metacognition— the awareness and understanding of one's thought processes. As learners assess others' work, they reflect on their own understanding and learning strategies.
Increased Engagement	Learners may become more engaged in the learning process when they know their peers will review their work. This heightened engagement can lead to a deeper exploration of concepts to present their understanding effectively.
Feedback Ownership	Learners may be more receptive to feedback from their peers, as it comes from someone who is experiencing the same learning journey. This ownership of the feedback can lead to a greater commitment to improving conceptual understanding.
Different Perspectives	Peers may have different approaches to understanding concepts, and by assessing each other's work, they expose each other to alternative perspectives. This broadens their understanding and enables them to consider multiple ways of approaching the same concept.
Explanation and Communication	When learners provide feedback, they must articulate their thoughts and explanations clearly. This exercise helps learners refine their own understanding of the concepts as they explain them to others.
Identification of Misconceptions	Peer assessment can help identify misconceptions or misunderstandings of the conceptual understanding. Addressing these misconceptions through feedback can lead to improved understanding.

Examples of Peer Feedback

Please note that peers can record their feedback using video or audio and it does not have to be in written form.

Peer Assessment on Conceptual Understanding of Earth's Natural Cycles with Feedback	
Setting the Scene	**Understanding Question:** How do Earth's natural cycles function? **Peer Assessment:** In this peer assessment, Grade 8 students assess each other's conceptual understanding of how Earth's natural cycles function. They provide feedback to their peers based on their observations, dialogue, and understanding.
Student A: Areas of Strength	Student A demonstrated a clear understanding of the water cycle and the role of evaporation, condensation, and precipitation. They were able to explain the concepts clearly and use relevant examples to support their understanding. Student A also made connections between the water cycle and the importance of water conservation.
Student A: Areas For Improvement	Student A could provide more connections to other natural cycles, such as the carbon cycle and the nitrogen cycle. It would be helpful if they included additional examples or real-world applications to enhance their explanation.
Peer Feedback (Student B to Student A):	Your understanding of the water cycle is impressive. You explained the concepts of evaporation, condensation, and precipitation clearly. I liked how you connected the water cycle to the importance of water conservation. To further improve, consider providing more details about other natural cycles like the carbon cycle or the nitrogen cycle. Additionally, adding more examples or real-world applications would make your explanation even stronger. Really interesting explanations.

Conclusion	In this example, Grade 8 students engage in peer assessment of their conceptual understanding of Earth's natural cycles. They provide specific feedback to their peers, highlighting strengths and suggesting areas for improvement. The feedback is constructive, supportive, and focused on helping peers enhance their understanding. The teacher then provides feedback to acknowledge the peer's effort in providing thoughtful feedback and affirms the validity of their suggestions. The teacher's feedback reinforces the value of peer assessment and recognizes the student's ability to provide meaningful feedback. This process promotes a collaborative learning environment and encourages students to actively engage in assessing and supporting each other's learning.

Peer Assessment in Grade 9: Viewing an Artwork Through the Concept of Perspective	
Setting the Scene for Feedback	**Understanding Question:** How does an interpretation of artworks develop perspective and opinions? **Peer Assessment:** In this peer assessment, Grade 9 students view an artwork through the lens of perspective and provide feedback to their peers, focusing on their understanding of the concept.
Student A: Areas of Strengths	Student A effectively used a one-point perspective in their artwork to create a sense of depth and space. They demonstrated an understanding of how to make objects appear smaller as they recede into the distance. The converging lines and placement of objects accurately depict perspective.
Student A: Areas For Improvement	Student A could explore more variety in the scale of objects to enhance the illusion of depth. It would be helpful if they experimented with different perspectives, such as two-point perspective, to further develop their understanding.

Peer Feedback (Student B to Student A):	I can see that you have a clear understanding of one-point perspective. Your artwork effectively demonstrates depth and space through the use of converging lines. To enhance your process, consider exploring more variety in the scale of objects. This can create a stronger illusion of depth and make the artwork more engaging. Additionally, I encourage you to experiment with different perspectives, like a two-point perspective, to expand your understanding and further develop your skills.
Conclusion	In this example, Grade 9 students engage in peer assessment by viewing each other's artwork through the concept of perspective. They provide feedback to their peers, focusing on strengths and areas for improvement. The feedback is constructive and specific, highlighting the effective use of perspective and offering suggestions for further development. The teacher then provides feedback to the peer, acknowledging their thoughtful feedback and affirming the validity of their suggestions. The teacher's feedback reinforces the importance of peer assessment and fosters a supportive learning environment. It provides an opportunity for the student artist to gain a deeper understanding of their thinking and receive guidance for continued growth in their artistic expression.

Protocols for Giving Peer Feedback

When offering feedback to peers, it's crucial to strike a balance between constructive criticism and encouragement. Here are some protocols that learners can follow to provide effective peer feedback. These also support a learning environment where feedback is part of classroom culture:

Start with positive feedback—Begin by highlighting what the peer did well. Acknowledge their strengths or the parts of their learning that impressed you. This sets a positive tone for the conversation.

Be specific—Provide detailed feedback rather than general statements. For instance, instead of saying, "Good job," say, "I appreciated how you incorporated real-life examples to support your points in the presentation."

Use "I" statements—Frame feedback based on your own observations and experiences. This approach can prevent the feedback from sounding like judgement or absolute truth. For example, say, "I found this section a bit unclear," instead of "This section is confusing."

Offer suggestions for improvement—After discussing strengths, provide suggestions for areas that could be enhanced. Be clear, actionable, and respectful in your suggestions. Phrase them as opportunities for growth rather than as criticism.

Be respectful and kind—Maintain a respectful and supportive tone throughout the feedback process. Remember, the aim is to help each other grow, not to criticize or demean.

Focus on the learning, not the learner—Ensure feedback is centred on the specific piece of work or task, not on the individual personally. This helps separate the critique from the person's identity.

Encourage reflection—Encourage your peer to reflect on the feedback received and ask for clarification if needed. Open a dialogue to discuss areas of improvement or any points they want to delve deeper into.

End on a positive note—Conclude the feedback session with encouragement or a positive remark. This helps reinforce the idea that feedback is intended to support growth and improvement.

Follow up—If appropriate, follow up later to see how your peer has incorporated the feedback and to offer further assistance if needed.

A culture that supports feedback protocols makes it clear that feedback is a normal and valuable part of the process, not a personal attack. This helps learners feel safe to share and receive feedback, fostering open communication and collaboration. A safe culture for sharing feedback nurtures positive relationships. When feedback is given respectfully and constructively, it strengthens trust and cooperation among the community of learners.

Learner Reflection Proformas for Peer Feedback

The following tools have been around for many years; perhaps you have seen adaptations of them. While we do not take any credit for their development, we wanted to share them here because they provide clear and practical guidelines that you can use with your learners.

Two Stars and a Wish	
Star One Something I think you are doing really well at in your learning is . . .	
Star Two Another area in your learning you are doing well at is . . .	
Wish In thinking about your learning, a "wish" I have as a way for you to improve your learning is to . . .	

TAG Feedback	
T—Tell your peer a positive about their learning in connection to the criteria.	
A—Ask a question that will get your peer thinking about their learning and possible next steps in their learning connected to the criteria.	
G—Give your peer an idea for next steps in their learning in connection to the criteria.	

Glow and Grow Peer Feedback	
Things Learned	
Lingering Questions	
2 Glows I like how you . . . What is interesting about your learning is . . . This is amazing learning because . . .	
1 Grow Next time try to . . . One idea might be . . . It might be useful to . . .	

Two Stars and a Wish	
I like . . . Peers indicate what it is they like about the learning and why.	
I wish . . . Peers indicate a wish they have about learning as a way to improve it.	
I wonder . . . Peers ask a question about the learning that they have or that will guide toward further improvement.	

Start-Stop-Continue	
Choose a concept or understanding question to reflect on. Brainstorm and review with your peers.	
What should we **start** doing? What new situations should we adapt to? What other ways should we try? What ideas have not yet been considered?	
What should we **stop** doing? What is not working very well? What is not having the desired outcome? What is feeling impractical? What "roadblocks" or obstacles are in our way?	
What should we **continue** doing? What do we like and want to keep? What do we want to keep trying or testing? What is helping us make progress? Group and prioritize your ideas.	

THE ROLE OF SELF-REFLECTION IN EMPOWERING LEARNER AGENCY AND VOICE

Self-reflection is an essential tool for continuous assessment. As students reflect on their learning and understanding, the insight gained can then be used by educators to inform quality feedback. This type of assessment helps educators evaluate and understand the learner's strengths and weaknesses and provide targeted support. Self-reflection also helps learners to identify areas where they need to improve and focus their efforts. Ultimately, the connection between learner self-reflection and continuous assessment is one of mutual reinforcement, because both approaches can help build a deeper understanding and improve learning outcomes.

Using I Can *Statements for Self-Assessment*

For learners to be competent in understanding the expectations, they need to know and experience what success looks like. They need models and examples to view and discuss. By embedding *I can* statements into the rubric, we are ensuring that the expectations are clear. Using their language, as Moss and Brookhart (2012) state, is important: "To be effective, the language we use must be descriptive, specific, developmentally appropriate, and written in a learner friendly language."

In terms of self-assessment, the *I can* statements empower learners to respond to the following questions:

1. Where do I need to go?
2. Where am I right now?
3. What do I need to do to close the gap between where I need to go and where I am right now?

When learners understand what they are supposed to be learning and what that learning might look like, they are better able to reflect on and review their progress, and determine next steps.

Learner Self-Reflection

"The reflection process informs the inquiry, guides goal setting, informs next steps, and suggests new directions. It is also key to ensuring that educators identify and address the differentiated needs of their learners'"

— Andrea Müller and Tania Lattanzio, *Taking the Complexity Out of Concepts*

Learner self-reflection is a process in which learners reflect on their own learning and assess their understanding. With regard to developing understanding, self-reflection is a critical and valuable aspect of the learning process.

To make time and space for learner self-reflection, educators can incorporate journaling, guided reflections, group discussions, and dedicated reflection times after specific learning experiences. By integrating self-reflection into the learning journey, learners can develop a deeper and more meaningful understanding of the concepts, fostering their growth as independent learners.

Self-reflection allows learners to think deeply about their learning experiences and insights. The practice fosters growth, leading to enhanced conceptual understanding and long-term retention.

 Make sure to plan time for learner self-reflection and provide tools for documenting their thinking.

What Learners Are Doing During Self-Reflection

When you ask learners to spend time in self-reflection, they are engaging in deep work. Consider the description of what is going on during each type of reflection.

Thinking About Their Thoughts and Feelings—Pause to consider personal experiences, thoughts, and emotions and how these might provide conceptual perspective.

Evaluating Learning—Analyse previous learning to understand where adjustments might need to be made to deepen conceptual understanding.

Setting Goals for Next Steps—Determine goals based on reflections and insights gained. Decide how to develop steps to get there and take ownership of the learning.

Identifying Strengths and Areas for Improvement—Assess personal strengths, possible obstacles, and areas for development.

Examining Values and Beliefs—Consider personal values and beliefs and how these guide understanding and connections to the concepts.

Considering New Perspectives—Seek out new perspectives, challenge assumptions, and broaden understandings related to the learning outcomes (understanding questions).

Cultivating Lifelong Learning—Become more self-directed in seeking knowledge and refining understanding throughout their lives.

Following are examples of learners' self-reflection processes; their reflections and evaluation of their learning and the decisions informed by educator or peer feedback determine what their next steps might be.

Self-Reflection by a Learner Explaining Changes in Understanding of Energy Transfer	
Throughout my learning journey, my understanding of energy transfer has evolved significantly. Initially, I had a limited grasp of this concept, but with the further learning, guidance, and feedback from my teacher, I have developed a deeper understanding.	
Self-Reflection on My Changing Perspective:	
Before	In the past, I used to think that energy transfer only occurred when one object physically touched another. I believed that energy could only be transferred through direct contact, such as when a person touches a hot stove and feels the heat. I didn't consider the idea that energy could be transferred without direct physical interaction.
Now	As a result of feedback connected to my learning, I have come to realize that energy transfer goes beyond direct contact. I have learned that energy can be transferred through various mechanisms, such as radiation, conduction, and convection. For instance, I now understand that heat energy from the Sun can reach the Earth through radiation, even though there is no physical contact between the two.

Teacher Feedback 	My teacher played a crucial role in expanding my understanding of energy transfer. Through their feedback, they encouraged me to explore beyond my initial beliefs and consider different ways in which energy can be transferred. They provided examples and explanations, such as the concept of thermal radiation, which broadened my perspective and challenged my previous assumptions.
	Additionally, my teacher provided opportunities for hands-on inquiry and small-group collaboration. They guided us in exploring real-life scenarios and encouraged us to analyse energy transfers in different contexts. The feedback received during these learning engagements helped me refine my understanding and reinforced the concept of energy transfer beyond direct contact.
	The constructive feedback I received from my teacher allowed me to reflect on my misconceptions and guided me toward a more accurate understanding of energy transfer. Their guidance fostered a sense of curiosity and a desire to explore the concept further.
Next Steps	Moving forward, I will continue to seek feedback from my teacher to deepen my understanding of energy transfer. I am excited to continue learning and apply this understanding to various scientific phenomena, knowing that my teacher's feedback will guide me toward a more comprehensive understanding.
	In summary, my understanding of energy transfer has transformed from a narrow view of direct contact to a broader understanding that includes various mechanisms. The role of my teacher's feedback in challenging my initial beliefs and providing guidance has been instrumental in shaping my evolving understanding of this concept.

Using Connect Extend Challenge (Visible Thinking Routine) as a Tool for Self-Reflection and Peer Assessment

Grade 3 Student Reflecting on Understanding of the Power of Social Media

Understanding Question: How might the power of social media influence decisions we make?

Connect	I can connect the power of social media to my life by understanding how it allows people to connect and communicate with others from around the world. I have seen my family and friends use social media platforms like Instagram and Facebook to share photos, videos, and messages with people who are far away.
Extend	To extend my understanding, I can learn more about the positive and negative impacts of social media. I can explore how it can be used to spread awareness about important issues or promote kindness and empathy. I also want to understand the challenges and responsibilities that come with using social media, such as cyberbullying or sharing personal information.
Challenge	One challenge for me is using social media responsibly. I want to learn how to be safe online, protect my privacy, and be mindful of the content I share or engage with. I also want to understand how to identify reliable information and avoid falling for misinformation or fake news on social media.
Peer Feedback (Student B)	
Connect	Student A, I can connect with your understanding of social media. Like you, I have seen my family and friends use social media to connect with people they can't see in person. It's a great way to stay in touch and share important moments.
Extend	To extend your understanding, you could explore more about how social media can impact our emotions and self-esteem. Sometimes, people compare themselves to others on social media, which can make them feel bad about themselves. It's important to be aware of this and practice self-care.

Challenge	I think your challenge of using social media responsibly is important. We should all be cautious about what we post and share online. It would be interesting to learn more about the consequences of cyberbullying and how we can prevent it.
Teacher Feedback	Your self-reflection on the power of social media shows a clear understanding of how it connects people and allows for communication across distances. Your connection to the experiences of your family and friends is relatable and provides a personal touch.
	To extend your understanding, I encourage you to explore the positive and negative impacts of social media in more depth. Understanding how it can be used for spreading awareness and promoting empathy will help you become a responsible digital citizen. Additionally, your curiosity about challenges such as cyberbullying and misinformation showcases your awareness of the potential pitfalls of social media.
	I value the peer feedback from Student B. Their connection to your understanding of social media and their suggestion to explore the emotional impacts of social media on self-esteem is insightful. It's crucial to be mindful of our feelings while using social media and to practise self-care.
	Your challenge of using social media responsibly aligns with the importance of digital citizenship. Exploring the consequences of cyberbullying and learning about strategies for prevention will empower you to navigate social media safely.
	Overall, your self-reflection and the peer feedback demonstrate critical thinking and an understanding of the complexities of social media. Keep up the great learning, and continue to explore the ideas with curiosity and responsibility. Remember to reach out if you have any questions or concerns regarding online safety or digital well-being.

FEEDBACK TECHNIQUES AND STRATEGIES FOR LEARNER REFLECTION AND EVALUATION

"Most effective teachers ask students to explain the process they used to answer the questions, to explain how the answer was found. Less successful teachers ask fewer questions and almost no process questions."

— Rosenshine, "Principles of Instruction"

Questions are used throughout the learning process to guide and promote reflective thinking, seek clarification, search for understanding, provide context for making connections, and support learners in identifying next steps in their conceptual learning.

The suggested questions we've suggested here promote reflective thinking. These open-ended questions engage learners as active participants. As you consider these questions, remember that to be effective in shaping the learning process, feedback must be timely, meaningful, and constructive. Plan to allow time for reflection so learners can pause to make connections to their learning, explore the concepts in various contexts, and then provide evidence of their understanding.

Questions to Promote Reflective Thinking		
Questions Before a Learning Engagement	**Questions During a Learning Engagement**	**Questions After a Learning Engagement**
• What do you already know? • What would you like to know? • What do you expect you will learn? • What do you notice?	• What might you do next? • What question do you still have? • What are you wondering about? • What still puzzles you? • Can you connect this to something else?	• What made you say that? • What helps you learn? • What might you do differently? • How can you use what you have learnt? • How might you explain to another person what you have just learnt? • Why do you think you needed to learn this?

Educators play a pivotal role in guiding learners toward self-reflection through thoughtful questioning techniques. Reflective questions used in classroom settings help learners think deeply about their own learning.

Equally, learner questioning plays a crucial role in self-reflection. When learners ask questions, they engage in a process of inquiry that encourages critical thinking, curiosity, and deeper understanding.

Below are examples of questions that can be used to guide learner self-reflection and educator feedback. These types of questions elicit learners' understanding and assist the educator to gain insight into what was comprehended within the learning.

We've included examples of tools and strategies that can be used for self-reflection in tandem with these questions. Notice how self-reflection is used to guide and promote reflective thinking, to seek clarification, to search for understanding, to provide contexts for making connections, and to support learners' in identifying next steps in their conceptual learning.

Educator

Questions to Highlight Learners' **Areas of Strength**

- What aspects of your response demonstrate a clear understanding of the concept/s?
- Can you identify specific examples or evidence in your learning that show your understanding?
- How did you effectively apply the knowledge or concepts you have learned in this learning?

Self-Reflection Tool: Brainstorming

Brainstorm: Using an understanding question from a unit

How and why are rules made for communities?

Individually learners record their thinking using words, drawings, or symbols. They come to a consensus on three to four key points that illustrate their current understanding.

Self-Reflection: When conferencing or dialoguing with the educator, the questions above can be used to highlight learners' **areas of strength.**

Learners individually can reference their thinking but also, importantly, be able to record any adjustments to their current understanding.

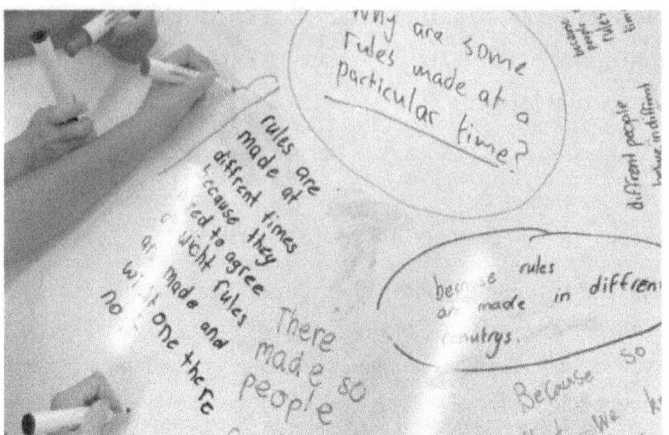

Year 5 St Francis of Assisi Calwell ACT, Australia

Educator

Questions to Highlight Learners' Areas of Strength

- What aspects of your response demonstrate a clear understanding of the concept(s)?
- Can you identify specific examples or evidence in your learning that show your understanding?
- How did you effectively apply the knowledge or concepts you have learned in this learning?

Self-Reflection Tool: Journaling

Journaling as a reflective practice can be done in various formats, such as written journals, digital blogs, audio recordings, or visual journals. It is a personal and flexible tool that supports learners in gaining deeper insights into their learning processes and becoming more self-directed and autonomous. Journaling is a form of self-expression and self-assessment, in which learners can document their progress, challenges, and achievements in a personal and introspective way.

Self-Reflection and Feedback

When conferencing or dialoguing with the educator, the questions above can be used to highlight learners' *areas of strength.*

If the learner has raised questions or uncertainties in their journal, the feedback might provide clarifications or direct them to seek answers in specific areas. The feedback would validate the learner's reflections and insights, indicating that their thoughts and observations are valued and meaningful. The educator might suggest learning strategies that align with the learner's reflections and preferred learning approaches.

Educator

Questions to Highlight Learners' **_Areas of Strength_**

- Are there any areas where your response shows a lack of understanding or misconceptions? Can you pinpoint specific examples?
- Which parts of the task require further clarification or practice to enhance your understanding?

Self-Reflection Tool: Index Cards Summaries and Questions

Distribute index cards and ask learners to fill them in according to the following prompts:

- Side 1: List or draw what you understand about the concept, then word your understanding as a summary statement.
- Side 2: Identify what you do not yet understand about the concept and word it as a question.

Self-Reflection and Feedback

When conferencing or dialoguing with the educator, the questions above to highlight learners' **_areas for improvement_** can be used.

As the educator collates the index cards, on which all learners would have annotated their thinking in some way, feedback can be given to learners where there might be some confusion or misconception about the concept. This tool can also provide feedback for the educator as to where they may need to make some adjustments or refocus on the concept.

Educator

Questions to highlight learners' **areas for improvement:**

- Are there any areas where your response shows a lack of understanding or misconceptions? Can you pinpoint specific examples?
- Which parts of the task require further clarification or practice to enhance your understanding?

Self-Reflection Tool: One-Minute Q and A

Educators engage with the learners by asking a question about a concept (e.g., *What is biodiversity?*)

The learners are given one minute to answer the questions. At this time, the educator is listening and observing to determine the learners' current understanding of the concept.

Self-Reflection and Feedback

Using the evidence through observing and listening to the learner, the educator engages in a deeper conversation to allow opportunity for the learner to provide examples of what they are currently understanding (e.g., *How biodiversity provides essential resources such as food, medicine, clean water, and air purification, as well as cultural and recreational value*).

Remember, this format is designed for quick and concise responses to provide a brief explanation of the concept.

Educator

In following up on areas for improvement, use questions to support learners in identifying strategies for improvement.

- Based on your current conceptual understanding, what strategies or approaches could you employ to strengthen this in the future?
- Are there additional resources or learning opportunities that you could explore to further develop your understanding?
- How can you use the feedback to deepen your understanding?
- What insights have you gained from this self-reflection that will inform your future learning strategies?

Self-Reflection Tool

Observation of Learner Engagement in Conceptual Invitations

Key to effective continuous assessment is the power of observation. Educators walk through the learning space and observe learners as they explore and investigate the concepts. Look for how learners are expressing their understanding of the concepts and the misconceptions connected to the concepts. Record what 'you hear and see' through anecdotal notes, checklists, and photos.

Self-Reflection and Feedback

Ongoing conversation between individual learners and the educator occurs as learners engage in the invitations.

Educators use critical questioning to unpack the thinking further. For example, "What made you say that?" can be a powerful teaching strategy to help learners delve deeper into their thinking, make connections, and articulate their thought processes.

Specific feedback on conceptual learning when educators are observing focuses on the depth of understanding and the learner's ability to grasp and apply abstract ideas or principles. It goes beyond surface-level knowledge and assesses the learner's capacity to think critically and make connections between concepts.

EDUCATOR'S VOICE

"I'm so glad that everything is not resting on summatives and find that practical application and transfer gives students more agency and me better insights into their learning."

— Lucy Elliott, PYP Coordinator, ICS Addis Ababa

Educator

In following up on areas for improvement, use questions to support learners in identifying strategies for improvement.

- Based on your current conceptual understanding, what strategies or approaches could you employ to strengthen this in the future?
- Are there additional resources or learning opportunities that you could explore to further develop your understanding?
- How can you use the feedback to deepen your understanding?
- What insights have you gained from this self-reflection that will inform your future learning strategies?

Self-Reflection Tool: Goal Setting

Reflecting on Learning Process: The learner regularly reflects on their learning process and progress toward the goal. As a result of that reflection, they can set smaller, incremental goals that build on each other. This approach helps them make steady progress toward the larger conceptual understanding goal. As they set goals, it is important for learners to also consider how they will achieve that goal and what success for that goal will look like.

Develop a process for ongoing self-assessment to monitor their progress and adjust their strategies as needed.

Self-Reflection and Feedback

When learners are setting new goals to improve their conceptual understanding, feedback should provide targeted strategies that focus on enhancing their ability to grasp abstract ideas, think critically, and deepen their comprehension.

Feedback that offers specific and actionable strategies for improvement empowers learners to take ownership of their learning and make meaningful progress in their conceptual understanding. Providing guidance tailored to the individual's needs helps foster a deeper and more meaningful learning experience.

Educator

In following up on areas for improvement, use questions to support learners in identifying strategies for improvement.

- Based on your current conceptual understanding, what strategies or approaches could you employ to strengthen this in the future?
- Are there additional resources or learning opportunities you could explore to further develop your understanding?
- How can you use the feedback to deepen your understanding?
- What insights have you gained from this self-reflection that will inform your future learning strategies?

Self-Reflection Tool: Exit Cards

A timely and relevant tool to inform effective feedback is the Exit Card. This can be used throughout the learning process or as a way to reflect after the exploration of a concept or concepts. The specific reflection provides the educator with evidence of understanding and, therefore, can be used to engage with the learner to determine next steps based on insights gained. This tool could also be used as learner feedback to inform the adjustments the educator might need to make to the planned teaching and learning.

Self-Reflection and Feedback

Exit Card

Name _____

What do you now understand about the concept?

What are you still trying to understand about the concept?

What is the most important thing that you have learnt about the concept?

Exit Card

Name _____

Three things I have learnt about the concept . . .

Two things I found interesting . . .

One thing I still want to know . . .

Additional approaches that learners can use for self-reflection and educators can use to inform feedback:

Clarifying Key Concepts: If the learner has identified specific concepts they struggle with, offer strategies to clarify those concepts. This might include recommending additional readings, videos, or interactive resources that explain the ideas in different ways.

Relating Concepts to Real-World Examples: Encourage the learner to connect the abstract concepts to real-world examples or scenarios. Provide suggestions on how they can find practical applications of the concepts to deepen their understanding.

Encouraging Self-Explanation: Advise the learner to explain the concepts to themselves or others in their own words. This self-explanation process helps solidify understanding and identify areas that need further exploration.

Seeking Diverse Perspectives: Encourage the learner to seek different perspectives on the same concepts. This exposure can help them develop a more comprehensive understanding of the topic.

Identifying Knowledge Gaps: Help the learner identify any knowledge gaps or prerequisites that might hinder their understanding. Suggest filling these gaps through pre-reading or background research.

Promoting Questioning and Inquiry: Encourage the learner to ask questions and explore further to deepen their understanding. Provide guidance on where they can find reliable sources of information or resources to deepen their inquiries.

Reviewing and Summarising: Encourage the learner to review and summarise the concepts regularly. Summarising in their own words can reinforce understanding and retention.

In summary, feedback and reflection are integral components of conceptual learning within the framework of continuous assessment, offering valuable insights and opportunities for growth. Feedback provides learners with specific information and guidance from external sources, such as instructors or peers, enabling them to understand their strengths and areas for improvement in grasping complex concepts.

Actionable feedback helps learners adjust their strategies, deepen their understanding, and refine their conceptual frameworks over time. In parallel, reflection encourages learners to engage in introspection and critical analysis of their own learning processes, facilitating self-awareness and metacognitive skills development. Through reflection, learners can explore the underlying assumptions, connections, and implications of conceptual knowledge, fostering deeper understanding and application. Together, feedback and reflection form a dynamic feedback loop that supports continuous learning and improvement, enhancing the effectiveness of conceptual learning in a continuous assessment context.

Learner Proformas and Ideas for Self-Assessment of Conceptual Understanding

Reflective Journal—Learners keep a regular journal in which they record their ongoing ideas and thoughts about the concept. Educators may want to monitor the journals to keep track of how learning and understanding evolves throughout the unit and use this to engage in constructive feedback.

Sentence Starters—Make these available to learners to help support their self-assessment. These are a few examples:

Before Sentence Starters

I already understand . . .

I am wondering about . . .

This is what I think might happen . . .

This is what I plan to do . . .

I'm not sure about . . .

I feel . . .

After Sentence Starters

I have learnt . . .

The most important thing I have understood is . . .

I can now . . .

This is important to me because . . .

If I was doing this again, I would change . . .

I would have liked to . . .

Setting Personal Goals or Identifying Next Steps—This proforma can be adapted to use with elementary and middle school learners. A structure to help plan and annotate their thinking and ideas is a useful tool to map their progress.

Step 1: Identify a focus for your learning or some aspect of your learning you would like to improve on.

What do I want to learn?	
What do I already know and understand about the learning?	

Step 2: Make a plan. Decide on how you will achieve your goals or next steps.

What can I do to reach my goal or next steps?	
What might stop me from reaching my goal or next steps?	
What could I do to deal with those challenges?	
How will I make a start on reaching my goals or next steps?	
Who and what can help me achieve my goal?	

Step 3: Self-reflect. Reflect on your progress toward your goals or next steps.

What actions have I planned and done?	
Have I achieved my goal or next steps?	
What might I do differently next time?	

Rubric for Understanding—Using the levels and criteria, learners reference the *I can* statements and assess their progress using those criteria. They can collect information about their learning, analyse what it reveals about their progress toward conceptual understanding, and plan the next steps for their inquiry.

Stop and Pause—This strategy provides an opportunity for learners to stop and reflect on the concepts that they have been learning about. The teachers pause the class and have the learners work in small groups to discuss their current understanding of the concept. Sentence starters to prompt discussion could include the following:

- I changed my ideas about . . .
- I now know . . .
- I was surprised about . . .
- I felt . . .
- I connected to . . .
- I still want to know . . .

Student Conference—The teacher conducts a one-on-one conversation with each learner, using carefully designed questions to check their level of understanding. This is particularly good for young children who may not have developed the necessary writing skills to transcribe their thoughts.

Hand Signals—Ask learners to display a designated hand signal to indicate their understanding of the concept:

- Thumbs up: I understand and can explain it.
- Thumbs down: I do not yet understand.
- Thumb midway: I'm not completely sure about it.

Concept Map—Learners create a concept map that shows the connections between ideas and links to concepts. Words are used to describe the relationship between the ideas. Concept maps enable learners to continuously add their ideas and build their understanding of the concepts.

Index Card Summaries and Questions—Throughout the unit, distribute index cards and ask learners to fill them in according to the following prompts:

- Side 1: List what you understand about the concept, then word your understandings as a summary statement.
- Side 2: Identify something about the concept that you do not yet fully understand and word it as a question.

Four Corners—Have *I can* statements written on paper in four corners of the classroom. Learners decide where their current understanding is in connection with the understanding question. As a group they discuss why they are in this group and what they might do to move along in their current understanding.

Where am I now?

Lines of inquiry	Level 1: Recalling	Level 2: Describing	Level 3: Explaining and connecting	Level 4: Analysing and applying
How and why is the earth continuously changing?	Identify the changes in the earth -continents -landforms ✓	Describe how and why the earth is changing over time -movement of plates ✓ -natural disasters	Explain similarities and differences in how the earth has changed over time (eg slow processes and fast processes) ✓	Hypothesise how these changes can impact future generations

Grade Four, St. Joseph's Institution International School, Singapore

Learners examine their learning and together with a peer decide where they are in connection to the levels in the rubric. They tick off the levels based on evidence and agreement from their peers that their learning does demonstrate the understanding.

What Have You Learnt?   **Name:**

How have you understood the concepts?

What resources were useful in your learning?

What were the significant conceptual understandings?

How did you apply and transfer your conceptual understandings?

What questions did you have at the start?

What new questions do you have from your conceptual inquiry?

Examples of Exit Ticket

Exit Ticket

Name _____

I was surprised to learn . . .

I will always remember . . .

I'm still not sure about . . .

Exit Card

Name _____

The understanding question I understand the most is . . .

This is because . . .

The understanding questions I still need to know more about is . . .

This is because . . .

EXIT CARD

Name _____

What do you now understand about the concept?

What are you still trying to understand about the concept?

What is the most important thing that you have learnt about the concept?

EXIT CARD

Name _____

Three things I have learnt about the concept ...

Two things I found interesting about the concept ...

One thing I still want to know about the concept ...

TRANSFER & APPLY	What strategies or tools do you use to support student self-reflection?	How do you use these to inform both teacher and peer feedback?
	What might you need to do more or less of?	

PLANNING IN RESPONSE TO LEARNERS TO DIFFERENTIATE THE LEARNING

Planning in response to evidence and differentiating learning after feedback are crucial components of effective teaching and learning. They are essential practices that enable you to personalise instruction, address misconceptions, promote learner growth, foster engagement and motivation, and continuously improve your teaching practices. By incorporating feedback into the planning process, you can create meaningful learning experiences that empower all learners to succeed.

Responding to learners' needs and planning for different pathways involves recognizing and addressing individual strengths, challenges, and interests. This includes offering various instructional strategies, resources, and support mechanisms tailored to accommodate diverse learning preferences and paces. By flexibly adapting the learning and instruction, educators can empower learners to engage meaningfully in their learning journey and achieve success through personalised pathways aligned with their unique needs and goals.

EDUCATOR'S VOICE

"This gives you a multitude of data points to triangulate and also data to inform the next steps in learning and how to differentiate to meet learners' needs. It provides ongoing data to inform learning. It helps me address misconceptions as they occur and also see students who may need extending. Without this kind of data, teaching is in a vacuum and not personalised to learner needs."

— Lucy Elliott, PYP Coordinator, ICS Addis Ababa

The process of continuous assessment plays a crucial role in supporting differentiation by providing ongoing feedback and data that further informs instructional decisions tailored to individual learner needs.

If educators and learners are gathering evidence of understanding, analysing that evidence, and deciding next steps in the learning, then it should follow that the learning will be differentiated to respond to the needs of students.

The examples below show different ways in which educators can plan in response to learners' needs. Educators provide strategies that specifically focus on moving learners forward in their understanding and depth. Therefore, you will notice in the examples below the learning engagements are different based on where learners' current understanding might be.

By considering the options and choices, the various modes in which learners can demonstrate their understanding at the planning stage ensures the pathways learners might require are accessible and personalised.

Understanding Question: How can you demonstrate that organisms are cellular systems?
Differentiating the Learning

Conduct an experiment to provide evidence that living things are made of cells, either one cell or many different numbers and types of cells.	Develop and use a model to describe the function of a cell as a whole and ways the parts of the cell contribute to the function.	Use argument supported by evidence for how the body is a system of interacting subsystems composed of a group of cells.

Understanding Question: How and what is identity?
Differentiating the Learning

Interview Task: Learners can be tasked with conducting interviews with family members, friends, or community members to explore different perspectives on identity. Differentiation can be achieved by providing interview question prompts at varying levels of complexity, in connection to the Rubrics for Understanding, offering support in conducting interviews for learners who may need assistance, and allowing flexibility in the format of the interview (written, audio, video).

Collage Task: Learners can create collages or visual representations of their identities using images, words, and symbols. Differentiation can involve providing a variety of materials and tools for creating the collage, offering templates or guidance for learners who may struggle with creativity or organisation, and allowing flexibility in the final product (physical collage, digital collage, multimedia presentation). Complexity of levels can be developed through the explanation of the collage.

Storytelling Task: Learners can write or orally share personal narratives or stories that illustrate key aspects of their identity and how they have evolved over time. Levels of complexity in the task involve providing scaffolding and support in narrative writing for learners who may struggle with storytelling, offering prompts or guiding questions to help learners identify meaningful experiences to share, and allowing flexibility in the format of the storytelling (written, oral, multimedia).

Representation Task: Learners can create artistic representations of their identities through media such as painting, drawing, sculpture, or digital art. Differentiation can include providing a variety of art materials and tools, offering support in developing artistic skills and techniques for learners who may struggle with art, and allowing complexity of understanding in the interpretation and expression of identity through art.

Understanding Question: What is the impact of sustainability?
What solutions are there for sustainability?

Differentiating the Learning

Sort the images and identify which scenes promote sustainability and which do not with an explanation.	Place images in order from those that you think have the biggest impact on sustainability to those that have the least. Explain your thinking.	Looking at the images, propose possible solutions to the issue. Explain how your solution will assist in sustainability.

Understanding Question: How are the elements of music interpreted and recognised in instrumentation and composition?

Differentiating the Learning

Listening Stations: Set up listening stations where learners can listen to music examples that exemplify different elements such as melody, harmony, rhythm, dynamics, tempo, and form. Differentiate by providing a variety of music genres and styles to cater to diverse preferences and backgrounds. Offer graphic organisers with guiding questions at varying levels of complexity to accompany the listening experience.

Music Analysis Task: Assign learners to analyse a piece of music, focusing on specific elements. Differentiate by providing music selections at varying levels of complexity and offering support in identifying and analysing elements for learners who may need it. Learners can present their findings through written reports, multimedia presentations, or oral discussions.

Instrument Exploration: Allow learners to explore different musical instruments and how they contribute to various elements of music. Differentiate by providing opportunities for hands-on exploration of instruments, offering resources and guidance for learners who may need assistance, and allowing flexibility in the choice of instruments based on learners' interests and abilities to connect to their current level of understanding.

Composition Tasks: Learners are given the opportunity to compose short musical pieces, focusing on specific elements such as melody, harmony, or rhythm. Promote levels of complexity by providing composition templates or starter melodies/chords for learners who may need support in getting started. Offer opportunities for peer feedback and collaboration during the composition process.

Understanding Question: How do we communicate and respond in different contexts? **Differentiating Learning**			
Play games and songs that involve using greetings.	Role play different scenarios for students to greet different people.	Role playing at a restaurant, students order food and engage in conversations at the restaurant.	Questions and answers. Students are given questions from different contexts. One asks the question, and the other answers.
Differentiated Learning for More Capable Language Learners Using the Same Understanding Question: How Do We Communicate and Respond in Different Contexts?			
You are at the shop, and you see different clothing. How do you say the names of the clothing?	You are at the shop, and you want to buy a piece of clothing. What would you say?	You are at the shop, and you want to find out whether they have a piece of clothing you are interested in in a different size or colour. What would you say?	You are at the shop, and you want to ask about the variety of clothes they have connected to design, size, and colour. What would you say?

Understanding Question: How is interdependence identified in natural ecosystems?
Differentiating the Learning

Field Observation Task
Learning Engagement: Take learners on a field trip to observe a local ecosystem (e.g., a forest, wetland, or grassland). Ask them to identify and document examples of interdependence among organisms within the ecosystem.

Levels of Complexity
- Provide field guides or identification charts to support learners in identifying different species.
- Offer visual aids or checklists with simplified descriptions for learners who may struggle with identifying organisms.
- Assign roles within groups to ensure that all learners are actively engaged, such as recorder, observer, and reporter.

Case Study Analysis Task
Learning Engagement: Assign learners to analyse a case study of an ecological disturbance (e.g., deforestation, pollution, invasive species) and its impact on interdependent relationships within an ecosystem.

Levels of Complexity
- Provide case studies of varying levels of complexity and with different ecological contexts.
- Offer guided questions or prompts to help learners analyse the cause-and-effect relationships within the case study.
- Allow learners to work in pairs or small groups to facilitate peer discussion and collaboration.

Simulation or Game Task
Learning Engagement: Engage learners in a simulation or game that simulates interactions within a natural ecosystem (e.g., a predator–prey simulation, an ecological board game).

Levels of Complexity
- Provide simplified versions of the simulation or game for learners who may struggle with complex rules or concepts.
- Offer additional challenges or extensions for learners who require more advanced tasks.
- Allow learners to work in pairs or small groups to provide peer support and collaboration during the simulation.

In conclusion, feedback and reflection are integral components of continuous assessment, particularly in conceptual learning, because they promote deeper understanding, metacognitive development, personalised learning experiences, and continuous improvement for learners. By incorporating feedback and reflection into the learning process, educators can facilitate meaningful learning experiences that enhance conceptual understanding and promote lifelong learning skills.

Included in this is planning in response to learners' current understanding. Reflecting with learners to consider their next steps ensures that we are planning in response to our learners and not for them.

CHAPTER SIX

Transfer and Application for Authentic Learning

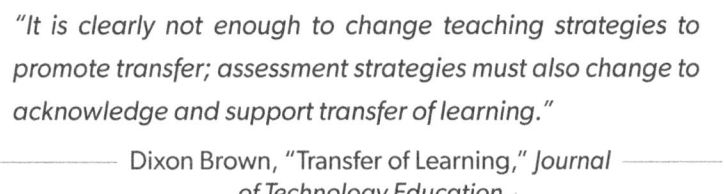

"It is clearly not enough to change teaching strategies to promote transfer; assessment strategies must also change to acknowledge and support transfer of learning."

Dixon Brown, "Transfer of Learning," *Journal of Technology Education*

This chapter looks at the role of authentic learning. We examine the shift from using the terminology of summative assessment to transfer and application, where learners **transfer and apply** their learning to different contexts. Rather than focus on what the final assessment for the learning will be, we look at how learners transfer and apply what they have learnt to an authentic context. This transfer and application can take place throughout the unit and is not always designed to be an end product.

In an attempt to ensure learning has application beyond the school, we look at ways to connect with your community. Likewise, we consider the question, "So what?" as a means of moving knowledge to understanding to application in broader contexts.

AUTHENTIC LEARNING FOR TRANSFER AND APPLICATION

The connection between authentic tasks and continuous assessment lies in the fact that authentic tasks can serve as a means of conducting continuous assessment. By using authentic tasks to assess learner performance, educators can get a more accurate and comprehensive picture of what a learner knows and can do with their understanding. In other words, how can they apply what they have learnt?

We have moved away from using the language of summative assessment to *Transfer and Application,* which gives consideration to how learners use what they have understood and learnt. This is a significant shift in thinking. Previously, we focused on the end of a learning journey and had learners produce evidence of what they learnt. Now we are looking at transferring and applying their learning to authentic situations, not exclusively at the end of the learning but throughout the entire experience.

THE ROLE OF "SO WHAT?"

As we want to ensure authenticity of Transfer and Application, we advocate for what we refer to as the "So What?" This final understanding question promotes the transfer and application of the learning. It is not enough for learners to acquire information. What they do with their learning is what matters. We want them to ask, "Now that I have learnt this, what can I do with it?"

Answering "so what?" is key to bringing relevance to learning. If we and our learners can't answer this crucial question, then the next question must be, *why are we teaching this?*

The "so what" in learning refers to the significance, relevance, or practical application of the knowledge or understanding being acquired. It questions the purpose and importance of what is being learned and seeks to understand the broader implications or value of the conceptual understanding.

When someone asks "so what" in the context of learning, they are essentially asking why they should care about or invest their time and effort into acquiring certain knowledge or understanding. It prompts learners to consider how the conceptual ideas they are gaining can be applied in real-life situations, how they can contribute to personal or professional growth, or how they can make a difference in the world.

By understanding the "so what" of their learning, learners can find motivation and meaning in their educational pursuits. It helps them connect the dots between what they are learning and how it can be useful or impactful in various aspects of their lives. Additionally, recognizing the "so what" can encourage critical thinking and a deeper understanding of the concepts, as learners strive to uncover the underlying reasons and implications behind what they are learning.

The "so what" also provides opportunities for learners to take action. By keeping the learning at a local level, particularly for young children, they are able to use their learning positively in their community, realising that they can contribute and make a difference.

Following are some possibilities for employing "so what?" to the final understanding question.

Last Understanding Question to Promote "Transfer and Application," the SO WHAT of the learning.
How can I use authors' verse and devices in my writing?
How can we meet the needs of our community?
How can we promote sustainability in our community?
How can we effectively contribute to our team?
How can I express my identity artistically?
How can we use our understanding of energy to create a sustainable product?
How can I use critical thinking to solve mathematical problems?

How can I curate historical evidence to tell a story of the past?
How can I help others develop a sense of belonging?
How can we pose a creative solution for our natural environment?
How can we develop habitats for living things?
How can we build structures that have a purpose?
How can we be successful in the marketplace?
How can we use our understanding of measurement to create games in our community?
How can I develop an effective business plan to sell a service?

Knowing our community, the people, organisations, and the opportunities that exist within it, leads to authentic learning experiences. Connecting learners to real people, places, and issues within their own community promotes action and authenticity of learning. When collaborating with schools and developing the "transfer and application" part of the learning, we always consider these:

Who in our community does this?

What are their roles and occupations in the community?

How might we connect with them?

How does what they are doing connect to what we are doing?

How does that make what we are learning authentic?

How are they contributing to the community?

How can we contribute to the community?

When learners see what they are learning connects to the roles of people in their community, it provides relevance and meaning to their "so what." It is not something that is only done in school; it does "mimic the roles" of people in the community. For young learners, the community may be their school community; for older learners, it may be their school community and beyond.

AUTHENTIC TASKS FOR TRANSFER AND APPLICATION

When discussing authentic learning, Audrey Rule (2006) states that it is "an activity that involves real-world problems and that mimics the work of professionals; the activity involves presentation of findings to audiences beyond the classroom."

Authentic tasks are real-world activities that reflect understanding and knowledge in a meaningful context. Assessment for understanding is a form of evaluation that focuses on the process of learning rather than simply measuring the outcome. When used in conjunction, authentic tasks and assessment for understanding can provide a more complete picture of a learner's abilities because learners are required to apply their knowledge and understanding in meaningful, relevant ways. This approach to assessment is thought to lead to deeper under-standing and long-term retention of information.

> *Authentic assessment also promotes learners as active citizens, where they have the opportunity to contribute to the community through genuine authentic action. It promotes learners as problem solvers, where they are examining problems and issues and considering how they might go about developing solutions for them.*
>
> *In a world where so much is going on in young people's lives, we feel it is important to be solution-oriented, providing learners with opportunities to contribute or solve problems in their community as a way to see that small or large contributions and ideas can make a difference—focusing on hope.*

Characteristics of an Authentic Task That Promotes Transfer and Application

When developing authentic tasks that promote transfer and applica-tion, we use the following criteria:

Is connected to what people in the community do	• The task connects people in the community to learners. Introducing learners to the variety of roles in the community that support and contribute to the community enables learners to see value in their own learning, seeing that what they are doing extends beyond the school walls. Examples: Volunteers, community members who bring joy through what they do, people who work at organizations that contribute to the community, vocations that exist in the community
Has real-world relevance	• The task is relevant because it requires the application of learning to an authentic context that resembles real-life scenarios, providing learners with genuine and meaningful experiences.
Involves an authentic audience	• The task involves an audience beyond the classroom. This could involve the school community or going beyond to include the local or global community. An authentic audience promotes motivation for learning.
Provides opportunities for learners to demonstrate (action) their knowledge and understanding	• The task involves learners demonstrating what they have learned and understood. It requires them to respond and act on their learning.
Is connected to the learning	• The task is directly connected to the learning; it is not an add-on at the end or an additional piece of the learning. It requires a demonstration of what has been learnt by the learner.
Provides options and choices for learners	• The task provides options and choices for learners. It is not a task where at the end there will be twenty-five of the same product. Learners within the task get to choose how they will demonstrate what they have learnt.

Requires a level of planning	• The task requires a level of planning. It is not something that can be actioned immediately, because there is a level of complexity that requires learners to consider how they may go about it. This doesn't necessarily have to be formal; however, there is a level of thinking required to transfer and apply the learning.
Encourages learners to consider various perspectives	• The task requires learners to think about various perspectives. When developing the task, learners have to consider varying viewpoints. This could be because of the task itself and the impact it has or the perspective of an audience or group member.
Promotes a range of solutions and applications	• The task does provide a variety of solutions or applications that learners can consider. There is not only one way the task can be approached. It requires learners to think and consider what is most suitable for what they want to do.
Promotes active citizenship	• The task promotes learners to contribute positively to their community, through their own actions or by solving problems, being solution oriented.

"PRACS" DEVELOPING AUTHENTIC TASKS THAT PROMOTE TRANSFER AND APPLICATION

When developing transfer and application tasks, our starting point is the final understanding question. Working backward, we develop what we refer to as a "PRAC" task, adapted from the GRASPS model designed by Jay McTighe and Grant Wiggins.

The "PRACs" provide learners with options and choices in connection to how they may go about the situation. They also may provide opportunities for learners to apply their thinking and understanding of concepts, and application of their skills throughout the learning; apply and transfer may not take place only at the end of the learning.

This will be dependent on what the PRAC is and how it connects to the learning.

Purpose and Context
Role
Audience
Criteria

Purpose	• What is the purpose of and context for the task? • Consider your last understanding question, the *so what*? • Select a real-world context connected to the question. • Choose a context that is relevant to learners and broad vocational opportunities they will encounter in the real world. • Define the task. • Clearly articulate how the learners are expected to apply and transfer their learning. • Clearly define what learners are expected to know and be able to as a part of the task.
Role	• What is the role required for the task? • Where appropriate, the first step is to connect learners to people in the community who carry out this role. • How are their roles described? • How does that connect to what we want to do? • What role will we take on? • Can members of the community be used as mentors for the task?
Audience	• Who is the audience? • Consider who the audience might be. How will the audience go beyond the classroom? • How can you connect the task to the local or wider community?
Criteria	• What will success in the task look like? • Determine the criteria for success: Specify the criteria that will be used to evaluate the quality of learners' work. • Learners and educators can construct the criteria together and then use this to peer- and self-evaluate, providing constructive feedback that assists them in being successful in the task.

It is also important to provide support and resources: We need to ensure that learners have access to the resources and support they need to be successful in the task, such as access to technology or mentoring from relevant experts from various sections or fields within the local and wider community, such as industry, the arts, design, environmental science, medical fields, nonprofit businesses, volunteering, and so forth. Often learners will also access resources that have already been used in the unit, so making these accessible throughout the learning process is significant.

Examples of PRACs

Understanding Question: "So what?"	How can we meet the needs of the community through problem solving?
Purpose and Context	**Purpose:** To meet the needs of the community through solving community problems. **Context:** You have been asked to consider your community and examine problems that may exist in it. You have to define what you think the problem is, the issues in the community, the problem it is causing, and how your solution will assist in solving the problem. You need to transfer your understanding of the problem and apply a reasonable solution.
Role	To be decided based on the chosen problem and solution. To be partnered (where appropriate) with a community member to mentor them through the process.
Audience	Local community

Criteria	<ul><li>The problem has been identified.</li><li>The problem needs a solution because . . .</li><li>The problem is one that exists in the community (we know this because…).</li><li>A plan is developed that includes<ul><li>What the solution is</li><li>How the solution will assist in addressing the problem</li><li>A process for how the solution will be put into place</li><li>Resources (including people) required to solve the solution</li><li>What would equate as being successful</li><li>How the solution will address the problem long-term</li></ul></li><li>Once the solution has been put into action, the plan will be reviewed, considering how successful it was and what if any changes are or would be needed.</li></ul>

Understanding Question: So what?	How can we use our understanding of sustainability in our community?
Purpose and Context	**Purpose:** To design and create a sustainable solution (A solution may be learners deciding that they will take action themselves in response to their learning.) **Context:** You have been asked to develop a sustainable solution for your community that will contribute to the sustainability of the community.
Role	Sustainable Advisor Connect to the community and access people who are in this role and invite them to come in to discuss with learners what they do and why.
Audience	Community
Criteria	<ul><li>My sustainable solution is . . .</li><li>It will help with sustainability by. . .</li><li>It is a short-term/long-term solution because . . .</li><li>I know it will be a success if . . .</li></ul>

Understanding Question: So what?	How can we develop a business plan and implement a service to meet the needs of our community?
Purpose and Context	**Purpose:** To create a successful business plan that focuses on a service. **Context:** You have to develop a business plan and a service to meet the needs of the Year 7 learners. You have to do market research to determine what services Year 7 learners are interested in and then devise a business plan based on this. Your business plan has to include a cost analysis, marketing, and how you will know your service will be a success.
Role	Service provider, business leader, or entrepreneur Have people who have drawn up business plans come in and discuss business development with learners.
Audience	Year 7
Criteria	The Plan • My business plan includes . . . • Market Research: Determine what service will meet the needs of the community. • Marketing and Advertising: How will we market and advertise our service? • Cost Analysis: All costs involved in setting up the business (human capital, physical capital, natural resources) • Service Fee: What the service fee will be as a way to ensure that a profit is made After the service day . . . • The business plan was effective or not effective because . . . • How did the service meet or not meet the needs of the audience? • Factors that contributed positively or negatively to our success were . . . • Things we would do differently are . . .

Understanding Question: So what?	How can we modify and create games for others to play?
Purpose and Context	**Purpose:** To develop a net game for Grade 2 to play. **Context:** You have been asked to create a net game to include rules and teach it to the Grade 2 learners. You need to find out what skills Grade 2 has to be able to devise a game that will be appropriate for the age group.
Role	Game Designer
Audience	Grade 2
Criteria	Our Game: <ul><li>The rules made sense to the learners.</li><li>Learners were able to use and follow the rules.</li><li>Learners understood how to use the techniques required in the game.</li><li>Learners were able to play the game successfully once they understood the rules and what they had to do.</li><li>Learners participated in the game.</li><li>The best thing about the game was . . .</li><li>If we were to change the game, the thing we would change is . . .</li><li>This is because of . . .</li></ul>

Understanding Question: So what?	How can we use our understanding of area and scale to create?
Purpose and Context	**Purpose:** To create games in the playground for other learners to use. **Context:** You have been asked to design games that can be painted on the school or community centre's outside area. Your design will be entered into a competition where the winners' games will be announced and painted in the school grounds.
Role	Mathematician, Designer

Audience	School Community
Criteria	Our game is called: • Our game is designed to fit into the allocated area. • The area our game takes up is . . . • The model of our game is to scale. • The rules for our game are . . . • Our game can be played by __ people. • Our game is interesting because . . . • People will want to play our game because . . .

Understanding Question: So what?	How can we tell stories of migration to build understanding?
Purpose and Context	**Purpose:** To tell the story of a migration. **Context:** You have been asked to tell the story of a person's migration. You have to choose a person you wish to interview, devise interview questions, and then tell that story. You can choose how it is you want to tell the story. The story needs to focus on building understanding of that person's journey of migration. The stories will be shared with the school community.
Role	Storyteller or Journalist
Audience	Community
Criteria	My story: • Includes why the person migrated • Articulates the journey of a person who migrates • Focuses on the migration journey from point of origin to where the person migrated to • Includes challenges the person went through when migrating • Includes the impact of the migration the person went through (positive/negative) • Builds understanding with the audience

Understanding Question: So what?	How can we curate historical sources to tell a story of the past?
Purpose and Context	**Purpose:** To curate historical sources to tell a story of the past. **Context:** You have been asked to curate the story of a person/place or event from history. Your curation has to be put together to tell a story of that person or event from the past.
Role	Museum Historian Contact people in the community whose role it is to curate artefacts. They come and discuss the role of a museum curator with learners so they have real experiences to connect their learning to.
Audience	School Community
Criteria	• To be developed by learners. • Learners visit different museums where there is curation. • As learners visit the museums, they begin to create criteria as to what they think will be effective curation in connection to telling a story of the past. • They interview curators to further develop the criteria. • The criteria will be used to peer- and self-assess their stories of the past.

Understanding Question: So what?	How can we design and build a structure for a purpose?
Purpose and Context	**Purpose:** To design and build a structure that has a purpose. **Context:** You have been asked by the school to build a structure that has a purpose. You have to explain what the purpose of your structure is, how it could be used, and what materials and tools you will need to build your structure.

Role	Builder/Designer
Audience	School Community
Criteria	My structure is . . . • The purpose of my structure is . . . • The structure is linked to the purpose because . . . • The materials I have chosen are . . . • I have chosen these materials because . . . • The tools I will need are . . . • The skills I will need are . . . • My structure will be a success if . . .

Understanding Question: So what?	How can we use our understanding of forces to create?
Purpose and Context	**Purpose:** To create, using an understanding of forces. **Context:** You have been asked to create and design using forces (e.g., toy, Rube Goldberg machine, arcade game). Using the design process, you plan and design your creation.
Role	Engineer
Audience	Community
Criteria	• Name of my creation: • Picture of my creation: • Materials required for my creation: • Tools and techniques required to make my creation: • I planned and made a creation that uses forces to work. • The force(s) I used in my creation is/are . . . • I correctly used the stages of the design cycle when making my creation by . . . • I made changes and adaptations to my creation as required in connection to the design cycle when I . . .

Understanding Question: So what?	How can we protect local environments?
Purpose and Context	**Purpose:** To take an active role and voice in protecting the local environment. **Context:** Through your ongoing investigations of the local environment, what issues have you noticed? You have to think as scientists and conservationists as to how you might take steps to communicate this issue to the community, how you might be able to find a solution to improve the quality of the environment, and who you might need to help with this to ensure the survival of living things that depend on that environment.
Role	In small groups, you are scientists and conservationists. You will use different people from the community to guide you in your plan and possible solutions.
Audience	Local community and environmental organisations
Criteria	• As a result of on-site investigations, there is an issue identified. • The evidence of this issue has been analysed (we understand this because . . .) • Sources that include science journals, videos, photos, and books are referenced to provide the rationale and steps for how to make a difference. • Check-ins: • What are we hoping to sort out? • How will we do this? • Who might we need to connect with to help us? • How will we know we have made a difference? • Ongoing observations can be made to see whether your ideas and solutions were successful.

Understanding Question: So what?	How can we connect people to the local community so there is a sense of belonging?
Purpose and Context	**Purpose:** To connect people to the local community. **Context:** You and your peers have been asked to consider how you can connect people that are new to the community. You have to consider the places in the community people may need to know about or may be interested in and devise a welcome pack that they can be given. (Can be a focus on people new to the school community.)
Role	Community Volunteers
Audience	People new to the school

Criteria	• Your package needs to include
	  ◦ A map of specific places in the community that might be of interest
	  ◦ How and why these places are significant
	  ◦ Contact details of people within the community who new people can connect to
	  ◦ Specific phrases or words that would assist people in connecting to others in the language of the community

Understanding Question: So what?	How can we promote well-being in our community?
Purpose and Context	**Purpose:** To promote well-being in the community. **Context:** You have been asked to choose a feature of well-being (emotional, physical, occupational, social, spiritual, intellectual, environmental, and financial) you have learnt about and want to focus on. You will be sharing what you have learnt with the school community on a well-being morning.
Role	Well-Being Ambassador People from the community who focus on the well-being of others will be asked to come into the school to discuss with learners what they do.
Audience	School community
Criteria	• Choose a factor that contributes to well-being. • Plan how you will share this with the community. • Include why what you have chosen contributes to well-being and how it does this. • Include short-term and long-term impacts of your well-being feature. • Plan how you will promote your well-being feature prior to the well-being morning.

Understanding Question: So what?	How can we save energy in our school?
Purpose and Context	**Purpose:** You have been asked to develop a plan to save energy in the school. **Context:** You have been asked to find ways to save energy in the school and present it to the School Leadership Team for consideration.
Role	Energy Advisor
Audience	Leadership Team

Criteria	• Your presentation needs to include
	◦ Ways your school can save energy
	◦ The impact and results that saving energy will have
	◦ Graphs or statistics that reinforce your ideas about energy saving
	◦ Other case studies in which places have saved energy using similar ideas

Understanding Question: So what?	How can we effectively create poetry for an audience?
Purpose and Context:	**Purpose:** To write a poem for the class collection. **Context:** You have been asked to contribute to a collection of poetry that will be made into a book and placed in the school library.
Role:	Poet
Audience:	School Library
Criteria:	Poem: Criteria to be developed by learners as they read poems as models of excellence, poems that appealed to them as learners. As they read poems, they start to develop criteria on what elements or features make an effective poem and what devices they need to use when writing their poem. This will be used as they draft their poem in their critique groups of 3, where they will give each other continuous feedback leading up to the publishing of the poem.

Understanding Question: So what?	How can we communicate about who we are?
Purpose and Context	**Purpose:** To create a webpage in the target language that provides people with an understanding of who we are. **Context:** You have been asked to create a website all about you. It will be a year-level website, and you will have a page dedicated to just you. The page will need to be written in the target audience's language.
Role	Autobiographer
Audience	School Community
Criteria	Your webpage includes: • A photo of you • A description of what you look like • Who is in your family • What you like to do and why • What things you do not like and why • One interesting thing about you

Understanding Question: So what?	How can we effectively perform as a group?
Purpose and Context	**Purpose:** To perform music at the local community centre. **Context:** You have been asked to perform at the local community centre.
Role	Performer
Audience	Community

Criteria	• Criteria to be developed by learners as they practise their composition.
	• It will include individual roles within the performance and what they need to do as well as how the group can work together for a successful performance.
	• The criteria will be used by the group leading up to the performance as a way for them to consider the feedback (peer/self/teacher assessed) to improve their performance.

Understanding Question: So what?	How can we observe and represent our world?
Purpose and Context	**Purpose:** To create a portrait of the Grade 5 children. **Context:** Grade 5 has been looking at the concept of identity. Your role is to create a portrait of one student, using either painting or drawing.
Role	Artist
Audience	Grade 5 student
Criteria	• Likeness: The portrait resembles the person being depicted.
	• Composition: The portrait draws attention to the subject's face.
	• Expression and Mood: The portrait captures the subject's personality and mood through facial expressions and conveys a sense of the person's identity.
	• Detail and Texture: The portrait has enough detail to make it interesting.

In summary, the power of continuous assessment becomes apparent when learners demonstrate their deep understanding through purposeful and meaningful authentic contexts. Many of these examples show the scope and diversity that provide learners with the opportunity to transfer and apply their understanding.

Transfer and application in continuous assessment are vitally significant processes. They go beyond simply measuring knowledge acquisition; they gauge a learner's ability to use their knowledge and understanding in varied contexts and real-life situations. This process assesses the depth of comprehension and the practical application of learned concepts.

When evaluating transfer and application in continuous assessment, educators gain insights into a learner's critical thinking, problem-solving skills, and the extent to which they can adapt knowledge to new scenarios. This ability to apply learned concepts in different contexts showcases a deeper level of understanding and proficiency, which are essential skills in today's dynamic and evolving world.

Overall, transfer and application hold immense significance in continuous assessment as they measure the true effectiveness and practicality of education, ensuring that learners can apply their understanding beyond the confines of a classroom setting. It also provides learners with the opportunity to genuinely contribute to their community.

TRANSFER & APPLY Can you create a PRAC task that is authentic around an understanding question that promotes the *So what?*

Purpose	What is the purpose of and context for the task?
Role	What is the role required for the task?
Audience	Who is the audience?
Criteria	What will success in the task look like?

CHAPTER SEVEN

Changing Assessment Practices

In this final section, we review some strategies for changing assessment practices. To equip you in this endeavour, we have included tools and questions you can use to evaluate your current assessment practices and consider what next steps to take as you move, plan for conceptual learning, and assess for conceptual understanding. Let's begin by looking at best practices for sustainable change.

GUIDELINES FOR SUSTAINABLE CHANGE

Find a Purpose

Begin with Current Assessment Practice

Guidelines for Sustainable Change

Pursue Ongoing Professional Learning

Build a Culture of Collaboration

Deep change and pedagogical shifts require substantial intention and effort. Following these guidelines will help ensure your success as you shift from content to concept learning and assessment.

Find a purpose.

Identify a few assessment practices that are relevant to you and then reflect on your current teaching. What aspects of your practice do you want to improve on? When working as an educational team, consider allowing each person to identify what practice assessment they find most essential to change. Doing so empowers and respects the different perspectives of educators' philosophies, interests, individual needs, and approach to change.

Begin with current assessment practice.

Starting with an understanding of current assessment practices rather than by looking to an idealised concept of "best practice" provides a foundation for educators to evaluate their effectiveness and gradually transition toward more effective and learner-centred assessment approaches.

Encourage educators to pilot new assessment practices in their classrooms. This step allows for experimentation, observation, and gathering real-world data on the effectiveness of these new practices. This step involves a cyclical process of improvement and refinement in which educators continuously reflect on the effectiveness of their new assessment practices and make adjustments based on ongoing feedback and data analysis.

Build a culture of collaboration.

Building a culture of collaboration and trust involves creating an environment where individuals feel empowered, respected, and encouraged to learn together toward shared goals.

This guideline is core to embedding the change to practise. It is essential that time is dedicated to building a culture of collaboration and trust, which involves creating an environment in which individuals feel empowered, respected, and encouraged to work together toward shared goals.

Below are significant features that support a culture of collaboration.

Characteristics for a Culture of Collaboration	
Open Communication	Encourage open and transparent communication among the education community. This includes active listening, sharing ideas, and providing constructive feedback without fear of judgement.
Shared Vision and Goals	Ensure everyone understands and aligns with the school's or team's vision around assessment. When goals are clear and collectively owned, it fosters a sense of unity and purpose.
Supportive Leadership	Leaders play a crucial role in fostering collaboration and trust. Supportive leadership involves empowering educators, providing guidance, and being accessible and approachable.
Respect for Diversity	Value diverse perspectives, experiences, and ideas. Acknowledging and appreciating differences fosters an inclusive environment in which everyone feels heard and respected.
Collaborative Decision-Making	Involve educators in decision-making processes whenever possible. This creates a sense of ownership and commitment to the decisions made.
Recognition and Appreciation	Acknowledge and celebrate achievements, both big and small, within the team. Recognizing contributions boosts morale and encourages continued collaboration.
Establishing Clear Roles	Ensure that everyone understands their roles and responsibilities within the education community. Clarity helps avoid misunderstandings and encourages accountability.
Continuous Improvement	Embrace a culture of continuous learning and improvement, encouraging experimentation, learning from failures, and adapting strategies based on feedback and outcomes.

Pursue ongoing professional learning.

Change can be challenging. Ongoing professional learning provides the necessary support and resources to navigate and embrace change effectively. Workshops, courses, conferences, and books studies can provide the tools, knowledge, and understanding needed to implement new practices successfully. Embracing ongoing professional learning fosters a culture of continuous improvement within educational settings. This culture becomes ingrained, encouraging a proactive approach to staying updated and adaptable in the face of change.

In essence, ongoing professional learning is a cornerstone for individuals and organisations seeking to evolve and adapt to changing practices. It empowers all of us as professionals to grow, innovate, and effectively implement change for improved and sustainable outcomes..

SELF-ASSESSMENT TOOLS FOR EDUCATORS

Reflective Tool for Educators: Shifting Assessment Practices: Moving Away From . . . Moving To . . .

Based on the ideas we have shared in this book, we have developed the table below to indicate what we feel we need to move away from to what we need to be doing more of.

The following table can be used as a reflective tool on assessment practices. The practices could be cut up and educators can be asked to make two columns—practices they want to move away from and another with practices they want to embrace.

This provides opportunity for critical dialogue around current assessment practices and gives educators the chance to really consider what they believe and what is important in connection to assessment practices.

From there they can start to think about what they need to do less of and what they need to do more of.

Changing Assessment Practices

Moving Away From . . .	Moving To . . .
Using the language of summative and formative assessment	Using continuous assessment and check-ins as language for assessment
Standardised tests as the sole measure of student performance	Diversified set of assessments that are considered over time instead of one performance
Assessment as the final judgement of a student's abilities	Assessment as a tool for feedback and improvement
Summative assessments that primarily assess content knowledge	Emphasising real-world applications and evaluating students based on their ability to solve problems and think critically, so that students are transferring and applying their understanding in an authentic context
Individual educators deciding on assessments and criteria	Moderation of criteria in which educators and learners collaborate with each other to ensure there is a clear understanding of criteria
Prioritising grades so students see them as the value of who they are as learners	Emphasising the importance of learning, effort, and improvement over time. Encouraging students to view challenges as opportunities for growth rather than failure
Assessment decisions made solely by teachers	Involving students in the assessment process, encouraging self-assessment, goal setting, and reflection, fostering a sense of ownership and accountability for their learning

Providing assessments at fixed points in the curriculum	Offering ongoing, continuous assessment that adapts to students' progress, allowing for timely feedback and personalised support so that planning is responding to the needs of students
Collecting evidence of learning at certain points in the learning	Evidence of learning is collected throughout the learning, and each learning moment is seen as an opportunity for assessment
Everyone doing the same assessment at the same time	Tailoring assessments to accommodate diverse learning styles, allowing students to demonstrate understanding in a variety of ways that align with their strengths and interests
Focusing assessment on rote memorization of facts and information	Focusing assessment on students analysing, synthesising, and evaluating information critically, fostering deeper understanding and analytical skills
A single letter or number grade accurately represents a student's knowledge, skills, and potential.	Assessment as a comprehensive approach that includes qualitative feedback and a variety of evidence

TRANSFER & APPLY Considering the table above, what is it you need to do in connection to assessment? Can you consider what you need to do less of in connection to assessment practices and therefore what you need to do more of?

Less of	More of

Shifting Assessment Practices: Teacher Self-Assessment Tool

The following assessment tool can be used by individual educators or teams of educators to consider their current practices in connection to continuous assessment. Educators can self-assess in connection to the practices and consider what they may need to work on further or how they may be able to assist others in the practices they feel they are doing well on. From here, educators can develop personal goals for improvement in connection to continuous assessment.

Teacher Self-Assessment Tool	No Evidence	Beginning to Use	Embedded in My Practice	Able to Mentor Others
Provide timely feedback.				
I use a variety of strategies for feedback to clarify learners' understanding of concepts.				
I provide regular feedback to learners to assist them in making connections to concepts.				
I support learners in identifying "next steps" in deepening their conceptual understanding.				
Identify learning gaps.				
I actively dialogue with learners to clarify misconceptions or confusions around concepts.				

I engage learners with the concepts by providing a range of resources to build their understanding.				
I plan for and use a variety of assessment strategies to scaffold and personalise the learning process.				
Collecting and Analysing Data				
I reflect on the evidence of understanding to adjust and shift my teaching.				
I often revisit a concept or concepts to support learners in making deeper connections.				
I provide additional support, scaffolding, and opportunities for learners to make sense of the concepts.				
Student Engagement				
I provide choice to increase learner engagement and motivation in how they can explore the concepts.				
I use and acknowledge learner voice as a lead for redesigning learning.				

I engage learners in meaningful and authentic experiences.				
Support Evaluation				
I use evidence of learners' understanding for reporting and evaluative purposes.				
I respect learner voice and agency in the acknowledging the diversity of the learners understanding.				
I use evaluative data to inform planning of conceptual learning for ongoing teaching and learning.				
Student Contribution				
I develop criteria with my learners so all are aware of expectations of the learning.				
I provide opportunities for learners to be in critique groups and offer each other feedback based on the criteria.				
I provide learners with opportunities to reflect on their learning and consider their own next steps.				
I discuss the next steps with learners so we can plan together how they can further be challenged in their learning.				

I have given learners the opportunity to unpack the command terms so that they understand the difference between the terms and how they can be successful in connection to the command terms.				

Goal Setting

Based on the self-assessment tool, my goals are:

ASSESSMENT PROCESS FOR LEARNING: A TOOL FOR EDUCATORS

This following diagram represents stages and cyclical nature of continuous assessment. It invites educators to consider how they can go through an "assessment process for learning." This process focuses on educators considering the steps involved in assessment as a way to assist them with their assessment practices. By following this process educators will ensure that they are focusing on continuous assessment and ensuring learning and evidence are at the forefront of the learning.

Reflection Questions for the Assessment Process

You will see that we have also developed questions to consider at each phase of the process. These questions can be used as a self-reflection tool for educators because they consider how they are embedded in the phases of the process. These questions also promote important dialogue for teaching teams around assessment.

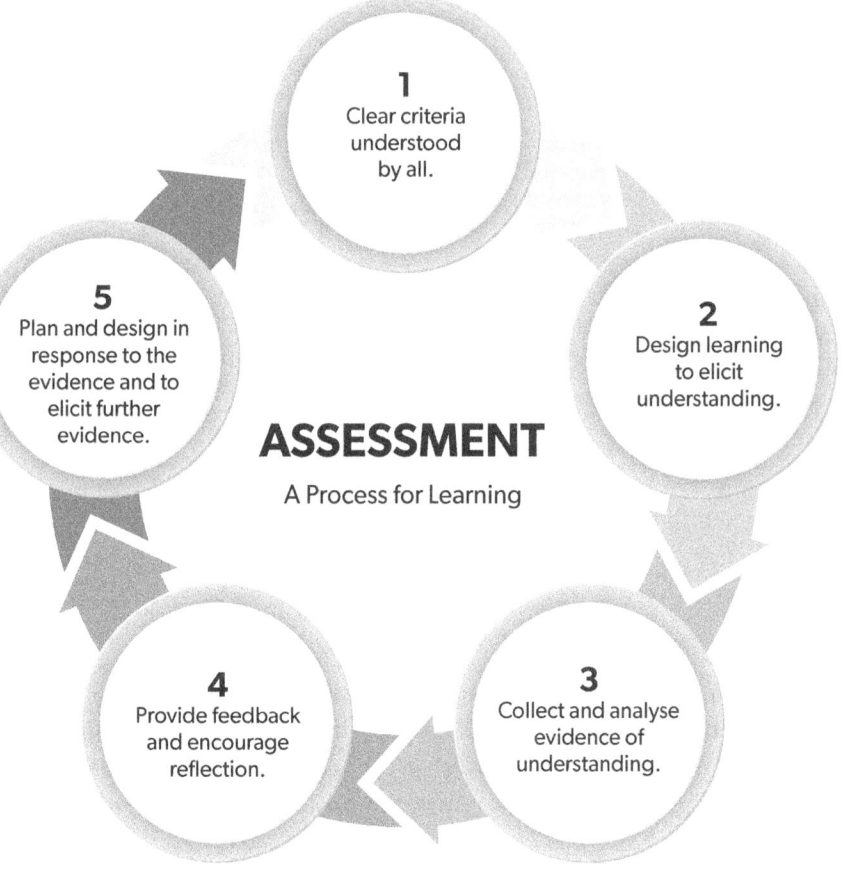

1 Clear criteria understood by all.

2 Design learning to elicit understanding.

3 Collect and analyse evidence of understanding.

4 Provide feedback and encourage reflection.

5 Plan and design in response to the evidence and to elicit further evidence.

ASSESSMENT

A Process for Learning

Continuous Assessment: A Process for Learning	Questions to Consider
Clear Criteria Understood by All	• Is there a clear progression of understanding in the Rubric for Understanding? • Does the Rubric for Understanding connect to developing deep learning over time for students? • How have I moderated the criteria in the Rubric for Understanding with other teachers teaching the same subject/year level? • How have I moderated the criteria in the Rubric for Understanding with students? • How have I assisted in ensuring students understand the command terms used in the Rubric for Understanding?
Design Learning to Elicit Understanding	• Do the invitations I have planned connect to my understanding questions? • Have I ensured the invitations will elicit evidence of understanding that I am looking for? • Do the invitations provide an entry point for all learners? • What prior knowledge tool/s will I use to gather evidence of understanding? • Can I use the prior knowledge tool/s as a continuous assessment tool throughout the learning?
Collect and Analyse Evidence of Understanding	• Am I providing learners with multiple ways to demonstrate their understanding at the different levels in the Rubric for Understanding? • What tools am I or learners using to gather evidence of understanding? • How many pieces of evidence do I need to collect? • How am I and learners analysing the evidence? • What does the evidence tell me about learners' current understanding? How do I know?

Provide Feedback and Encourage Reflection	• Where am I providing opportunities for learners to reflect on their learning? • How can I encourage peer-to-peer feedback? • Is the feedback I give connected directly to the learning? • How am I giving feedback, and is that feedback being used by learners? • Is the feedback and reflection being used by learners to consider next steps in the learning? • Is the feedback timely and constructive?
Plan and Design in Response to the Evidence and Elicit Further Evidence	• How am I adapting the learning in connection to the evidence? • How am I using the levels in the Rubric for Understanding to adapt the learning so all learners are challenged? • How is the learning differentiated to meet the needs of all learners? • How am I developing learning that provides all learners with the opportunity to be challenged and deepen their understanding? • How am I planning in response to learners and not for them?

LEARNER REFLECTION TOOLS

A valuable tool for learner self-reflection is a structured reflection journal. Adjustments can be made to suit different subjects, grade levels, or specific learning objectives. Depending on the learner's development level and needs, some of the reflection could be annotated by the educator and visuals could be inserted, which can be used to reflect on the learning.

This structured reflection journal format provides a framework for learners to systematically reflect on their learning experiences, challenges, and growth. It encourages self-awareness, critical thinking, and goal setting, fostering a habit of continuous self-improvement.

EDUCATOR TOOL: SELF-REFLECTION JOURNAL

Educators: Ideas to Assist You in Using a Self-Reflection Journal	
Subheadings	Reflection Process
Date and Time	Encourage learners to date each entry to track their progress over time.
Objective/ Understanding Question	Specify the objective, understanding question, or learning engagement being reflected on.
What I Did	Have learners summarise the task or learning they engaged in.
What I Learned	Ask learners to reflect on the key insights or knowledge gained from the learning experience. Encourage them to consider both their level of understanding and personal growth.
Challenges I Had	Prompt learners to identify any difficulties or obstacles encountered during the learning.
Strategies I Used	Encourage learners to list the strategies, methods, or approaches they used to tackle challenges or complete the learning engagement.
What Worked Well	Have learners highlight the aspects of their learning or actions that were successful or effective.
What I Would Do Differently	Ask learners to consider what they might change or improve on if faced with a similar learning engagement in the future. Encourage critical thinking and problem-solving.
How I Feel About My Progress	Invite learners to reflect on their feelings about their progress, achievements, or growth throughout the learning experience.
Goals for Improvement	Have learners set specific, actionable goals based on their reflections. These goals should be achievable and related to areas they've identified for improvement.

LEARNER TOOL: SELF-REFLECTION JOURNAL

This is a template in student voice, a structure to guide their reflection to deepen their understanding of their success, their approaches to learning, and next steps.

Student: Self-Reflection Journal Template	
Subheadings	Learner Reflection
Date and Time	Insert date and time
Objective/ Understanding Question	• What is informing my reflection? • What is the understanding question? • What is the learning outcome?
What I Did	• What have I been learning? • What was I doing?
What I Learned	• What new learning have I gained? • What do I now understand? • How do I know I have understood? • Are there ways I know I have gotten better as a learner?
Challenges I Had	• What challenges/obstacles/difficulties did I have with my learning? • How did I know I had challenges/obstacles/difficulties with my learning?
Strategies I Used	• How did I manage the challenges I had? • What strategies/approaches did I use? • Did these strategies/approaches work? How do I know?
What Worked Well	• What worked well for me? • How did I put into action my learning? • How do I know my learning was successful?
What I Would Do Differently	• If I were doing this learning engagement again, what would I change? • Why would I change your approach? • What strategies would I use?

How I Feel About My Progress	• How did I feel about my learning? • Can I identify where I made progress with my understanding?
Goals for Improvement	• What goals or next steps have I actioned? • How are my goals or next steps connected to learning? • How will I put into action my goals or next steps?

In summary, changing assessment practices holds significant value in various aspects. Assessments tailored to evaluate thinking and understanding encourage deeper learning. They shift the focus from rote memorization to comprehension, application, and critical thinking.

Integrating the components of continuous assessment that we have shared throughout the book provides an approach to ongoing, dynamic understanding of progress, fosters personalised learning, encourages timely feedback, and provides approaches to ensure as educators we adapt to meet evolving needs of our learners, ultimately maximising educational growth and development.

Ensuring a sustainable model for improving assessment practices is essential to achieve the planned changes. Reflective practice serves as a catalyst for sustainable change by fostering continuous learning, self-awareness, and adaptive strategies. It empowers individuals and schools to evolve, learn from experiences, and make informed decisions, laying the foundation for lasting and meaningful transformations.

Appendix

Rubric for Understanding Example

This is another example that details the steps you would take when developing the Rubric for Understanding.

Unit: Understanding Force and Motion

STEP 1: Insert your understanding questions.

What an Understanding Question Is	What an Understanding Question Is Not
How do people investigate forces?	Can you name three different types of forces (e.g., pushing, pulling, gravity)?
What is the connection between forces and motion?	What force do you use when riding a bicycle or kicking a soccer ball?
How do people use their understanding of forces to solve problems or create?	Can you make a lever?

Level 1: Recalling	Level 2: Describing
Learners recall and identify knowledge that relates to the conceptual questions.	Learners describe in some detail information related to the conceptual questions. Learners begin to make inferences and interpret their understandings.

Understanding Question: How do people investigate forces?

Understanding Question: What is the connection between forces and motion?

Understanding Question: How do people use their understanding of forces to solve problems or create?

Level 3: Explaining and Connecting	Level 4: Analysing and Applying
Learners make comparisons between existing knowledge and the concepts. They are able to explain in detail what they have learnt and the connections within it, with reasoning and evidence.	Learners analyse and evaluate through reasoning and application. Learners make new connections and justify their analysis using evidence and reason.

STEP 2: Brainstorm possible evidence of understanding.

Using the following brainstorming map or another planning tool, brainstorm what evidence of understanding could look like at each of the four levels.

Brainstorm Map For Evidence of Understanding

Level One
What might be evidence at this level?

- Identity a force.
- Identity a motion.
- Recognise a force.
- Recognise a motion.

Level Three
What might be evidence at this level?

- Explain why a force causes motion.
- Compare and contrast various forces in connection to motion and explain similarities and differences between them.
- Formulate theories that connect forces to motion with reasoning.

WHAT IS THE CONNECTION BETWEEN FORCES AND MOTION?

FORCES CONNECTION

Level Two
What might be evidence at this level?

- Describe different types of forces.
- Describe how a force causes motion.
- Compare different types of forces in connection to motion.

Level Four
What might be evidence at this level?

- Analyse theories in connection to forces and motions through further investigations.

Brainstorm Map For Evidence of Understanding

Level One
What might be evidence at this level?

- Identify where forces are used to slove problems.
- Identify where forces are used to create.

Level Three
What might be evidence at this level?

- Use forces to solve a problem and explain what forces are being used and why.
- Explain how it will be a solution to a problem Use forces to create and explain what forces are being used.

HOW DO PEOPLE USE THEIR UNDERSTANDING OF FORCES TO SOLVE PROBLEMS AND CREATE?

FORCES CREATIVITY

Level Two
What might be evidence at this level?

- Describe where forces are used to solve problems.
- Describe where forces are used to create.
- Use forces to create.
- Use forces to solve a problem.

- **Level Four**
- What might be evidence at this level?
- Analyse others' creations and problem solving using forces, evaluating how effective they are in connection to forces with evidence.
- Transfer and apply their understanding of forces to solve and or create in unfamiliarsituations.

Brainstorm Map For Evidence of Understanding

Level One
What might be evidence at this level?

- Identify what forces are.
- Describe what might be used to investigate forces.
- Illustrate different ways to investigate force.

Level Three
What might be evidence at this level?

- Compare and contrast the different ways forces are investigated.
- Interpret and explain the ways forces function in various situations and contexts.
- Investigate the effect of forces in the physical world citing evidence as to how they are used.

HOW CAN I INVESTIGATE FORCES?

INVESTIGATION

Level Two
What might be evidence at this level?

- Explain and demonstrate an investigation into forces.
- Make observations about forces.
- Investigate different forces.

Level Four
What might be evidence at this level?

- Analyse and critique how forces are investigated in real-world contexts.
- Transfer the understanding of forces in real-world contexts by providing reasons for how these connections exist.

STEP 3: Start developing the rubric.

Beginning at Level 3, consider what evidence would enable you to know learners understand the questions. Use the command terms to assist you.

What might this evidence look like for the learners in your classroom?

Level 1: Recalling	Level 2: Describing
Learners recall and identify knowledge that relates to the conceptual questions.	Learners describe in some detail information related to the conceptual questions. Learners begin to make inferences and interpret their understandings.
Understanding Question: How do people investigate forces?	
Understanding Question: What is the connection between forces and motion?	
Understanding Question: How do people use their understanding of forces to solve problems or create?	

Level 3: Explaining and Connecting	Level 4: Analysing and Applying
Learners make comparisons between existing knowledge and the concepts. They are able to explain in detail what they have learnt and the connections within it, with reasoning and evidence.	Learners analyse and evaluate through reasoning and application. Learners make new connections and justify their analysis using evidence and reason.
Learners **explain** and **demonstrate** the variety of ways they can investigate forces, using **evidence** to show the investigation process.	
Learners **compare and contrast** the connection between forces and motions, **explaining** which forces and motions are similar, why, and what impacts a force and motion.	
Learners **create** and or **solve** a problem using forces, **explaining** the types of forces and motions they have used.	

STEP 4: Decide on the success criteria for Level 2 and command terms that will be effective to scaffold the thinking toward the level of understanding expected at Level 3.

Level 1: Recalling	Level 2: Describing
Learners recall and identify knowledge that relates to the conceptual questions.	Learners describe in some detail information related to the conceptual questions. Learners begin to make inferences and interpret their understandings.
Understanding Question: How do people investigate forces?	
	Learners **explain** and **demonstrate** the variety of ways they can investigate forces, using **evidence** to show the investigation process.
Understanding Question: What is the connection between forces and motion?	
	Learners **compare and contrast** the connection between forces and motions, **explaining** which forces and motions are similar, why, and what impacts a force and motion.
Understanding Question: How do people use their understanding of forces to solve problems or create?	
	Learners **create** and or **solve** a problem using forces, **explaining** the types of forces and motions they have used.

Level 3: Explaining and Connecting	Level 4: Analysing and Applying
Learners make comparisons between existing knowledge and the concepts. They are able to explain in detail what they have learnt and the connections within it, with reasoning and evidence.	Learners analyse and evaluate through reasoning and application. Learners make new connections and justify their analysis using evidence and reason.
Learners **explain** and **demonstrate** the variety of ways they can investigate forces, using **evidence** to show the investigation process.	
Learners **compare and contrast** the connection between forces and motions, **explaining** which forces and motions are similar, why, and what impacts a force and motion.	
Learners **create** and or **solve** a problem using forces, **explaining** the types of forces and motions they have used.	

STEP 5: Decide on the criteria for Level 1 and command terms that will be effective to scaffold the thinking toward the level of understanding expected at Level 2.

Level 1: Recalling	Level 2: Describing
Learners recall and identify knowledge that relates to the conceptual questions.	Learners describe in some detail information related to the conceptual questions. Learners begin to make inferences and interpret their understandings.
Understanding Question: How do people investigate forces?	
Learners **investigate** forces.	Learners **explain** and **demonstrate** the variety of ways they can investigate forces, using **evidence** to show the investigation process.
Understanding Question: What is the connection between forces and motion?	
Learners **identify** forces and motions.	Learners **compare and contrast** the connection between forces and motions, **explaining** which forces and motions are similar, why, and what impacts a force and motion.
Understanding Question: How do people use their understanding of forces to solve problems or create?	
Learners **identify** where forces are used to solve problems.	Learners **create** and or **solve** a problem using forces, **explaining** the types of forces and motions they have used.

Level 3: Explaining and Connecting	Level 4: Analysing and Applying
Learners make comparisons between existing knowledge and the concepts. They are able to explain in detail what they have learnt and the connections within it, with reasoning and evidence.	Learners analyse and evaluate through reasoning and application. Learners make new connections and justify their analysis using evidence and reason.
Learners **explain** and **demonstrate** the variety of ways they can investigate forces, using **evidence** to show the investigation process.	
Learners **compare and contrast** the connection between forces and motions, **explaining** which forces and motions are similar, why, and what impacts a force and motion.	
Learners **create** and or **solve** a problem using forces, **explaining** the types of forces and motions they have used.	

STEP 6: Consider how learners will demonstrate their conceptual understanding through analysing and applying.

This level is an evaluative process in which learners apply, analyse, evaluate, and transfer their deeper learning.

Level 1: Recalling	Level 2: Describing
Learners recall and identify knowledge that relates to the conceptual questions.	Learners describe in some detail information related to the conceptual questions. Learners begin to make inferences and interpret their understandings.
Understanding Question: How do people investigate forces?	
Learners **investigate** forces.	Learners **explain** and **demonstrate** the variety of ways they can investigate forces, using **evidence** to show the investigation process.
Understanding Question: What is the connection between forces and motion?	
Learners **identify** forces and motions.	Learners **compare and contrast** the connection between forces and motions, **explaining** which forces and motions are similar, why, and what impacts a force and motion.
Understanding Question: How do people use their understanding of forces to solve problems or create?	
Learners **identify** where forces are used to solve problems.	Learners **create** and or **solve** a problem using forces, **explaining** the types of forces and motions they have used.

Level 3: Explaining and Connecting	Level 4: Analysing and Applying
Learners make comparisons between existing knowledge and the concepts. They are able to explain in detail what they have learnt and the connections within it, with reasoning and evidence.	Learners analyse and evaluate through reasoning and application. Learners make new connections and justify their analysis using evidence and reason.
Learners **explain** and **demonstrate** the variety of ways they can investigate forces, using **evidence** to show the investigation process.	Learners **analyse** the effectiveness of their investigations and **evaluate** these to make adjustments and improve how they investigate.
Learners **compare and contrast** the connection between forces and motions, **explaining** which forces and motions are similar, why, and what impacts a force and motion.	Learners **analyse** theirs and others' creation or problem-solving connected to forces and motion and **evaluate** them, making suggestions for how it can be improved, with **evidence.**
Learners **create** and or **solve** a problem using forces, **explaining** the types of forces and motions they have used.	*Please note that the two understanding questions at this level have been merged to transfer their understanding of the connection between forces and motion.

Additional Examples: Rubrics for Understanding

The following rubrics are examples collected from a variety of schools. They represent a range of subject areas and year levels. Reflect on these examples and consider whether or how they could be adapted to serve you and your students.

Several of these rubrics can be revisited throughout the year as learners take on different individual pursuits. Additionally, they are flexible enough to be used across grade levels and to give students the opportunity to choose what areas of interest they want to focus on.

Physical Education

Level 1: Recalling	Level 2: Describing
Learners recall and identify knowledge that relates to the conceptual questions.	Learners describe in some detail information related to the conceptual questions. Learners begin to make inferences and interpret their understandings.
Understanding Question: How do people develop techniques for individual pursuits? (This is based on the individual pursuit each year level is focused on.)	
Learners **recognise and demonstrate** the specific techniques used in individual pursuits.	Learners **describe and demonstrate** the key components and steps involved in developing a technique.
Understanding Question: How do people persevere and improve in individual pursuits? (based on the individual pursuit each year level is focused on)	
Learners **recognise** the importance of perseverance and improvement in individual pursuits.	Learners **describe** the specific actions and strategies that can be employed to persevere and improve in individual pursuits.

Level 3: Explaining and Connecting	Level 4: Analysing and Applying
Learners make comparisons between existing knowledge and the concepts. They are able to explain in detail what they have learnt and the connections within it, with reasoning and evidence.	Learners analyse and evaluate through reasoning and application. Learners make new connections and justify their analysis using evidence and reason.
Learners demonstrate and transfer techniques in individual pursuits, comparing and contrasting techniques across individual pursuits. Students **explain** the importance of developing technique and **how it relates** to personal growth and improvement.	Learners **analyse** the effectiveness of their technique and strategies and **evaluate their impact** on performance, making **suggestions for how they could improve.**
Learners **explain and demonstrate** how perseverance is **linked to** progress and growth in individual pursuits and how improvement can be achieved through consistent effort and dedication.	Learners **analyse** the effectiveness of different approaches to perseverance and improvement and **evaluate** their impact on their personal growth and achievement in individual pursuits.

Music

Level 1: Recalling	Level 2: Describing
Learners recall and identify knowledge that relates to the conceptual questions.	Learners describe in some detail information related to the conceptual questions. Learners begin to make inferences and interpret their understandings.

Understanding Question: How can I use the elements of music when I play a musical instrument? (based on what each year level is focusing on)

Name the elements of music used when playing.	**Recount and demonstrate** how each element of music applies to your instrument and its **connection** to the overall performance.

Understanding Question: How and why do musicians apply instrumental technique? (based on the instrument being focused on in different year levels).

Recognise the various instrumental techniques used in playing musical instruments.	**Recount and demonstrate** how each element of music applies to your instrument and its **connection** to the overall performance.

Understanding Question: How can I use the elements of music when I play a musical instrument? (based on what each year level is focusing on)

Name the elements of music used when playing.	**Recount and demonstrate** the specific application of instrumental techniques.

Level 3: Explaining and Connecting	Level 4: Analysing and Applying
Learners make comparisons between existing knowledge and the concepts. They are able to explain in detail what they have learnt and the connections within it, with reasoning and evidence.	Learners analyse and evaluate through reasoning and application. Learners make new connections and justify their analysis using evidence and reason.
Express and demonstrate how the skilful application of musical elements **connects** to and enhances your playing, improves musical communication with others, and conveys emotions through the instrument, with **justification.**	**Analyse** your performances to identify areas where the elements of music can be further utilised and **evaluate** how effectively you incorporate these elements to achieve desired musical outcomes.
Express and demonstrate how the skilful application of musical elements **connects** to and enhances your playing, improves musical communication with others, and conveys emotions through the instrument, with **justification.**	**Analyse** your performances to identify areas where the elements of music can be further utilised and **evaluate** how effectively you incorporate these elements to achieve desired musical outcomes.
Explain and demonstrate how instrumental techniques **connect** to producing specific sounds and effects, enhancing musical expression.	**Analyse** the effectiveness of instrumental techniques in conveying musical ideas, **evaluating** their impact on overall performance quality, and identifying areas for improvement.

Music

Developed with the music team at Anglo American School Moscow

Level 1: Recalling	Level 2: Describing
Learners recall and identify knowledge that relates to the conceptual questions.	Learners describe in some detail information related to the conceptual questions. Learners begin to make inferences and interpret their understandings.

Understanding Question: What are musical notation systems?

Students can **understand *or* demonstrate** that symbols (notes) can represent music.	Students **understand and demonstrate** that symbols can represent music in **connection** to rhythm and pitch.

Understanding Question: How do performers organise themselves?

Students **describe and demonstrate** there are different roles within an ensemble that contribute to the success of a performance.	Students **explain and demonstrate** there are different roles within an ensemble (that is made up of sections), and **connect** this to how each individual contributes to the success of a performance.

Level 3: Explaining and Connecting	Level 4: Analysing and Applying
Learners make comparisons between existing knowledge and the concepts. They are able to explain in detail what they have learnt and the connections within it, with reasoning and evidence.	Learners analyse and evaluate through reasoning and application. Learners make new connections and justify their analysis using evidence and reason.
Students **understand, organise, and demonstrate** that symbols can represent music with regard to rhythm and pitch, **using appropriate technique.**	Students **understand, organise, demonstrate, create,** and **explain** symbols that represent music with regard to rhythm and pitch, **using appropriate technique.**
Students can **identify** the group leader, **understand** the changing roles of accompaniment, soloist, and instruments throughout the form of a musical piece, and **connect** this to how it contributes to the success of a performance.	Students can **identify, explain, and demonstrate** the various roles in musical settings, and **demonstrate** each component through **transfer and application.**

Art

Level 1: Recalling	Level 2: Describing
Learners recall and identify knowledge that relates to the conceptual questions.	Learners describe in some detail information related to the conceptual questions. Learners begin to make inferences and interpret their understandings.

Understanding Question: What is the role of an artist's intention when creating artwork?	
Students **name** the artist's intent.	Students make **connections** between the artwork, elements of art, and the artist's intent.
Understanding Question: How do artists make choices when creating artworks?	
Students **identify** their intent.	Students **describe** and **connect** their choice of tools, materials, and the elements of art to their intent.
Understanding Question: How can we explore and experiment with different art techniques?	
Students **identify** and **use** different techniques in their artworks.	Students **explore** and **experiment** with different art techniques, **describing** which they would/will use for their artworks.

Level 3: Explaining and Connecting	Level 4: Analysing and Applying
Learners make comparisons between existing knowledge and the concepts. They are able to explain in detail what they have learnt and the connections within it, with reasoning and evidence.	Learners analyse and evaluate through reasoning and application. Learners make new connections and justify their analysis using evidence and reason.
Students examine artworks, **explaining** in **detail** the artist's intent in **connection** to the elements with **justification.**	Students **evaluate** their and others' artworks in connection to intent, the elements of art, and techniques used, and **analyse** how they feel the art piece could be improved and why this would improve it, with **reasoning.**
Students **explain** in detail throughout the artmaking process their choice of materials, tools, and the elements of art to their intent.	
Students **explore** and **experiment** with different art techniques, **comparing** them and **explaining** which they would/will use for their artworks and why **(justification).**	

Physical Education

This rubric can be used throughout a year, unlike other units of learning, in which there can be a start and finish point. A unit like this could take place all year, as learners are involved in different types of movement, such as dance and gymnastics. Educators and learners may use this unit twice within a year for a unit on dance and for a unit on gymnastics. It can also be used across year levels because the understanding can be connected specifically to the movements being focused on. By having this type of assessment, there is also the opportunity for learners to have choice in their learning. Learners can choose the type of movement they wish to use to create sequences. This can be done after educators have built up their repertoire of sequences.

Level 1: Recalling	Level 2: Describing
Learners recall and identify knowledge that relates to the conceptual questions.	Learners describe in some detail information related to the conceptual questions. Learners begin to make inferences and interpret their understandings.
Understanding Question: How do we develop and refine our movement composition skills?	
Students **demonstrate** techniques (e.g., control, balance) required for different movement skills.	Students **demonstrate effective** techniques (e.g., control, balance) required for different movement skills.
Understanding Question: How can movements be combined to create a sequence?	
Identify movement sequences.	**Demonstrate** movement sequences by **copying** movements and **connecting** them.
Understanding Question: Why is reflection important?	
Identify what reflection is.	**Reflect** on performance and **make suggestions** for how movements skills and sequences can be improved.

Level 3: Explaining and Connecting	Level 4: Analysing and Applying
Learners make comparisons between existing knowledge and the concepts. They are able to explain in detail what they have learnt and the connections within it, with reasoning and evidence.	Learners analyse and evaluate through reasoning and application. Learners make new connections and justify their analysis using evidence and reason.
Students **apply accurately** the technique (e.g., control, balance) required for different movement skills, **outlining** the **development** of their technique and how they have improved.	**Transfer and apply** ongoing reflection to continually improve movement skills and sequences.
Demonstrate and **independently** develop movement sequences that **combine** movements to **create a flow** of a sequence.	
Reflect on performance and **make informed decisions** for how movements skills and sequences could be improved, with **justification and action.**	

Art

Level 1: Recalling	Level 2: Describing
Learners recall and identify knowledge that relates to the conceptual questions.	Learners describe in some detail information related to the conceptual questions. Learners begin to make inferences and interpret their understandings.

Understanding Question: How can I explore, compare, and contrast different tools and materials used in art?

Students **explore** materials and tools and **identify** effects.	Students **explore** materials and tools used in art and **define** the different effects they make.

Understanding Question: How can I develop technique when using a variety of art tools and materials?

Students experiment with art tools and materials and **identify** different techniques.	Students **demonstrate** different techniques associated with art tools and materials.

Level 3: Explaining and Connecting	Level 4: Analysing and Applying
Learners make comparisons between existing knowledge and the concepts. They are able to explain in detail what they have learnt and the connections within it, with reasoning and evidence.	Learners analyse and evaluate through reasoning and application. Learners make new connections and justify their analysis using evidence and reason.
Students **compare and contrast** different materials and tools used in art; they **critique** the different effects they make and **connect** this to when they would use that effect with **reasoning.**	Students **create** artwork and **transfer and apply** their technique and understanding of effects to their artwork, **interpreting** their artistic intention and how they **reflected** on and **improved** their technique.
Students **demonstrate** different techniques associated with art tools and materials and **reflect** to **determine** the steps needed for improvement of technique.	

Literacy Middle School

*Developed with the literacy team at International Community School
of Abidjan, Ivory Coast*

This rubric can be used throughout the unit. Whilst you will see in the rubric we have referred to literature, this can be used for poetry, short stories, novels, or any other type of literature learners are involved in exploring. It enables learners to really focus on and build their understanding of the understanding questions over time and through a variety of literature, ensuring transfer and application of learning.

Level 1: Recalling	Level 2: Describing
Learners recall and identify knowledge that relates to the conceptual questions.	Learners describe in some detail information related to the conceptual questions. Learners begin to make inferences and interpret their understandings.
Understanding Question: How do we read literature as a form of expression?	
Students **read** literature, using different forms of expression.	Students read literature, using a **variety of expressions** and **describe** how it changes the meaning.
Understanding Question: How do writers use literary forms and devices as a form of expression?	
Students **point out** literary forms and devices in literature.	Students **recall** literary forms and devices and **connect this** to how the device and form adds to the expression of the literature.
Understanding Question: How do we use literary forms and devices to express ourselves through literature?	
Students **plan** for and **use** literary devices and forms in their own writing,	Students **plan** for and **use** literary devices and forms in their own writing and **connect** this to why they have used them.

Level 3: Explaining and Connecting	Level 4: Analysing and Applying
Learners make comparisons between existing knowledge and the concepts. They are able to explain in detail what they have learnt and the connections within it, with reasoning and evidence.	Learners analyse and evaluate through reasoning and application. Learners make new connections and justify their analysis using evidence and reason.
Students **compare and contrast** the different ways they can read literature. They **explain** how the way they read can change the expression of the literature and decide which is the **most effective, with justification.**	Students **evaluate** how literature is being read and **analyse the effectiveness** of how it is expressed and make **suggestions** for how it could be more effectively expressed.
Students **compare and contrast** different literary forms and devices and **explain** how the device and form add to the expression of the literature and its effectiveness, with **justification.**	Students **evaluate** their and others' poems in connection to literary devices and forms and intended audience response. They **analyse** them and **make suggestions** for how they could be improved, with **justification.**
Students **plan** for and **use** literary devices and forms in their own writing. They **clarify** why they have used them and the intended response from the audience, with **evidence.**	

Social Studies: History

Developed with the middle years' educators at International Community School of Abidjan

This unit is focused on what it means to be an historian. The educator in this situation did not determine what the content of the learning would be; he instead focused on historical sources and what they tell us about the past and how we know whether they are valid not. This provides learners with many opportunities to follow their own interest in connection to history, providing motivation for learning.

Level 1: Recalling	Level 2: Describing
Learners recall and identify knowledge that relates to the conceptual questions.	Learners describe in some detail information related to the conceptual questions. Learners begin to make inferences and interpret their understandings.
Understanding Question: What is the role of a historian?	
Students **recall** what historians do.	Students **describe** the role of a historian and what they do.
Understanding Question: How do historical sources provide insight into the past, and whose story do they tell?	
Students **identify** historical sources.	Students **categorise** historical sources and **provide details connected** to what the sources tell us about the past.
Understanding Question: What is the role of validity in connection to historical sources?	
Students **note** what validity of evidence is.	Students **categorise** sources into valid or not valid and **describe** their reasons for this.

Level 3: Explaining and Connecting	Level 4: Analysing and Applying
Learners make comparisons between existing knowledge and the concepts. They are able to explain in detail what they have learnt and the connections within it, with reasoning and evidence.	Learners analyse and evaluate through reasoning and application. Learners make new connections and justify their analysis using evidence and reason.
Students **connect** what historians do to their role and **explain** why the role is important, with **evidence.**	Students **transfer and apply** their understanding of being a historian and **evaluate** how effective they are at being an historian, with reasoning.
Students **compare and contrast** historical sources and provide **detailed explanations** of what they tell us about the past, whose story they tell, and why.	Students **evaluate** historical sources and **analyse** their **bias and validity, explaining** the **perspective** of the bias and lack of validity.
Students **explain** the role of **perspectives** in connection to validity of evidence and **give details** of when sources are valid or not, **with examples**.	

Languages

Developed with the language teacher at Beacon School Philippines
This rubric can be used in any language setting. As learners are acquiring their oral skills to communicate through the language, the rubric can be reference throughout the year to guide their understanding of communication and provide them with the proof of progress as they see their communication skills developing.

Level 1: Recalling	Level 2: Describing
Learners recall and identify knowledge that relates to the conceptual questions.	Learners describe in some detail information related to the conceptual questions. Learners begin to make inferences and interpret their understandings.
Understanding Question: How can we effectively orally communicate in different contexts?	
Students **interact** with others at school (use **simple greetings** and words).	Students interact with others in different contexts. (using sentences).

Level 3: Explaining and Connecting	Level 4: Analysing and Applying
Learners make comparisons between existing knowledge and the concepts. They are able to explain in detail what they have learnt and the connections within it, with reasoning and evidence.	Learners analyse and evaluate through reasoning and application. Learners make new connections and justify their analysis using evidence and reason.
Students **interact** with others as appropriate in **different contexts** sharing relevant information **(follow and engage in conversation).**	Students analyse the context and can accurately interact with different people in that context, exchanging information clearly and effectively (formal/informal).

Design

This rubric for design can be used across different contexts. It focuses on learners being able to connect to a problem or issue that is significant to them and then design a solution. It also provides learners with options in making connections to what the problem and solution may be. For instance, it could be looking at a global problem such as *sustainability* and asking learners to consider the problem from this context and to develop a solution.

Level 1: Recalling	Level 2: Describing
Learners recall and identify knowledge that relates to the conceptual questions.	Learners describe in some detail information related to the conceptual questions. Learners begin to make inferences and interpret their understandings.

Understanding Question: What design solution will be the most effective for the problem?	
Students **state** what the problem is and know a solution is required.	Students **outline** and **describe** the solution to a problem.

Level 3: Explaining and Connecting	Level 4: Analysing and Applying
Learners make comparisons between existing knowledge and the concepts. They are able to explain in detail what they have learnt and the connections within it, with reasoning and evidence.	Learners analyse and evaluate through reasoning and application. Learners make new connections and justify their analysis using evidence and reason.
Students **explain** the solution and how this will assist in solving the problem.	Students analyse the context and can accurately in Students **explain** and **justify** the need for the solution in connection to the problem and **analyse** why their solution will be effective, with **reasoning.** teract with different people in that context, exchanging information clearly and effectively (formal/informal).

Math

This rubric can be used throughout the year because it is focussed on how learners communicate their mathematical understanding. As learners are provided with opportunities to communicate their thinking, they use the rubric to consider where they are in their understanding and what their next steps may be.

Level 1: Recalling	Level 2: Describing
Learners recall and identify knowledge that relates to the conceptual questions.	Learners describe in some detail information related to the conceptual questions. Learners begin to make inferences and interpret their understandings.
Understanding Question: How can we use mathematical language and communicate effectively when explaining our representations?	
Students **point out** the math in their representations.	Students **give context** to the math in their representations.
Understanding Question: How can we represent our mathematical information logically and in an organised way?	
Students **use a** representation to demonstrate mathematical information.	Students use **different forms** of representation and **give context** their organisation of their mathematical information.

Level 3: Explaining and Connecting	Level 4: Analysing and Applying
Learners make comparisons between existing knowledge and the concepts. They are able to explain in detail what they have learnt and the connections within it, with reasoning and evidence.	Learners analyse and evaluate through reasoning and application. Learners make new connections and justify their analysis using evidence and reason.
Students **justify** the math in their representations, **making connections** using **mathematical language.**	Students **analyse** their representations, **explaining** patterns and relationships **using advanced mathematical terminology.**
Students **compare and contrast** the ways in which they can represent mathematical information and **explain** how their representation and organisation in the most effective way to show the information with **reasoning.**	Students **evaluate** their and others' mathematical representation of information and how it is organised and are able to **make logical and reasoned** suggestions for how they can be improved to better demonstrate the information.

TRANSFER & APPLY Develop a rubric of understanding, using your understanding questions.

Level 1: Recalling	Level 2: Describing
Learners recall and identify knowledge that relates to the conceptual questions.	Learners describe in some detail information related to the conceptual questions. Learners begin to make inferences and interpret their understandings.
Understanding Question:	
Understanding Question:	
Understanding Question:	

Level 3: Explaining and Connecting	Level 4: Analysing and Applying
Learners make comparisons between existing knowledge and the concepts. They are able to explain in detail what they have learnt and the connections within it, with reasoning and evidence.	Learners analyse and evaluate through reasoning and application. Learners make new connections and justify their analysis using evidence and reason.

Citations

Absolum, Michael. *Clarity in the Classroom: Using Formative Assessment for Building Learning-Focused Relationships.* Auckland, NZ: Hodder Education, 2006, pp. 28–46.

AITSL. "Using Learner Data." 2020. https://www.aitsl.edu.au/teach/improve-practice/practical-guides/using-learner-data.

Ausubel, David Paul. *Educational Psychology: A Cognitive View.* New York: Holt, Rinehart and Winston, 1968.

Blythe, Tina, and Associates. *The Teaching for Understanding Guide.* San Francisco: Jossey-Bass, 1998.

Boaler, Jo. "'Big Ideas' Issued by the State of California." *Youcubed Stanford University, Youcubed,* 2021. mailchi.mp/youcubed/big-ideas-de-tracking-and-online-course-news.

Bransford, John D., Ann L. Brown, and Rodney R. Cocking (eds). *How People Learn: Brain, Mind, Experience and School,* revised edition. Washington, DC: National Academy Press, 2000, p. 17.

Bronke, Chris. (2023). "Deeper Learning: Empower Students to Think, Collaborate, and Problem-Solve." 2023. *www.novakeducation.com.* Accessed 20 July 2023. https://www.novakeducation.com/blog/deeper-learning-empower-students-to-think-collaborate-and-problem-solve

Bruner, Jerome. *The Process of Education.* Cambridge, MA: Harvard University Press, 1960.

Bruner, Jerome, Jacqueline J. Goodnow, and George A. Austin. *A Study of Thinking,* revised edition. New Brunswick: Transaction Publishers, 1956.

Claxton, Guy. *What's the Point of School?: Rediscovering the Heart of Education.* Oxford: Oneworld, Imp., 2013.

Coutts, N. (2020, December 1). "Reimagining Education for Uncertain Times with Perkins, David." *The Learner's Way.* https://thelearnersway.net/ideas/2020/8/23/reimagining-education-for-uncertain-times-with-david-perkins.

Dixon, Raymond A. and Ryan A. Brown. "Transfer of Learning: Connecting Concepts During Problem Solving." *Journal of Technology Education* 24, no. 1 (2012): 2-17.

Eysink, Tessa H. S. and Kim Schildkamp. "A Conceptual Framework for Assessment-Informed Differentiation (AID) in the Classroom." *Educational Research* 63, no. 3 (2021): 261-278; doi: 10.1080/00131881.2021.1942118.

Frey, Nancy, Douglas B. Fisher, and John Hattie. "Developing 'Assessment Capable' Learners." *ASCD,* 2 February 2018. www.ascd.org/el/articles/developing-assessment-capable-learners.

Hattie, John A.C. and Gregory M. Donoghue. (2016). "Learning Strategies: A Synthesis and Conceptual Model." *Science of Learning* 1, no. 1 (2016). doi: 10.1038/npjscilearn.2016.13.

Hattie, John, and Helen Timperley. (2007). "The Power of Feedback." *Review of Educational Research* 77, no. 1 (2007): 81-112.

McTighe, Jay, and Harvey F. Silver. "Instructional Shifts to Support Deep Learning" September 2020. http://www.ascd.org/publications/educational-leadership/sept20/vol78/num01/Instructional-Shifts-to-Support-Deep-Learning.aspx.

McTighe, Jay, and Grant Wiggins. "Developing Performance Tasks: Constructing a Task Scenario." *Jaymctighe.com*, 2010, jaymctighe.com/downloads/GRASPS-Design-sheets.pdf. Accessed 8 Oct. 2024.

Main, Paul. "Webb's Depth of Knowledge." n.d. *www.structural-learning.com*. https://www.structural-learning.com/post/webbs-depth-of-knowledge.

Masters, Geoff. "The Role of Evidence in Teaching and Learning." *Australian Council for Educational Research*. 2018. https://research.acer.edu.au/columnists/39/.

Maxwell, Graham S., and J. Joy Cumming. "Managing Without Public Examinations: Successful and Sustained Curriculum and Assessment Reform in Queensland." In: *Australia's Curriculum Dilemmas: State Cultures and the Big Issues.* Melbourne University Publishing, 2010.

Moss, Connie M, and Susan M. Brookhart. *Learning Targets: Helping Students Aim for Understanding in Today's Lesson*. Alexandria, VA: ASCD, 2012.

Müller Andrea, and Tania Lattanzio. *Taking the Complexity out of Concepts.* Moorabbin, Vic., Hawker Brownlow Education, 2015.

Murdoch, Kath. (2020). "Planning for Inquiry — JustWondering." 2020. https://www.kathmurdoch.com.au/blog/category/planning+for+inquiry

Murdoch, Kath. *The Power of Inquiry.* Melbourne, Australia: Seastar Education, 2015.

National Research Council. National Science Education Standards. 1996. Washington, DC: The National Academies Press. https://doi.org/10.17226/4962.

Open Colleges. "How To Make Learning Relevant to Your Learners (And Why It's Crucial to Their Success)." *Open Colleges*, 4 October 2014. www.opencolleges.edu.au/informed/features/how-to-make-learning-relevant/.

Perkins, David. *Making Learning Whole: How Seven Principles of Teaching Can Transform Education*. San Francisco, CA: Jossey-Bass, 2009.

Perkins, David. *Teaching for Understanding: Linking Research with Practice*. San Francisco: Jossey-Bass, 1998.

Pettit, Casey, and Claudia Bicen. "Engaging Learners in Personally Meaningful SEL." *ASCD*, 24 June 2021. https://www.ascd.org/el/articles/ engaging-students-in-personally-meaningful-sel.

Popham, W. James. "All About Accountability / The Lowdown on Learning Progressions." *Educational Leadership* 64, no. 7, (2007): 83-84. Retrieved from http://www.ascd.org/publications/educational-leadership/apr07/ vol64/num07/The-Lowdown-on-Learning-Progressions.aspx.

Rosenshine, Barak. "Principles of Instruction: Research-Based Strategies That All Teachers Should Know." *American Educator* 36, no. 1 (2012): 12-39.

Rule, Audrey. "Editorial: The Components of Authentic Learning." *Journal of Authentic Learning*. 3 (2006).

Sbar, Eric. "Schemas Are Key to Deep Conceptual Understanding." *blog. mindresearch.org*. Accessed 5 July 2023. https://blog.mindresearch.org/ blog/schemas-deep-conceptual-understanding.

Stiggins, Rick, & Jan Chappuis. "Using Student-Involved Classroom Assessment to Close Achievement Gaps." *Theory into Practice* 44, no. 1 (2005): 11-18. http://www.jstor.org/stable/3496986.

Tomlinson, Carol Ann, Tonya Moon, and Marsha B. Imbeau. (2015). "Assessment and Student Success in a Differentiated Classroom: White Paper." *ASCD*. 2015. Accessed 15 April 2023. https://www.polzleitner.com/epep/Uni/PPS3/ articles-and-chapters/assessment-and-di-whitepaper.pdf

Tomlinson, Carol Ann and Caroline Cunningham Eidson. *Differentiation in Action: Implementing the Differentiated Classroom*. Association for Supervision and Curriculum Development, 2003.

Tomlinson, Carol Ann, and Tonya R. Moon. *Assessment and Student Success in a Differentiated Classroom*. Alexandria, VA: ASCD, 2013.

Treadwell, Mark. *The Future of Learning*. New Zealand: Global Curriculum Project, 2017.

Treadwell, Mark. *The Conceptual Age and the Revolution: Schoolv2.0*. Heatherton, Vic., Australia: Hawker Brownlow Education, 2008.

Webb, Norman L., and others. "Web Alignment Tool." *Wisconsin Center of Educational Research. University of Wisconsin-Madison*. 24 July 2005.

Weller, Martin, and Michelle Appleby. "What are the benefits of interdisciplinary study?" 2021. https://www.open.edu/openlearn/education-development/ what-are-the-benefits-interdisciplinary-study#:~:text=Interdisciplinary%20 study%20allows%20for%20synthesis.

Wiliam, Dylan. *Embedded Formative Assessment*, 2nd ed. Bloomington, IN: Solution Tree Press, 2011.

Ye, Peiqi, and Xionghu Xu. "A Case Study of Interdisciplinary Thematic Learning Curriculum to Cultivate '4C Skills.'" *Frontiers in Phycology* , vol. 14, 7 Mar. 2023.

More From

ELEVATE BOOKS EDU

Outsmarted
The Changing Face of Learning in the Era of Smartphones and Technology
By Lisa Green

In Outsmarted, educator Lisa Green considers the impact of today's rapidly advancing technology on children's and teens' mental and emotional development. Green navigates the complex journey of preparing learners to succeed in a high-tech world. She offers practical approaches to smartphone management, skill-building, and assessment in today's classroom.

Dive into Inquiry
Amplify Learning and Empower Student Voice
By Trevor MacKenzie

Dive into Inquiry beautifully marries the voice and choice of inquiry with the structure and support required to optimize learning. With Dive into Inquiry, you'll gain an understanding of how to best support your learners as they shift from a traditional learning model into the inquiry classroom where student agency is fostered and celebrated each and every day.

Inquiry Mindset: Elementary Edition
Nurturing the Dreams, Wonders, and Curiosities of Our Youngest Learners
By Trevor MacKenzie and Rebecca Bushby

Inquiry Mindset: Elementary Edition offers a highly accessible journey through inquiry in the younger years. Learn how to empower your students, increase engagement, and accelerate learning by harnessing the power of curiosity. With practical examples and a step-by-step guide to inquiry, Trevor MacKenzie and Rebecca Bushby make inquiry-based learning simple.

Available in English, French, Latin American Spanish, and European Spanish

Inquiry Mindset: Assessment Edition
Scaffolding a Partnership for Equity and Agency in Learning
By Trevor MacKenzie

Trevor MacKenzie takes another deep dive into inquiry as he examines the role of assessment in education through the lens of co-designing and co-constructing with students. In *Inquiry Mindset: Assessment Edition*, he outlines the beliefs, values, and frameworks that allow teachers to scaffold assessments infused with student voice, understanding, and autonomy.

Inquiry Mindset: Questions Edition
Cultivating Curiosity and Creating Question Competence
By Trevor MacKenzie

The Question Routines and teacher insights in *Inquiry Mindset: Questions Edition* provide a framework that you and your students can use to craft, organize, and justify questions. Effective across grade levels and subject areas, the strategies MacKenzie provides will empower you to bring fresh excitement and engagement to the learning experience.

Getting Personal with Inquiry Learning
Guiding Learners' Explorations of Personal Passions, Interests and Questions
By Kath Murdoch

In *Getting Personal with Inquiry Learning*, world-renowned inquiry expert, Kath Murdoch, draws on decades of experience to offer a thorough, practical guide to supporting young learners' investigations into their passions, interests, and questions. Following on from the best-selling Power of Inquiry, this book invites teachers to take their thinking about inquiry to the next level and to truly honor both their own and their students' agency.

From Agency to Zest
A Journey through the Landscape of Inquiry
By Kath Murdoch

The delightfully thought-provoking words in this exploration of inquiry-based learning embody the essence of inquiry. Designed to be used to initiate reflection and to provoke professional dialogue amongst educators, *From Agency to Zest* offers insight into inquiry as an approach to teaching and learning. In addition to the explanations provided throughout, Murdoch offers practical advice on how to support and deepen professional learning experiences within and across schools.

Leading with a Lens of Inquiry
Cultivating Conditions for Curiosity and Empowering Agency
By Jessica Vance

Typical models of training and professional development focus on telling. It's a model that far too often trickles down to classrooms where the traditional way of "doing school" limits the way educators teach and students learn. Fortunately, there is a better way to learn: through wonder, agency, and inquiry. From *Leading with a Lens of Inquiry* administrators, educational instructors, and peer leaders learn how to cultivate learning spaces that ignite curiosity and inspire critical thinking in adult and student learners alike.

Taking the Complexities Out of Concepts
By by Tania Lattanzio and Andrea Muller

This practical resource designed by Innovative Global Education (IGE) helps educators shift from a content-based curriculum to a conceptual curriculum. Teaching through concepts provides context that leads to the transferability of knowledge. Using the strategies and ideas in *Taking the Complexities Out of Concepts,* students will develop connections to and a deep understanding of the material.

The AI Infused Classroom
Inspiring Ideas to Shift Teaching and Maximize
Meaningful Learning in the World of AI
By Holly Clark

With the right mindset, the right questions, and the right strategies, you can use AI to create and broaden meaningful learning experiences for every student. In *The AI Infused Classroom*, Holly Clark points out that students need well-trained educators now more than ever, to ensure they are prepared for the world of AI. This book equips you to navigate the latest iteration of edtech.

The Google Infused Classroom
A Guidebook to Making Thinking Visible and
Amplifying Student Voice
By Holly Clark and Tanya Avrith

This beautifully designed book offers guidance on using technology to design instruction that allows students to show their thinking, demonstrate their learning, and share their work (and voices!) with authentic audiences. *The Google Infused Classroom* will equip you to empower your students to use technology in meaningful ways that prepare them for the future.

The Microsoft Infused Classroom
A Guidebook to Making Thinking Visible and
Amplifying Student Voice
By Holly Clark and Tanya Avrith

Packed with ideas you can use in your classroom tomorrow, *The Microsoft Infused Classroom*, equips you to use powerful tools that put learning first. Edtech experts led by Holly Clark and Tanya Avrith show you how to use technology to increase engagement in your classroom and provide authentic opportunities for students to share their work and their voice.

The Chromebook Infused Classroom
Using Blended Learning to Create Engaging, Student-Centered Classrooms
By Holly Clark

Edtech expert and trainer Holly Clark serves as your guide to using Chromebooks effectively in the classroom. As with other books in the *Infused Classroom* series, *The Chromebook Infused Classroom* relies on proven pedagogical practices to create engaging and meaningful learning experiences for today's students. With its wealth of tools, ideas, and step-by-step instructions, this book equips you to empower your students for learning—and for life.

The InterACTIVE Class: Creation in a World of AI
Empowering Educators to Inspire Creativity and Innovation in an AI-Driven Classroom
By Joe and Kristin Merrill

Whether you are a seasoned educator or just beginning your teaching journey, this guide has the tools and insights you need to nurture the next generation of thinkers, creators, and innovators. With 40+ lesson plans and unlimited possibilities, you'll be prepared to navigate the ever-evolving technological landscape with confidence!

The InterACTIVE Class
Using Technology to Make Learning more Relevant and Engaging in the Elementary Classroom
By Joe and Kristin Merrill

In this practical and idea-packed book, coauthors, classroom teachers, and edtech experts Joe and Kristin Merrill share their personal framework for creating an interACTIVE classroom. You'll find new ways to inspire young learners to grow and to develop grit as they stretch their thinking and abilities.

Flipgrid in the InterACTIVE Class
Encouraging Inclusion and Student Voice in the Elementary
By Joe and Kristin Merrill

Classroom teachers Joe and Kristin Merrill have seen firsthand how the practical ideas shared in *Flipgrid in the InterACTIVE Class* impact learning.
By equipping teachers to design more opportunities for students to share their voices and create more equitable learning experiences, Flipgrid opens the door for interaction and discussion in the elementary classroom.

Sketchnotes for Educators
100 Inspiring Illustrations for Lifelong Learners
By Sylvia Duckworth

Sylvia Duckworth is a Canadian teacher whose sketchnotes have taken social media by storm. Her drawings provide clarity and provoke dialogue on many topics related to education. This book contains 100 of her most popular sketchnotes with links to the original downloads that can be used in class or shared with colleagues. Interspersed throughout the book are Sylvia's reflections on each drawing and what motivated her to create them, in addition to commentary from other educators who inspired the sketchnotes.

How to Sketchnote
Visual Note-taking Made Easy
By Sylvia Duckworth

Educator and internationally known sketchnoter Sylvia Duckworth makes ideas memorable and shareable with her simple yet powerful drawings.
In *How to Sketchnote,* she explains how you can use sketchnoting in the classroom and that you don't have to be an artist to discover the benefits of doodling!

40 Ways to Inject Creativity into Your Classroom with Adobe Spark
By Ben Forta and Monica Burns

Experienced educators Ben Forta and Monica Burns offer step-by-step guidance on how to incorporate this powerful tool into your classroom in ways that are meaningful and relevant. They present 40 fun and practical lesson plans suitable for a variety of ages and subjects as well as 15 graphic organizers to get you started. With the tips, suggestions, and encouragement in this book, you'll find everything you need to inject creativity into your classroom using Adobe Spark.

The HyperDoc Handbook
Digital Lesson Design Using Google Apps
By Lisa Highfill, Kelly Hilton, and Sarah Landis

The HyperDoc Handbook is a practical reference guide for all K–12 educators who want to transform their teaching into blended-learning environments. *The HyperDoc Handbook* is a bestselling book that strikes the perfect balance between pedagogy and how-to tips while also providing ready-to-use lesson plans to get you started with HyperDocs right away.